John Cage's Theatre Pieces

WITHDRAWN

Contemporary Music Studies

A series of books edited by Peter Nelson and Nigel Osborne, University of Edinburgh, UK

John Cage's Theatre Pieces

Notations and Performances

by William Fetterman

 harwood academic publishers
Australia • Canada • China • France • Germany • India • Japan
Luxembourg • Malaysia • The Netherlands • Russia
Singapore • Switzerland • Thailand • United Kingdom

Emmaplein 5
1075 AW Amsterdam
The Netherlands

British Library Cataloguing in Publication Data

Fetterman, William
　　John Cage's Theatre Pieces: Notations and
　　Performances. – (Contemporary Music
　　Studies, ISSN 0891-5415; Vol. 11)
　　I. Title II. Series
　　781.552092

　　ISBN 3-7186-5642-6 (hardback)
　　ISBN 3-7186-5643-4 (paperback)

Cover illustration: An excerpt from *Water Walk* (1959), showing the first thirty
seconds in the event's score-part. © 1961 Henmar Press Inc.

CONTENTS

INTRODUCTION TO THE SERIES

The rapid expansion and diversification of contemporary music is explored in this international series of books for contemporary musicians. Leading experts and practitioners present composition today in all aspects – its techniques, aesthetics and technology, and its relationships with other disciplines and currents of thought – as well as using the series to communicate actual musical materials.

The series also features monographs on significant twentieth-century composers not extensively documented in the existing literature.

NIGEL OSBORNE
PETER NELSON

ILLUSTRATIONS

ACKNOWLEDGEMENTS

I thank the following institutions and individuals for permission to include as textual illustrations:

1. The published scores by John Cage are reproduced through the courtesy of C. F. Peters Corporation on behalf of Henmar Press Inc.;

2. Unpublished materials by John Cage relating to the untitled event at Black Mountain College, *Music Walk, Water Walk, Cartridge Music, 0'00"*, *Variations III, Dialogue*, and *ONE*[12] appear courtesy of the Estate of John Cage, Bennet H. Grutman, Executor;

3. The editorial cartoon on the Cage Percussion Ensemble from the March 6, 1942 edition of the *New York World Telegraph* appears courtesy of the John Cage Archive at the Northwestern University Music Library;

4. The audience floorplan for John Cage's untitled event at Black Mountain College is reprinted from *TDR* Vol. 10, no. 2, "An Interview with John Cage" by Michael Kirby and Richard Schechner, by permission of The MIT Press, Cambridge, Massachusetts, copyright © 1965, *Tulane Drama Review*;

5. John Cage page 66 from *Empty Words* copyright © 1979 by John Cage and page 160 from *Silence* copyright © 1961 by John Cage are published by Wesleyan University Press, and appear by permission of the University Press of New England;

6. The "Horseshoe Spread" illustration from *Tarot Classic* is reproduced by permission of U.S. Games Systems, Inc., Stamford CT 06902 USA, copyright © 1972 by Stuart R. Kaplan;

7. The *HPSCHD* floorplan is reproduced courtesy of Frances Ott Allen;

8. The floorplan from the first performance of *Theatre Piece* is reproduced courtesy of Carolyn Brown;

9. The performer/audience floorplan for John Cage's untitled event at Black Mountain College is reproduced courtesy of M. C. Richards;

10. The examples of David Tudor's performance realizations of *Music Walk, Cartridge Music, Theatre Piece*, and an example of the notation-form from which he first performed *4'33"* appear courtesy of David Tudor.

In all the above cases, further reproduction is prohibited without the prior consent of the respective institutions or individuals.

Please note that the examples from scores (both unpublished manuscripts and published versions) are reproduced in this book in a different scale

than the original sources. Thus, when I discuss a space-equal-to-time notation, my text refers to the original dimensions, and not to the reformated scale
of the accompanying figure.

With research, my thanks to Frank Billack, Don Gillespie, and Lynn
Ozer of C. F. Peters for allowing access to scores, files, films, and sound recordings; Don Roberts and Deborah Campana for access to the John Cage Archive
at Northwestern University; David Vaughan for access to the Merce Cunningham Archive; and Laura Kuhn for arranging access to the unpublished scores
in the John Cage Estate. With writing, I thank Michael Kirby and Richard
Schechner for their critical input, and my editor Robert Robertson for allowing me a "free hand." Thanks also to Sarah Bayliss and Marybeth Bingham
for their kind patience with attention to details in publication preparation.

I have talked with several people over the years concerning John
Cage's work. All individuals who have been quoted from personal interviews
are noted in the list of references at the conclusion, and this blanket acknowledgement must suffice. In particular, however, I thank Merce Cunningham
for granting me a rare interview; Carolyn Brown for her information and wise
counsel; M. C. Richards and Ellsworth Snyder for our informative discussions
and gentle debates; and David Tudor for his patience in discussing various
performances and score realizations with me. Without the help of these
individuals this study would have been especially improverished.

I'm especially thankful to have been able to have interviews with
John Cage. His generosity with taking time out from his busy schedule to talk
with me, as well as allowing free access to materials in his possession,
provided both information and a more concrete focus. Much of his criticism
from reading early chapter drafts during the 1980s and early 1990s has been
incorporated in my final draft.

John liked the fact that I had "done my homework," and appreciated
that I asked questions that weren't always asked by others. I learned to never
try to second-guess him, and became clearer between my own personal
thinking and John's own interpretations of his work. John particularly liked
my questions about specific scores, but was often ambivalent concerning
actual performance. He wanted each individual reader/performer to find
his/her own performance realization from the indeterminately notated
scores; while my own concern was to document historical style and practice
as a departure for future inquiries into both practical performance and
intellectualizations of his scores. In hindsight, I realize that I was "in the right
place at the right time," and while my study is certainly subjective, I hope
that my writing is relatively free of any extraneous or untoward interpretation
that does directly relate to the topic under investigation.

Finally, I thank my parents for their support; Owen for suggesting I
put my research into writing; and Jack for urging its completion.

May, 1995

INTRODUCTION

John Cage (1912–1992) is an internationally acclaimed American composer, essayist and poet, mycologist (mushroom indentification expert), gourmet macrobiotic cook, and visual artist. He is known for his compositions for percussion ensemble, piano, prepared piano (where the tone is altered by inserting various objects between the strings), tape and live electronic music. His most famous and still-controversial work is 4'33" (1952), the "silent piece." Also in 1952, he presented an untitled performance event at Black Mountain College that has since become known as the first Happening. He has influenced the work of such diverse artists as Laurie Anderson, George Brecht, Earle Brown, Philip Corner, Merce Cunningham, Brian Eno, Morton Feldman, Jasper Johns, Allan Kaprow, Alison Knowles, Jackson Mac Low, Yoko Ono, Nam June Paik, Yvonne Rainer, Robert Rauschenberg, David Tudor, Robert Wilson, Christian Wolff, and La Monte Young. Of Cage's overall importance, Charles Hamm writes:

> He has been at the center of the avant–garde in the USA for several decades. The influence of his compositions and his aesthetic thought has been felt all over the world, particularly since World War II; he has had a greater impact on world music than any other American composer of the 20th century. (Hamm 1980, 597)

Cage is the author of several books of essays and poetry, including *Silence* (1961), *A Year from Monday* (1967), *M* (1973), *Empty Words* (1979), *Themes and Variations* (1982), *X* (1982), and *I–VI* (1990); co-author, with Kathleen Hoover, of *Virgil Thomson* (1959); co-editor, with Alison Knowles, of *Notations* (1969); and is the author of a children's book with illustrations by Lois Long titled *Mud Book* (1982). From 1978 through 1992 he made several series of prints and etchings for Crown Point Press. As a composer, Cage began writing music in the early 1930s and remained prolific until his death, producing approximately 350 works.

Cage also won several prestigious awards and honors, including a Guggenheim Fellowship and an award from the American Academy and Institute of Arts and Letters in 1949; election to the American Academy and Institute of Arts and Letters in 1968, to the American Academy of Arts and Sciences in 1978; was made a Commander of the Order of Arts and Letters by the French Minister of Culture in 1982; received an honorary Doctor of the Arts from the California Institute of the Arts in 1986; and the Kyoto Prize in 1989.

Throughout his career Cage also held several brief academic posts. He taught at the Cornish School in 1938–40, the Chicago School of Design in 1941–42, at Black Mountain College in 1948 and again in 1952, Wesleyan University in 1960–61 and again in 1970, the University of Cincinnati in 1967, the University of Illinois at Urbana in 1968–69, and the University of California at Davis in 1969. Towards the end of his life he delivered the prestigious Charles Eliot Norton lectures at Harvard University in 1988–89. In theatre his influence as a teacher was most prominent in the occasional classes given at the New School for Social Research from 1956 to 1960, with students including George Brecht, Dick Higgins, Allan Kaprow, and Jackson Mac Low.

Apart from his pervasive influence as a composer, teacher, and essayist, Cage is most often associated with theatre from his fifty years' collaboration with the dancer and choreographer Merce Cunningham (b. 1919). From the mid-1940s through the early 1950s Cage and Cunningham presented annual concerts of innovative music and dance. With the formation of the Cunningham Dance Company in 1953, Cage continued to be closely associated with Cunningham as a composer, performer, and musical advisor. Cage retired as a musical performer with the Company in 1988, but continued to served as a composer, and advisor until his death. The last Cage/Cunningham collaboration was the gentle, lyrical, romantic, and (atypically) naturalistic dance *Beach Birds* (1991) with Cage's score *FOUR*[3].

Specifically within theatre and performance art, Michael Kirby considers Cage's work to be "the backbone of the new theatre" (Kirby 1969, 77), and Richard Schechner considers Cage to be one of the two most important influences on theatre since World War II (Schechner 1973, 60). Yet, despite his pervasive influence and celebrity within the art world, Cage remains an under-studied figure. There have been several biographical studies (see Tomkins 1968, 69–144; Hamm 1980, 597–603; Stevenson 1982, 3–17; Revill 1992; and Hines 1994, 65–99), as well as general analyses of his work (see Snyder 1970; Griffiths 1981; and Pritchett 1993), but there remains much to be documented, analyzed and interpreted, or clarified. Several individuals are currently working on various studies of Cage's life and work, and the next few years promise several varied approaches to his legacy.

Many journalistic reviews of concerts or performances from the late 1930s through the present have expressed bewilderment, boredom, patronization, or outright hostility toward his work. Such writing tells little or nothing of Cage's aesthetics or of what occurred during a specific performance, but rather express only the personal opinions of the reviewer. The hostile critical interpretation of Cage and his work is summarily articulated by David Tame, who rejects Cage's use of chance procedures and Zen-influenced aesthetics in composition. Tame suggests that "we are invited to embrace a doctrine of aesthetics in which not only have morality and spirituality been disregarded as unnecessary, but no firm standards of any form whatsoever remain," finally concluding that Cage "deserves to be regarded as the arch-enemy of spiritual idealism" in music (Tame 1984, 128; 124).

Tame clings to the past, and tries to make the case that Bach and Beethoven are timeless composers who express universal spiritual values in their music, an ultimately ethnocentric and historically biased view of art which, in Tame's view, also excludes Mussorgsky, Tchaikovsky, Stravinsky, and Schoenberg! A completely opposite view of Cage, as exemplified most noticeably by Ellsworth Snyder, sees Cage's use of chance and Zen Buddhism as being one of the most truly profound expressions of spiritually in art since World War II (Snyder 1970).

Jacques Attali presents a mixed opinion of Cage's work. Attali first considers Cage's music to be a negation, a "contemptuous sneering at the meaning attributed to Art," which is then restated by noting that Cage "is regenerating all of music: he is taking it to its culmination." His conclusion is that Cage's work is "not the new mode of musical production, but the liquidation of the old" (Attali 1984, 136–7).

Attali's interpretation of Cage representing a "contemptuous sneer-ing" is questionable, for this attitude was absent in Cage's personality, nor is it to be found in his compositions, literary writings, or visual works (unless, of course, if one agrees with David Tame). The other charge, that Cage is not really an avant-garde artist but someone at the end of a tradition, is a more difficult matter to decide. Cage addressed this question with his usual optimistic attitude:

> People ask what the avant-garde is and whether it is finished. It isn't. There will always be one. The avant-garde is flexibility of mind. And it follows like day, the night from not falling prey to government and education. Without the avant-garde nothing would get invented. If your head is in the clouds, keep your feet on the ground. If your feet are on the ground, keep your head in the clouds. (Montague 1985, 210)

After Cage's death, it has become fashionable, and all too easy, for conservative critics to vent their judgmental sarcasm. In reviewing important events in classical music during 1992, Edward Rothstein would write:

> Argue that John Cage, whose death in August elicited no end of warm eulogies, was an amusing but overrated inventor. (Rothstein 1992)

(The invention that Rothstein refers is to the prepared piano from 1940, and such is a typical response to Cage's varied output.)

Richard Taruskin's 1993 essay "No Ear For Music" expands upon this patronizing view, which takes Cage's prepared piano works of the 1940s to be his most important music — charming, but comparatively mediocre.

Taruskin particularly faults Cage for being humorless and authoritarian. The charge of being authoritarian seems confused, for Taruskin does not recognize that Cage was — even when using chance procedures or indeterminate notation — fundamentally interested in accuracy, precision, clarity. Cage *could* write "scarey music" but he also composed several humorous works, such as the theatre pieces *Water Music* (1952), or *Water Walk* (1959). In person, Cage was a very charming, funny, often insightful presence. Being with him was a great lesson in etiquette, in tactful sociability. He could not "suffer fools," but was remarkably patient and rarely "lost his cool."

There are two basic views of what is important in Cage's work. Arthur Sabatini presents the first view, which states that the "[literary] writings of John Cage are destined to provoke more varied, and ultimately more enduring, responses than his music" (Sabatini 1989, 74). The other view is expressed by James Pritchett:

> *Considering the pervasive ignorance of Cage's works, we are justified in asking how, if we do not have sufficient knowledge of the music on its own terms, can it be written off as unimportant? It seems quite possible that the depreciation of Cage's music is a result of the imbalance in the critical writing, not a cause of it.* (Pritchett 1989, 251)

This question of interpretation was also answered by Cage:

> *. . .when we're writing music, that's what's important, and when we're writing ideas, that's what's interesting. And I would like to extend it to as many things in my life as I can — to cooking, to answering the telephone. And life actually is excellent at interrupting us.* (Kostelanetz 1988, 19)

I believe that Cage's most important work was in music composition, and that indeterminate notation was his most important invention. Several of the most interesting and complex examples of indeterminate notation are found in his theatre pieces. Theatre is only one aspect of Cage's total productivity, but it involves his work in music, literature, dance, and visual art.

The theatre pieces have not been systematically studied to date. The general interpretation, as exemplified by Henry Sayre, is to view Cage's own works as less important than the resultant influence on the work of others (Sayre 1989, 104–9). The only current essay that attempts to evaluate Cage's work in theatre is by Natalie Schmitt, who provides only an indirect definition of "theatre" and does not evaluate specific works or the development of Cage's ideas and practice over time. Schmitt makes the claim that his theatre is a contemporary correlation to Aristotle's *Poetics* and that Cage's aesthetics are a representation of twentieth-century physics and linguistic scientific models (Schmitt 1982, 17–37). The mental gymnastics involved in comparing Aristotle with Cage are fascinating, yet Schmitt admits that Cage's view is antithetical to Aristotle. Similarly, the use of ideas from physics, as in Einstein's

Relativity and Heisenberg's Uncertainty Principle makes for engaging read-ing, yet Schmitt notes that "in all likelihood Cage cannot understand the mathematics in which these discoveries are expressed and, if he can, he cannot literally translate them into theatrical terms" (Schmitt 1982, 18).

To date, only five of Cage's theatre pieces have been written about in any detail — Stephen Husarik's study of *HPSCHD* (1969) (Husarik 1983), Janetta Petkus's study of *Song Books* (1970) (Petkus 1986), Marjorie Perloff's study of *Roaratorio* (1979) (Perloff 1991), Laura Kuhn's study of *Europeras 1 & 2* (1987) (Kuhn 1992), and Charles Junkerman's study of a *Musicircus* (Junkerman 1993). My study is a general survey of the theatre pieces, first presenting a brief aesthetic background to Cage's first theatre piece *Water Music* (1952); and then discussing the basic theatre pieces arranged by variation or genre, with attention to both the score as well as performance. Ultimately, I have not been able to write about several pieces in desired detail, so the length of my writing on any particular composition thus has no relevance as to its "merit" within Cage's oeuvre.

1

EARLY COMPOSITIONS AND DANCE ACCOMPANIMENTS

The first mature period of John Cage's compositions dates from about 1936 to 1951. This period is marked by several works composed for percussion ensemble and prepared piano. It was also during this period that Cage became involved with modern dance, initially not from any conscious desire to be involved in theatre, but because he found modern dancers were more interested in modern music than classically trained musicians (Tomkins 1968, 83; 88).

Cage's interest in percussion composition was influenced by his studies with Henry Cowell, Arnold Schoenberg, and Oskar Fischinger from about 1934 through 1937. Cage is not the first Western percussion ensemble composer, but he was an early exponent of this genre. The first percussion work in the Western tradition is considered to be Amadeo Roldan's *Ritmicas* (1930), followed by Edgard Varèse's *Ionisation* (1931) (Sollberger 1974). From his studies with Henry Cowell in 1934, and from reading Cowell's book *New Musical Resources* (1935), Cage became interested in using percussion as a practical alternative to tonal composition. Cage would also have known Cowell's percussion ensemble works such as *Ostinato Pianissimo* (1934). Paul Griffiths notes that even in Cage's earliest tonal composition attempts (previous to his first percussion compositions) that the music is based on manipulations of structure rather than melody or harmony (Griffiths 1981, 3–5).

Cage would later recall that many of Schoenberg's classes were concerned with solving various problems and exercises in harmony:

> *Several times I tried to explain to Schoenberg that I had no feeling for harmony. He told me that without a feeling for harmony I would always encounter an obstacle, a wall through which I wouldn't be able to pass. My reply was that in that case I would devote my life to beating my head against that wall — and maybe this is what I've been doing ever since. (Tomkins 1968, 85)*

While Cage has not become known as a harmonic composer, he made several works that are harmonic as well as melodic throughout his career; and even in the percussion works made as formal reaction against Schoenberg's teaching there is a delicate use of various timbres.

While studying with Schoenberg, Cage was also working as an assistant for Oskar Fischinger, a film animation artist. Many of Fischinger's films were "visual music," complex sequences of abstract moving forms set to the music of classical composers such as Bach or Brahms. Fischinger's exploration of visualizing music through film technology also included experiments with synthetic sound tracks made by photographing geometric patterns or images directly onto the sound-track area of the film strip (Russett and Starr 1976, 57–65). Cage would later recall Fischinger's influence:

> He made a remark that impressed me: "Everything has a spirit, and that spirit can be released by setting whatever it is into vibration." That started me off hitting things, striking them, rubbing them, working with percussion, and getting interested in noise. (Montague 1985, 209)

Cage's first composition for percussion ensemble was *Trio* (1936), for three performers. *Trio* marks the first appearance of one of his most famous innovations, the water-gong. Cage had joined a modern dance group at U.C.L.A. as an accompanist and composer, and was asked to write a work for the swimming team's annual water ballet. During rehearsals he discovered that the swimmers could not hear the music underwater. His solution was to lower a gong into the water which, when struck, could be heard by the swimmers (Tomkins 1968, 88).

In 1938 Cage moved to Seattle as a faculty member of the Cornish School. At Cornish he was accompanist and composer for Bonnie Bird's dance company and also organized and conducted a percussion ensemble. It was also at the school that he first met Merce Cunningham, then a student with Bonnie Bird.

Cage first expressed his conceptual use of percussion in his 1937 lecture "The Future of Music: Credo." In this early essay, Cage writes that music will continue to employ not only traditional tonality but also noise and the entire spectrum of possible sounds, including use of electronics. He also is concerned with the formal, structural implications of sound, rather than tonality, in composition:

> The present methods of writing music, principally those which employ harmony and its reference to particular steps in the field of sound, will be inadequate for the composer, who will be faced with the entire field of sound. The composer (organizer of sound) will be faced not only with the entire field of sound but also with the entire field of time. The "frame" or fraction of a second, following established film technique, will probably be the basic unit in the measurement of time. No rhythm will be beyond the composer's reach.
>
> New methods will be discovered, bearing a definite relation to Schoenberg's twelve-tone system. . .and present methods of writing percussion music . . . and any other methods which are free from the concept of a fundamental tone. . . . The principle of form will be our only constant connection with the past. (Cage 1961, 4–5)

Aesthetically, this lecture was a very avant-garde statement in 1937 America, however, Cage's early adult essay was not an entirely new idea. It is still a "student piece," influenced from his recent studies with Schoenberg and Fischinger. The basic ideas are an echo of Luigi Russolo's 1913 Futurist manifesto "The Art of Noise" (in Kirby 1971, 166–174). Both Russolo and Cage stress the need for noise, including everyday sounds, as integral to music; the focus upon rhythm rather than tonality as a fundamental structuring principle; the employment of technology to create new sound sources; and the requirement to score these new musical elements with relative precision. While both essays are similar in content, Cage's lecture does not have Russolo's strident style and is more evocative of what such music might eventually become. Cage's essay, in retrospect, has been termed "prophetic" of his later development in composition (Tan 1989b, 39). In practice, however, Cage's later development into chance and indeterminacy can not be said to be an exact correspondence or alternative method to Schoenberg's twelve-tone system.

The new methods of noise composition that Cage initially explored through the percussion ensemble were basically practical considerations of performance. While the promise of film sound-tracks, wire recording, and electronic instruments such as the Theremin or Sonovox are alluded to in "The Future of Music: Credo," such rare and expensive technology was unavailable to Cage. Percussion instruments were a much more practical and economically feasible way of composing for a field of possible sounds.

At the Cornish School, Cage organized a percussion ensemble, promoting his own work as well as the work of William Russell, Lou Harrison, Ray Green, and J. M. Beyer. This ensemble performed in Seattle and on the West Coast. In a program note to a performance at Reed College on February 14, 1940, Cage wrote:

> *Listening to the music of these composers is quite different from listening to the music, say, of Beethoven. In the latter case we are temporarily protected or transported from the noises of everyday life. In the case of percussion music, however, we find that we have mastered and subjugated noise. We become triumphant over it, and our ears become sensitive to its beauties. (Cage 1940c)*

The percussion ensemble under Cage's direction during the latter 1930s and early 1940s mostly gave instrumental concerts, rather than dance accompaniment, however, the theatrical connotations of purely instrumental percussion performance were not overlooked during this period. Jack Avshalomoff would review the February 14, 1940 concert at Reed College by writing:

> *Performances of this kind should, I am convinced, be heard and not seen (at least until afterwards if the curious are insistent). The distraction caused by what is going on*

prevents the clear reception of the mass of sound as a whole, and this is most important.
(Avshalomoff 1940)

The unconventional instruments, and the performance of such compositions, were novel and thus created an added visual interest as well. Ironically, what Avshalomoff decried in these early percussion ensemble concerts — the interest in visual as well as aural aspects of musical performance — would later become a central component of Cage's own definition of theatre in the early 1950s.

Cage's own compositions for percussion ensemble during the latter 1930s and early 1940s were most influenced by the work of Henry Cowell and William Russell. Cowell's influence, as in his *Ostinato Pianissimo* (1934) or *Pulse* (1939), may heard in Cage's *Imaginary Landscape No. 1* (1939) or *First Construction (in Metal)* (1939). In both the mentioned works by Cowell and Cage, there is a delicate use of percussion instruments that, while structured rhythmically, provide the listener with an unexpected tonal content as well.

The influence of Cage's contemporary William Russell (1905–1992) is more subtle. Cage's percussion ensemble performed several of Russell's compositions, and it was largely with Russell's compositions that the ensemble gained some national attention and notoriety. Russell would cease composition in 1940 to concentrate on studying and documenting hot jazz and its origins in New Orleans, but both Russell and Cage would collaborate on a short essay "Percussion Music and Its Relation To The Modern Dance" published in 1939 (Cage and Russell 1939, 266; 274), where both the artistic, avant-garde, as well as popular, folkloristic roots of percussion are outlined.

Currently Russell is a neglected composer, but by 1932 he was one of the premiere American percussion ensemble composers. A complete retrospective of his work, including revisions, a new piece, and several first performances, was performed on February 24, 1990, by Essential Music at Florence Gould Hall in New York City for Russell's 85th birthday. A CD recording of his complete works was released in 1993.

Russell's compositions are usually brief, lyrical works of sophisticated structure and playful charm. His *Made in America* (1936) is scored for automobile brake drums, tin cans, suitcase, washboard, lion's roar, a drum kit made from found-objects, and a "Baetz' Rhythm Rotor" (an early electronic instrument that produced rhythmic ticks, similar to the contemporary drum machine or beat box) (Kennedy and Wood 1990). Russell's eclectic and innovative choice of instrumentation may also be seen in Cage's percussion works such as *Imaginary Landscape No. 1* (1939) for muted piano, cymbal, and two variable-speed turntables playing frequency records; or *Living Room Music* (1940) for speech quartet and furniture. Cage, like Russell and Cowell, composed for percussion as a practical way of including a field of sound rather than accepted harmonic tones as the province of musical composition and performance.

The three major dance productions that Cage was involved with while at the Cornish School were *The Marriage at the Eiffel Tower* (1938–39), *Imaginary Landscape* (1939), and *Bacchanale* (1940). Bonnie Bird recalls their collaborative process:

> It was mostly talking back and forth, but it wasn't simultaneous. It was as though he sat at the piano and I was on the floor working with the dancers. He would watch what I was doing, frequently, and then he was no doubt making mental notes — maybe he even fiddled around at the piano at times — but usually we talked and he wrote something, and then we tried it out. (Bird 1991)

The first major dance production that Cage was involved with as a composer and percussion conductor was for Bonnie Bird's production of Jean Cocteau's *Les Mariés de la Tour Eiffel* ("The Marriage at the Eiffel Tower"), first written and produced in 1921 (in Benedikt and Wellwarth 1964, 101–115). Various sections of music were composed by Cage, Henry Cowell, and George McKay (a local Seattle composer). The score has not been published, but Cage's manuscript is in the New York Public Library, and the sections by Cowell and McKay are in the music archive at Northwestern University. The music is scored for various toy whistles, sirens, and two pianos. In the surviving music one sees all three composers employing a purposefully comic and satiric mode of expression.

The choreography is not reconstructable, but the principal dancers were Syvilla Fort, Dorothy Herrman, and Merce Cunningham. Bonnie Bird and her husband Ralph Gundlach were the two narrators. An anonymous newspaper clipping reviews the production by noting that the set included mobiles and wooden caricatures of human beings ("Round About" ca. 1939). Bonnie Bird no longer recalls there being any mobiles, but describes the basic mise-en-scene:

> There were two things that looked like phonographs at the side of the stage, and those were supposed to be the record players. I was behind one and my husband was behind the other, and the two of us did the reading of the script.
> The set had a suggestion of the Eiffel Tower in that there were ropes that went from the side, up-stage way down in the corners, left and right, and they went up; and there were cross-bars that suggested the shape of the Eiffel Tower. And there was a ramp that went from up-stage right to about two-thirds of the way across the stage — it was probably about three feet deep, and pushed way up at the back of the stage. In addition, we had a table that was really a flat that was painted to look like it was a table set for a wedding breakfast, and it had a stand behind it so they [the dancers] could put their feet of it, appear as if they were behind, sitting at a table or standing, so that was a kind of life behind this flat, a life to their postures, really. We had a rather small stage, so we couldn't do an awful lot with it, and that was really the essential set piece.
> Then down-stage was the outline of a camera, a sort of old-fashioned tripod

kind of thing, which also looks a little like the front of an engine of a train. So the cow-catcher at the bottom was really like the bottom of the camera itself, and the camera lens was like the headlight at the front of the train. You thought of it as a camera as long as it was right up against the proscenium arch, but when it began to open and slowly move across, it looked like a train because there was this black accordian stuff behind it with little windows that began to open up as the people took off from the train.

And then, I didn't have enough men in the company at that time — these were all students, really — so I thought, well, I really don't need men, the men are like coat-racks, so I created some hat-stands with circular bottoms, and I put on the stand a wire coat-hanger and a buttoneer and a collar and a tie, and a hat on the top of the stand, you know, a top hat for a wedding. And that was the partner for the dancers, so the women danced with these and rolled them around (laughs). It worked wonderfully! It was a substitute for having males that couldn't dance very well anyway (laughs). (Bird 1991)

Imaginary Landscape (1939) was an even more innovative collaboration. Cage's score includes two variable-speed turnables playing frequency records, and is his first composition to incorporate electronic technology. Bonnie Bird recalls that he got the idea to use frequency records from her husband, who was doing research in psychological response to music. Bonnie Bird describes the production:

I had three triangles, and they had a stand. They stood about three feet high. Two were pointed and one was chopped-off at the top, and a figure could curl up behind it and not be seen. And you could lift it up also, so that you could cover your torso so that only your legs were seen, or only a leg if you could hide one leg behind it, and so on. It was really quite a contortion! And then I had a six-foot rectangle made that was just as wide as Merce, and it had a tiny step on it. That could also be held up — it was light, it was cloth-covered, and Merce could stand up and his head would appear at the top with nothing else showing, and he could slide his head down the side by tilting his body and holding everything in place. It was really quite a task!

We did this against a black curtain, and we used beamed lighting from the sides, from down-stage, that would pick up the head or legs, and they were very specific beams, very narrow and clean-cut. What was interesting was that I could move figures walking down-stage, and you would see only the legs walking. Or, I would stretch a body out so that there was a head at one end of the stage, and then you'd see between these triangles a piece of torso, another piece of torso, and legs at the other end — a sort of surreal landscape — and the body would break up. And suddenly it was only arms, or only a head, or a head and legs walking away, so there was a wonderful kind of disconnected quality to the whole thing.

We had quite a time with the music, because it had an arhythmic quality, and we were not used to working with music that we could not hold on to in some way. (Bird 1991)

While *Imaginary Landscape* was still a student production, the primary elements would later become central ideas in the Cage/Cunningham collaborations in the early 1950s, with Cunningham analyzing and breaking down movement into discontinuous parts, and Cage writing music that only shared a common total duration with the choreography.

The final major dance collaboration Cage did at the Cornish School was *Bacchanale* (1940), which marks his first composition for prepared piano. The prepared piano is considered to be Cage's own, original invention (Ripin 1980, 216), however there is some precedent. James Harding writes that at the first performance of Erik Satie's play *Le Piège de Méduse* ("The Ruse of Medusa") "sheets of paper were slipped between the strings of the piano for added musical effect" (Harding 1975, 134). It is unclear whether Harding means the private first performance in 1916 or the public first performance in 1921, however in either case this predates the first prepared piano works by Cage by about twenty years.

There are other precedents with altering the timbre of the piano strings. The Futurist Luigi Russolo invented keyboard instruments called "psofarmoni" which he would describe, in 1926, as being able to imitate sounds such as wind, water, frogs, and cicadas (Kirby 1971, 39). Also, early twentieth century American jazz pianists played the "tack piano," by inserting tumbtacks onto the felt of the hammers. The most familiar tack piano recording is heard in the soundtrack of the "Bojangles of Harlem" dance solo by Fred Astaire in the 1936 film *Swing Time*. It is reminiscent of the sound of a harpsichord. Cage may have used tack piano in the first performance of his *Credo in Us* (1942), discussed later in this chapter.

The Victorian era also had some apparent influence, although this is largely undocumentable. One type of music box had a lever which could raise or lower a bar onto the vibrating comb teeth. The music box sounds as usual with the lever raised — that is, the teeth will then vibrate for a sustained and naturally decaying duration. When the lever is lowered, the metal bar rests, with some pressure, on the tone rods which, when activated, sound and then are quickly muted. This effect was called "banjo."

The genesis of *Bacchanale* came from having to write an accompaniment for the senior recital of Syvilla Fort, a Black dancer and choreographer in Bonnie Bird's company. Bonnie Bird recalls:

> *This was really quite a magnificent dance. She was beginning to explore her own racial heritage, her own background. The dance was really not about being Black or anything like that, but it was about a kind of marvelous celebratory feeling, and had an almost Oriental quality to it. John looked at it, and he came to me and said "I have to have a gamelang orchestra" (laughs). I said, "Fat chance! We have fifty dollars for our entire budget." (Bird 1991)*

Both Cage and Bonnie Bird recall that the prepared piano was discovered by intuition and personal experimentation, but their recollections differ. Cage would recall:

At that time, because I had recently been studying with Arnold Schoenberg, I wrote either twelve-tone music or percussion music. I first tried to find a twelve-tone row that sounded African, and I failed. So I remembered how the piano sounded when Henry Cowell strummed the strings or plucked them, ran darning needles over them, and so forth. I went to the kitchen and got a pie plate and put a book on the strings and saw that I was going in the right direction. The only trouble with the pie plate was that it bounced. So then I got a nail, put it in, and the trouble was it slipped. So it dawned on me to wind a screw between the strings, and that was just right. Then weather stripping and so on. Little nuts around the screws, all sorts of things. (Montague 1985, 209)

Bonnie Bird recalls that the prepared piano was initially discovered by accident. While choreographing *The Marriage at the Eiffel Tower*, she wanted the dancers to come down a brass pole, but when she went to the factory where fire company poles are manufactured, discovered that it was too expensive. Nonetheless she was given a small piece of a brass pole, which she brought into class. As Bird tells the story:

I brought it back to the studio and said to John as I was about to teach a class, "Well, I have to give up that idea because I can not afford a brass pole, so I'll have to think of something else," and John put this on the tray on the piano that would hold the music (laughs). That was a very wobbly tray, and as he started to play the piano for class, it fell off onto the strings, and rolled up the strings that he was playing — in the bass, as I remember it. Well, he was so intrigued with this sound that he got totally involved in rolling this thing up and down and playing with sound. So I turned to the class and said, "We'll just let him go on, we'll go on with the class" (laughs). And so we proceeded to ignore him. . . What was happening was that he was beginning to get the idea for prepared piano. (Bird 1991)

Half of Cage's compositional output from 1940 through 1951 would be works for prepared piano. The earlier examples, such as *A Valentine out of Season* (1944), only use a small gamut of prepared tones and only prepared tones are used in the composition. Cage's most extensive and complex work for prepared piano is *Sonatas and Interludes* (1946–48), requiring 45 prepared tones and including unprepared tones in the composition as well. It is rather difficult to adequately describe the sound of any kind of music in words, but Virgil Thomson's assessment of Cage's prepared piano works has withstood the test of time:

The effect in general is slightly reminiscent, on first hearing, of the Balinese gamelang orchestras, though the interior structure of Mr. Cage's music is not oriental at all. (Thomson 1945)

Listening to the prepared piano works, one also hears a very intricately microtonal organization of sound that is very lyrical and emotionally expressive.

From 1941 through 1942 Cage taught at the Chicago School of Design on the invitation of Maholy-Nagy, and continued giving percussion ensemble performances with a newly organized group. It was through the percussion ensemble compositions and concerts that Cage first received national attention.

Audiences at these early percussion concerts were both bemused and cautious. One particular work, *Three Dance Movements* (1933) by William Russell, gained national newspaper coverage while Cage was still in Chicago. At the conclusion of the third dance, a Foxtrot, a bottle is broken. The concert performance of Russell's work, given at the Arts Club of Chicago on March 1, 1942, was deemed of enough news importance to be an Associated Press story, and in a few days would be the subject of an editorial cartoon in New York City (see Fig. 1). This cartoon reveals a problem of interpretation that continues through the present not only of Cage's work in general, but also of twentieth-century avant-garde music. The cartoonist expresses an amused detachment and patronization of the compositional aesthetics, however there is some wit and charm (usually lacking in later negative reviews of Cage's work), and the inferred political content is, in part, a prophetic statement of Cage's later social consciousness during the mid-to-latter 1960s.

Cage effectively ceased composing for the percussion ensemble after 1943, concentrating on the prepared piano, but two compositions from 1942 represent the high-point of his percussion ensemble accompaniment for theatrical presentation.

On May 31, 1942, radio station WBBM, C.B.S., Chicago presented the half-hour radio drama *The City Wears a Slouch Hat* by Kenneth Patchen with percussion music by John Cage as part of the "Columbia Workshop" series of experimental programming. The play was directed and produced by Les Mitchell, with the actors Les Tremayne, Madelon Grayson, Forrest Lewis, Jonathan Hole, Frank Dane, and John Larkin. The percussion ensemble, under Cage's direction, was Xenia Kashevaroff Cage, Cilia Amidon, Stuart Lloyd, Ruth Hartman, and Claire Oppenheim, who played a wide variety of instruments including tin cans, tom-tom, sandpaper brushes, a fire gong, brass gongs, a water gong, a Chinese rattle, tam-tam, and sound-effects recordings (La Hay 1942).

Patchen's drama is a collage of various vignettes of city life as experienced by a nameless Christ-like character identified only as "The Voice." It is bitter, but not entirely hopeless, view of the violence and hypocrisy in twentieth century society (Patchen 1977, 75–93). The play concludes with The Voice summarizing the previous events of the unconnected narrative with the moral that "...we need more love in the world..." While much of Patchen's script now seems to be somewhat dated and heavy-handed, *The City Wears a Slouch Hat* remains a still-relevant plea for passivism and personal enlightenment in the latter 1990s.

A recording of the broadcast still exists (Patchen and Cage 1942). Much of the acting is now rather dated, and is not a good example of the best

Fig. 1. An editorial cartoon of the Cage Percussion Ensemble (Johnstone and Suhl 1942). The hand-written annotations at the bottom are by Lucretia Cage, the composer's mother, and is included in a scrap-book which she made of her son's early career. Reproduced courtesy of the John Cage Archive, Northwestern University Library.

radio performance style of the period (as in the work of Orson Welles).

The recording is most valuable as a documentation of the way Cage's percussion ensemble sounded under his own direction. There is a great deal of nervous energy and emotion in the performance. The energy of the musicians is no doubt a reflection of the haste in which the score was composed and rehearsed. Cage would recently recall the circumstances of collaborating with Kenneth Patchen on the radio play:

[Question: How did this come about?]

I guess through the work with percussion orchestra. I had the idea that — and also from the radio — that the sound effects department of the radio was like an extension of a percussion orchestra — in my mind — and so I thought that the sounds of the play could be ambient to the activity in the play. If, for instance, if the play was about living in the country, then it could be birds, and so on.

[Question: How was it that you worked with Kenneth Patchen?]

My first choice was Henry Miller, and Henry Miller didn't want to write anything for the radio. The next person I asked was Kenneth Patchen, because I admired his book called The Journal of Albion Moonlight *[1940]. I don't have any impression that he wasn't satisfied with the result. I liked what he did.*

[Question: Were the sounds used in the play Patchen's idea or yours?]

That was my idea. So I wrote a whole score for that play, and I took it to the sound-effects department of the radio and they said it was impossible, and I said why, and they said it was too expensive, that I'd used too much compressed air — which was one of their things — and each time they used the compressed air it cost a certain amount of money — I forget how much — and I had used it a great deal, and so they said I had to write something else. So I gave up my first idea of using city sounds and went back to the percussion orchestra, which I had. I had a trained group in Chicago, and I sat up for three days and three nights and wrote the whole half-hour of music at the very last minute, and rehearsed it, and made the performance. (Cage 1987e)

The first score, unperformed, is no longer extant. The second, broadcast score was recently again performed with Patchen's script by Essential Music in New York City on October 23, 1990 with Jackson Mac Low as The Voice. The score has since been published by C. F. Peters (Cage 1942a).

Encouraged by the mostly positive mail response, Cage left Chicago and moved to New York City in the late spring of 1942. During that summer he lived in the apartment of Jean Erdman and Joseph Campbell. In exchange for paying rent for those few months, Cage composed his last major percussion ensemble accompaniment, *Credo in Us*.

Jean Erdman recalls that the genesis of this piece took place during a New Year Eve's party in 1941. Joseph Campbell suggested that Jean (his wife) and Merce Cunningham (now in New York as a principal soloist with the Martha Graham Company) should present a joint dance recital, and that John Cage should compose some music:

. . .So when the evening was over, we were decided, we were going to do this. So there was the plan, how would Merce and I work together? Well, neither of us wanted to be choreographed, we both wanted to choreograph, so what we did was to agree on two or three duet ideas, and then each of us compose our own parts. We just had a sketch of the opening and closing, and then each one choreographed his or her own part.

This was based on a script that Merce had written, but he didn't want anyone in the world to know he'd ever written anything, so we just pretended we'd gotten it out of a French magazine and translated it (laughs)! It was a kind of criticism of our own bourgeois backgrounds — the parents having a little too much trouble, or something — it was in the air that young people always had some criticism of the generation before. The script is the secret. We had words that we said, we had lines that we threw out, but it was all done as a dance piece. (Erdman 1989)

The script by Merce Cunningham apparently no longer exists, and one can not tell from Cage's score which sections were duets or solos, but the music is one of his stylistically most important works and foreshadows several later developments in his compositions.

Credo in Us is scored for pianist, two percussionists who play tin cans, gong, tom-tom and electric buzzer, and a fourth performer who plays the radio or a phonograph. There is no hierarchy of instrumentation, as in a conventional piano concerto, but all are equally represented. The pianist plays unprepared piano, and at times also mutes the strings or plays the body as a percussion instrument. Although there is no indication in the score, Jean Erdman also recalls that a tack piano was used (tacks inserted into the felt hammers) in the original performance, as a reference to early jazz (Erdman 1989). The conventionally notated piano part includes an Oriental-sounding theme, rhythmic structures in ostinati or block-chords, and jazz influenced boogie-woogie. The two percussionists play rhythmic figures as well as liminally melodic counterpoint. The fourth performer, on phonograph and/ or radio, has only a notated indication of duration and amplitude.

The opening bars appear in Fig. 2. In this example, one sees that the piano part is conventionally notated. The two percussionists are also in conventional notation, however the pitches are only relative indications of higher or lower timbres. The phonograph/radio part is the most indeterminate notation. In this example the performer is instructed to use a phonograph. Later in the score, page 18, one is instructed to use a radio. In his preface to the score, Cage writes of this part:

If Radio is used, avoid programs during national or international emergencies, if Phonograph use some classic: e.g. Dvorak, Beethoven, Sibelius or Shostakovich. (Cage 1942b)

The result is a notation indeterminate of its actual sound. The performer, rather than the composer, determines what actual recordings are to be played. In playing the radio, there is also an element of chance and nonintention that

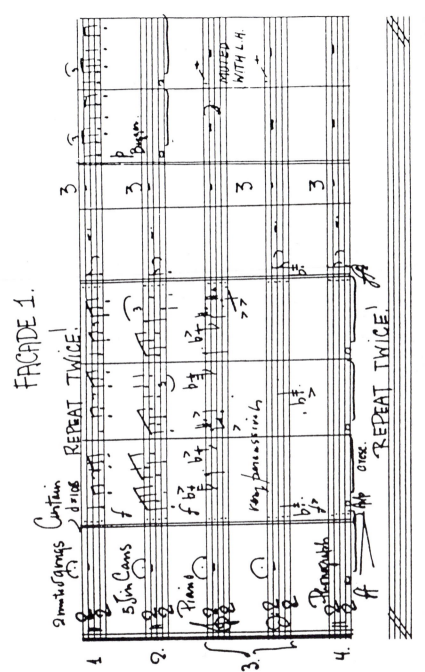

Fig. 2. The opening measures of *Credo in Us* (1942), showing an early use of indeterminate notation; © 1962 Henmar Press Inc.

can not be predetermined by either the composer or performer.

Cage would work with Jean Erdman again in 1946 (*Ophelia*) and in 1951 (*Imaginary Landscape No. 5*), as well as with Pearl Primus in 1944 (*Our Spring Will Come*), and Louise Lippold in 1948 (*In a Landscape*), but it is with Merce Cunningham that Cage has become most identified with music for dance accompaniment.

Cunningham dates their formal collaboration from their first joint solo recital in 1944 with pieces including *Totem Ancestor* and *Root of an Unfocus* (Cunningham 1982, 107). The choreography for the early Cage/Cunningham collaborations, including Cunningham's dance-play *Four Walls* (1944) and the ballet *The Seasons* (1947), is now unrecoverable, and only Cage's music remains. The exception is *Totem Ancestor*, with Cunningham's solo documented in Labanotation by Lena Belloc and edited by Ann Hutchinson (Cage 1942c). Detailed analysis of Cunningham's solo must wait for more specialized study by a Labanotation expert, but what one basically sees in the dance notation is a virtuosic use of body levels and asymmetrical gestures. Cage's score is for prepared piano, and is basically rhythmic in content.

Four Walls is now considered to be the first major Cage/Cunningham collaboration. Once thought to be a lost work, the score was rediscovered by Richard Bunger in the latter 1970s. A six-minute silent color film was taken of Cunningham and other dancers, but is too fragmentary from which to reconstruct the basic choreography (Cunningham 1944). It was initially performed only once, on August 22, 1944, at the Perry-Mansfield Workshop in Steamboat Springs, Colorado. Eric Salzman, in his notes to Richard Bunger's recording, writes:

> *Neither a complete script of the work nor a program of the performance seem to have survived but the subject was some kind of family psychodrama with a father, a mother (played by Leora Dana), a girl (Julie Harris), a boy (Merce Cunningham), a group of six "near-people" and another of six "mad-ones." (Salzman 1989)*

The second public performance of *Four Walls* was by Margaret Leng Tan (piano), Andrea Goodman (singer), with choreography and dance by Sin Cha Hong at the Asia Society in New York on May 17, 1985 (Program 1985). The music is written exclusively on the white keys of the piano, and has a remarkably thin but sustained sonic texture. Michele Porzio notes that Cage's score is representative of "not the four walls of a room but those of the mind," and that it is the first of Cage's compositions to use silence (a *tacet* of 44 bars in Number II) as integral to music and listening (Porzio 1992, 30; 34).

The concept used in these early collaborations is explained by Cunningham:

> *What was involved was a "macro-miscroscopic rhythmic structure" in which the large parts were related to the small parts in divisions of time. This was a way of working*

between the music and the dance that allowed them to be separate, coming together only at the structural points. . . This use of time structure allowed us to work separately, Cage not having to be with the dance except at structural points, and I was free to make the phrases and movements within the phrases vary their speeds and accents without reference to a musical beat, again only using the structural points as identification between us. (Cunningham 1982, 107–108)

Such compositions by Cage during the 1940s were made according to what he called the "square-root formula." A concrete example is in the first of *Two Pieces* (1946) for piano. It is written in ten sections of ten measures (or, 10 x 10, hence the designation "square-root"), with each of the ten sections subdivided into measures of three-five-two. There is a limited gamut of tones that are arranged in short harmonic or melodic fragments within the predetermined structures of measures. Figure 3 presents a thematic analysis of the first piece from *Two Pieces*. Each square on the graph of Fig. 3 equals one measure of music, and each letter from a through p represents a tonal event or theme. A horizontal line represents a sustained tone or tones from the previous measure. An S with a horizontal line represents silence. There are twenty measures of silence in total, and since the work is not for a dance accompaniment (as in *Four Walls*), silence becomes an even more integral

a	b	c	a	b	d---	----	----	e--	----
e	–	–	S	–	–	–	–	f	–
f_1--	----	f---	----	f_1--	----	----	----	a	b_1
a	b	c	a	b	d---	----	----	g	h
g---	----	----	g	h	g---	----	----	S--	----
i	j--	----	i	j_1--	----	i_1--	----	S--	----
i	j--	----	i--	----	----	S--	----	i_1-	----
i--	----	----	k	l	i_1--	----	k	S--	----
i_1	m	n	o	p---	----	p_1--	----	S--	----
o	p--	----	S--	----	----	----	----	o	p

Fig. 3. Thematic analysis by measures of the first piece from *Two Pieces* (1946). Lower-case letters are motifs; a letter with a number indicates a slight variation; letters followed by a long dash indicate a sustained tone or tones; the capital S is silence.

structural and aesthetic component in the process of composition, performance, and reception.

Another significant influence on Cage's work was his exposure to the work of Erik Satie, beginning in the mid-1940s. When Cage and Cunningham were first at Black Mountain College during the summer of 1948, Cage presented a series of lectures and performances of Satie's music. The finale was the production of Satie's proto-absurdist play *Le Piège de Méduse* ("The Ruse of Medusa") on August 14. The script was translated by Mary Caroline Richards, with sets by William and Elaine de Kooning, and direction by Arthur Penn and Helen Livingston. The cast included Elaine de Kooning as Frisette, Medusa's daughter; Merce Cunningham as Jonas, Baron Medusa's mechanical monkey; and Buckminster Fuller as Baron Medusa. John Cage played the piano accompaniment to the seven monkey dances, with Cunningham's own choreography (M. Harris 1987, 154–156).

Cage's work shares a common sensibility with Satie in compositions that may often irritate middle-class taste and sensibilities; an irrelevant (and sometimes irreverent) sense of humor; an interest in structure; a seemingly innocent yet mature insight into the significance of mundane or trivial events; a restrained although passionately engaged emotional content beneath the veneer of impersonality; and the inherent calligraphic beauty of their handwritten musical scores. Cage held Satie to be a model composer through the rest of his life. His last dance composition for Merce Cunningham was *FOUR*[3] (1991), which includes "chance determined variations of the cantus firmus and the counterpoints" of Satie's *Vexations* (Cage 1991b).

In 1945 Cage began to study Indian music and philosophy with Gita Sarabhai, who, when asked what was the purpose of music in Indian philosophy, told him: "To sober the mind and thus make it susceptible to divine influences" (Cage 1961, 158). Also during this time Cage read Ananda Coomaraswamy's book *The Transformation of Nature in Art*, which contained the statement: "Art is the imitation of nature in her operation" (Cage 1961, 100). These two ideas would be central to Cage for the rest of his life, however the application changed with chance and indeterminacy in the 1950s.

Cage initially used Coomaraswamy's "imitation of nature in her manner of operation" in reference to the nine Rasas or permanent emotions in traditional Indian aesthetics. Examples of compositions made in this manner include *Sonatas and Interludes* (1946–48) for prepared piano, the ballet score of *The Seasons* (1947), *String Quartet in Four Parts* (1950), and the score for Cunningham's *Sixteen Dances* (1951). *Sixteen Dances* is the last of Cage's compositions to be made from an intentional, subjective, intuitive, emotional expression. It is also, ironically, the first of Cunningham's works to employ chance procedures in making the choreography. Cunningham writes that he first made the rhythmic structures for the individual dances, which were then used by Cage to write the music (Cunningham 1982, 110). The emotionally based dances of *Sixteen Dances* are:

Solo:	*Anger*
Trio:	*Interlude*
Solo:	*Humor*
Duet:	*Interlude*

Solo:	*Sorrow*
Quartet:	*Interlude*
Solo:	*Heroic*
Quartet:	*Interlude*

Solo:	*Odious*
Duet:	*Interlude*
Solo:	*Wondrous*
Trio:	*Interlude*

Solo:	*Fear*
Quartet:	*Interlude*
Duet:	*Erotic*
Quartet:	*Tranquility*

For the composition of *Sixteen Dances*, as also in *Concerto for Prepared Piano and Chamber Orchestra* (1951), Cage made charts of musical elements, moving from square to square akin to the movements of pieces on a chessboard. The musical materials and moves on the graphs were made by personal, intuitive choice. William Brooks writes that in the third piece from *Sixteen Dances*, Cage "expresses 'humor' by means of extreme dynamic and timbral contrasts; while movement IX, the 'odious,' is pervaded by finicky ostinati" (Brooks 1984). The problem is that without recourse to a program, one does not necessarily perceive the music as being expressive of the intended emotional state. Cage himself would recognize this lack of communication through music as "a Tower of Babel" (Tomkins 1968, 97).

The solution to this crisis in composition was resolved through attending Daisetz T. Suzuki's lectures on Zen Buddhism at Columbia University from 1949 through 1951. Cage learned from Zen to avoid the ego, likes and dislikes, and to instead welcome the moment without the intervention of intention or desire, to transcend language, conceptual thought, and in the process gain enlightenment. The study of Zen altered Cage's initial understanding of Coomaraswamy which was amended as: "The highest purpose is to have no purpose at all. This puts one in accord with nature in her manner of operation" (Cage 1961, 155). The "manner of operation" that Cage found was chance operations structured through reference to the *I Ching*. The *I Ching*, or "Book of Changes," is an ancient Chinese sacred text for divination and meditation. It has been called "the cradle of Chinese culture," and has been given the authority and reverence bestowed on *The Bible* in the West (Jou 1984, 113). The *I Ching* consists of 64 hexagrams (six-line figures) made of broken (yin) and unbroken (yang) lines, with commentary on each hexagram and each individual line. The hexagrams are found by chance procedures, either manipulating yarrow sticks or tossing coins. The *I Ching*, in English translation by Cary F. Baynes from Richard Wilhelm's German translation, was given to Cage by Christian Wolff in late 1950. Cage immediately saw similarities between the structure of the *I Ching* and his intuitively made composition charts. The *I Ching* offered an intricate methodology based upon chance, rather than personal expression or intention. Chance procedures were first used by Cage as in composing *Imaginary Landscape No. 4* (1951) for twelve radios, and *Music of Changes* (1951) for piano.

Imaginary Landscape No. 4, composed in April, 1951, is a chance composition in determinate notation. It is scored for twelve radios, with two performers stationed at each radio, one playing the radio station dial, the other controlling the amplitude and timbre. The duration is written in conventional music notation, whole notes through sixteenth notes, placed on the conventional five-line staff. A note placed higher on the staff refers to a higher kilocycle frequency, and a note placed lower on the staff refers to a lower kilocycle frequency, with the frequency number written above the staff (Cage 1951b). While the notation is determinate, the actual performance of playing radio stations results in events which can not be foreseen, and thus each performance will differ.

The first performance of *Imaginary Landscape No. 4*, conducted by Cage at Columbia University's McMillin Theatre on May 2, 1951, is one of the most famous premieres of his entire career. When the piece was performed at the close of the program, it was around midnight, and several radio stations in the New York area had already gone off the air for the night. The resultant performance was thus much more silent than indicated in the score. Arthur Berger, reviewing the performance would write:

> *If anything was amusing, it was merely the sight of Mr. Cage earnestly conducting an ensemble of some of our finest musicians in a series of embarrassing silences and, at best, the shreds of broadcasts you get at home when you turn the dial rapidly. The word "Korea" recurred, and applause greeted bits of a Mozart violin concerto, which came as a balm to listeners eager for such pleasing sounds after an evening of "modernism." (Berger 1951)*

The audience's disappointment was also shared by Virgil Thomson and

Henry Cowell. Thomson later told Cage that he had "better not perform a piece like that before a paying public" (Tomkins 1968, 114), and Cowell would write that the radios "were unable to capture programs diversified enough to present a really interesting specific result," ultimately becoming a "failure to communicate" (Cowell 1952, 126).

Cage, however, was not dissatisfied with the performance, but welcomed the unintended silences. Several years later a journalist would report that Cage. . .

> . . .described it as a venture in "minimal art," and he compared it to a painting which incorporated only the most minute variations in color, a painting which, in other words, stood on the line between art and a blank wall. (Daseler 1970)

While Cage had not intended *Imaginary Landscape No. 4* to contain as much silence as actually occurred during the first performance, he was already concerned with silence and nonintentional content. In a March 14, 1951, interview with *The Hartford Times* made just previous to composing the work, Cage stated:

> Silence to my mind is as much a part of music as sound. Now, starting with the concept, we go on to the accepted qualities of music — pitch, timbre, volume and duration. Which of these partakes of both silence and sound? Only duration. Both silence and sound have duration.
>
> Therefore, I take my sounds when I have decided what they are going to be and place them in this background of silence. This reduces the structure of the composition to pure rhythm, nothing else.
>
> Also, I make no attempt to "say" anything. Beethoven wrote from a subjective emotion which he objectified in his work. It, and the sounds I use, exist solely for their own sake unrelated to anything else. ("Silence, Sound in Composition Are Stressed" 1951)

These ideas from *Imaginary Landscape No. 4* continue in *Imaginary Landscape No. 5*. The score is dated January 12, 1952, and was written for Jean Erdman's dance solo *Portrait of a Lady* (Cage 1952a). This is Cage's first work for magnetic tape, and continues the use of chance procedures, but in a less deterministic notation. The score is a block-graph. Each square equals three inches of tape. In total there are eight simultaneous tracks made from any 42 records. Notated is a duration and amplitude for each of the 42 records, however there is no indication of what the records should be. For *Portrait of a Lady* Cage used 42 jazz records that Jean Erdman used in her studio for jazz improvisation dance exercises (Erdman 1989).

The original tape version of the score has a rather dense sound, with only occasional silences of two to five seconds (Cage 1952b). The finished tape is a fixed and unalterable object, however the score could be realized with any 42 records, not necessarily 1940s jazz. Jean Erdman recalls that Cage did not initially want to use jazz material, and that it was through using the jazz records through chance procedures that he was able to avoid any decisions involved with personal taste or expressivity (Erdman 1989). The actual score of *Imaginary Landscape No. 5* is thus an instance of notation indeterminate of its performance. It is the performer of the score, rather than the composer, who finally determines what the content will be. The only basic contribution that the composer provides is how it is to be done.

Chance and indeterminacy are the two primary concepts involved with Cage's theatre pieces from 1952 through 1992. Neither is synonymous with the other, and both are at the center of Cage's still controversial reputation. The theatre pieces discussed in the following chapters are complex examples of chance and/or indeterminacy. To avoid any major confusion or disapproval by the reader, both terms must be briefly defined for this study.

"Chance" is perceptively defined as being two types by the poet Jackson Mac Low and the physicist Karl Popper. Mac Low distinguishes between "systematic" and "impulsive" chance. "Systematic chance" means using objective methods of random orders such as in using dice, cards, random-digit tables, or the *I Ching*. "Impulsive chance" is defined through the example of the painter Jackson Pollock:

> *He has often been said to have worked by chance, but his was a highly controlled kind of chance that had to do with his personality & how he flung things around. He was real careful where he was flinging things even though the exact placement & area of the drip or squiggle of paint was not entirely defined by him consciously. (Mac Low 1978, 171–172)*

Karl Popper also distinguishes between two types of chance. The first might be termed "causal chance," which Popper defines as. . .

> *. . .due to the independence of two causal chains which happen, accidentally, to interfere at some place and time, and so combine in bringing about the chance event. . .anybody furnished in advance with sufficiently full information about the relevant events could have predicted what was bound to happen. It was only* the incompleteness of our knowledge *which gave rise to this kind of chance.*

Popper's other type is "absolute chance":

> *According to quantum mechanics, there are elementary physical processes which are not further analyzable in causal chains, but which consist of so-called "quantum jumps"; and a quantum jump is supposed to be an absolutely unpredictable event which is controlled by neither causal laws nor by the coincidence of causal laws, but by probabilistic laws alone. (Popper 1982, 125)*

For the purposes of this study, Cage's use of chance refers to Mac Low's "systematic chance" and to Popper's "absolute chance," with the amendation by George Brecht that. . .

> . . .*events are defined as due to chance in a relative way. There is no absolute chance or random event, for chance and randomness are aspects of the way in which we structure our universe. (Brecht 1966, 2)*

Indeterminacy, or indeterminism, is defined by Webster's dictionary as "not determinate, inexact in its limits, nature, etc., not yet settled, concluded, or known," and as "the doctrine that the will is free or to some degree free, or that one's actions and choices are not altogether determined by a sequence or causes independent of one's will." The intellectual arguments for or against free will are entirely out of the scope or intent of this study. In this study, indeterminacy refers to the way in which Cage invents a variety of notation systems that provide a bounded, limited range of possible events or actions which are then to be determined by the individual performer or performers. The notations are indeterminate of a specific, repeatable content, but the resultant performance is finally a determinate act. Many of the works to be discussed are in indeterminate notation.

Cage has defined "theatre" this way:

> *I try to made definitions that won't exclude. I would simply say that theatre is something which engages both the eye and the ear. The two public senses are seeing and hearing; the senses of taste, touch, and odor are more proper to intimate, non-public situations. The reason I want to make my definition that simple is so one could view everyday life itself as theatre. (Kirby and Schechner 1965, 50)*

This is the definition of "theatre" used in selecting Cage's compositions designated here as "theatre pieces," that is, works which are not purely meant for dance accompaniment, but compositions which in themselves are aural as well as visual in performance.

Apart from his practical experience in writing dance accompaniments, the plays by Patchen and Satie, and the visual attention generated by using unconventional instruments in percussion concerts, Cage's early influences in theatre are unconcerned with "drama," "playwriting," or "acting." Cage would later recall:

> *I was among those dissatisfied with the arts as they were, and as Europe had given them to us. . . I just looked at my experience in the theatre, realized I bought a ticket, walked in, and saw this marvelous curtain go up with the possibility of something happening behind it and then nothing happened of any interest whatsoever. . . I can count on one hand the performances that struck me as being interesting in my life. They were* Much Ado About Nothing, *when I was in college [1928–30], it was done by the Stratford-upon-Avon Players. Nazimova in* Ghosts. *Laurette Taylor*

in Glass Menagerie. *The Habima Theatre's* Oedipus Rex *in 1950 or thereabouts.*
[Pause] I run out. . . (Kostelanetz 1980b, 53)

The final significant influence on Cage's development towards theatre is from the virtuoso musician and composer David Tudor. Tudor was born in Philadelphia in 1926, studied piano and composition with Irma and Stefan Wolpe, and moved to New York in 1947 to accompany modern dance groups. In the late 1940s he met composer Morton Feldman, who in turn introduced Tudor to Cage. Cage had returned from Europe in the fall of 1949 with the manuscript of the *Second Piano Sonata* by Pierre Boulez, and was looking for a pianist who could master the intricate and difficult score. Tudor performed the Boulez sonata in 1950 and became a specialist in avant-garde piano compositions, performing works by Boulez, Feldman, Karlheinz Stockhausen, Sylvano Bussotti, Christian Wolff, Earle Brown, and George Brecht, but it is with Cage's compositions that Tudor is most often recognized as a performer. It was Tudor's extraordinary prowess as a pianist that led Cage to compose *Music of Changes* in 1951. He has been the primary musician for Merce Cunningham from 1952 through the present.

During the early 1960s Tudor, along with Cage, was a pioneer in the performance of live electronic music. He also is an innovative composer and inventor of new music. Since the 1960s he has designed and manufactured his own electronic sound-sources, and has composed works such as *Rainforest* (1968), *Pulsars* (1970), and *Five Stone Wind* (1988). He has taught at various colleges in the United States, Europe, and India, and was one of the four core artists who collaborated on the Pepsi Pavillion for Expo '70 in Osaka, Japan. He has also collaborated with the visual artist Jacquiline Monnier on several environmental installations.

David Tudor has rarely performed as a pianist since the 1960s, concentrating instead on live electronic music, but as a pianist he is known for his extraordinary ability at sight-reading, his meticulous and thorough intellectual approach to the score, and an unsurpassed technical execution in performance (Schonberg 1960, 49–50). When listening to Tudor's recordings of Cage's *Concert for Piano and Orchestra* (1957–58) in 1958 or Earle Brown's *December 1952* (1952) released in 1974, one hears precise control of disparate dynamics with widely separated keyboard areas, performed with incredible speed. In audial/visual works, such as Cage's theatre pieces, Tudor's physical agility became noticeable not only from his meticulous approach, but from the efficient and understated quality of gesture as well. One review of Tudor performing aural/visual compositions in the late 1950s notes that he ". . .is not only an excellent pianist, but also a good acrobat" (Siff 1959).

Tudor's approach to gesture is not to use gesture for it's own sake (unless this is integral to the specific composition) but as a means of sound-production. Harold Schonberg, in his essay on Tudor, writes:

> *Most people consider him a strange character. Words used to describe him are "enigmatic," "mystical," "an enigma," "permanently concentrated." On stage he goes about his business with a poker face, no matter how wildly his fingers are flying, no matter where he may be located physically (inside the piano, say). On the rare occasions he smiles, the extreme corners of his lips turn up literally up at right angles. It is a very mysterious, inner smile. (Schonberg 1960, 53–54)*

Many who know of Tudor's work speak of him in awe. Philip Corner has said:

> *We can take his virtuosity and intelligence for granted. It's never self-expressive, there's nothing gratuitous, there's nothing extra, it's just this thing getting done. It's not personal in any of the ordinary senses that we talk about personality, it is maybe personality at its most restricted, least out-going before it becomes impersonal. It's not only not playing to the audience, he's not playing to himself either. He's just playing. (Corner 1989)*

It must also be mentioned that David Tudor is a very warm, gentle, and selfless person beneath his usual shyness. For all of his reputation for dissonant and noisy music performance, Tudor uses his ears in a remarkably sensitive, subtle, and emotional as well as cerebral manner.

Many of the works by Cage discussed in the following chapters were first performed by David Tudor. John Cage has said of him:

> *In all my works since 1952, I have tried to achieve what would seem interesting and vibrant to David Tudor. Whatever succeeds in the works I have done has been determined in relationship to him. . . David Tudor was present in everything I was doing. . . Today [1970] he is present in himself. And I am truly very happy about that. (Cage and Charles 1981, 178)*

The first of Cage's theatre pieces — which fulfills Cage's own definition of "theatre" — is *Water Music* (1952). It is here that this study will address Cage's work in more detail.

2

WATER MUSIC, WATER WALK, AND SOUNDS OF VENICE: EARLY VARIATIONS ON CHANCE COMPOSED THEATRE PIECES IN DETERMINATE NOTATION

Water Music

Water Music, composed in the spring of 1952 (Cage 1952d), is the first example of John Cage's theatre pieces, theatre being, according to Cage, "something which engages both the eye and the ear" (Kirby and Schechner 1965, 50). The six minute and forty second composition is for a pianist who, in addition to using the keyboard, also employs a radio, various whistles, a deck of cards, containers of water, a wooden stick, four piano preparation objects, and a stop-watch. The piece is generally programmed as *Water Music*, although it may be identified as the date or place of performance (Cage 1952d). It was first performed by David Tudor on May 2, 1952 at the New School for Social Research, New York City, and was programmed as "66 W. 12" (the street address for the performance); when Tudor next performed it, at Black Mountain College on August 12, 1952, it was titled "Aug. 12, 1952" (Dunn 1962, 43).

David Tudor would perform *Water Music* at least nine times from 1952 through 1960 (Dunn 1962, 43). Of his performance, he recalls:

> It was very enjoyable, and not so easy to do — you know, the sounds are very special — like the sound of the duck whistle in a bowl of water [from 0.30 through 0.525 in the score], and the duck is supposed to die, so you had a whistle with a wide mouth. It's a very special sound.
>
> I remember that the sounds are very important, and how difficult the radio was to play because of the timing. And each radio is different, and where to tune it.
>
> One of the nicest things that happened was when I was playing it in London in 1954, and there is an occurrence where you turn on the radio for three seconds and then turn it off [at 3.505 in the score], and I turned it on — (laughs) — 'These sounds are coming to you through the courtesy of the British Broadcasting Corporation" (laughs).
>
> I wouldn't hesitate to smile, but I was a very dedicated performer. I made a point of making it very straight, because that's what it is. (Tudor 1989a)

David Tudor's straight-faced, no-nonsense performance style with *Water Music* and the many other compositions that he has performed through the present, has become the standard for all later performers of Cage's work in general.

After David Tudor, the three significant performances of *Water Music* have been by Ellsworth Snyder, Don Gillespie, and Margaret Leng Tan. Ellsworth Snyder wrote the first doctoral dissertation on Cage (1970), and is one of the most reliable and insightful scholars in Cage studies. Snyder recalls performing *Water Music* several times during the 1960s and early 1970s at colleges through the mid-West. He especially remembers using the radio, noting it must be conveniently placed in relationship to the keyboard (Snyder 1989).

Perhaps the most important of Synder's *Water Music* performances was on April 6, 1991, at the First Unitarian Church in Madison, Wisconsin. On that occasion, he premierred *ONE* [5] (1990), a solo piano work which Cage composed for Synder in recognition of his scholarly work, as well as his deft, subtle pianism. The basic floorplan of score-poster, piano, and objects appears in Fig. 4. Synder's physical arrangement is basically the same as used by the other performers, the only difference that he had two posters mounted for better readability by the audience.

Ellsworth Snyder's performance persona in playing *Water Music* is almost transparent, simply and accurately following the score. There is nothing purposefully self-expressive or overtly "theatrical" in his approach, and his performance may well be the most "David Tudoresque" in comparison with the other contemporary pianists. Snyder's persona is understated, lyrical, and intense without seeming forced. His gestures are small and efficient, and do not call attention to themselves apart from the sounds. For

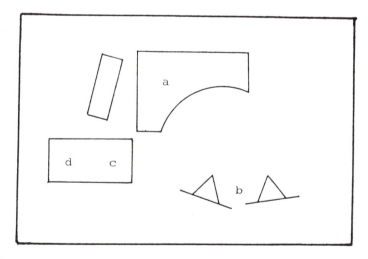

Fig. 4. Ellsworth Snyder's floorplan for *Water Music* at the First Unitarian Church, Madison, Wisconsin, on April 6, 1991. The symbols refer to: a is the piano; b shows the two score posters, each mounted on an easel; c is the radio; and d is the position of the two containers to pour water.

instance, when Snyder shuffled and dealt playing cards onto the open piano strings at 2.195, his attention was in doing the required event within the time-frame and not in making any overtly visual statement. Perhaps the most memorable moment during this performance was when at one point he tuned the radio dial, and a 1940s jazz piano-solo recording of "It Had To Be You" was heard. Many in the audience were not sure whether to respond with laughter or silence, but John Cage, also in attendance, laughed with great delight at this unforeseen occurrence.

Don Gillespie, Cage's publication editor at C. F. Peters, performed *Water Music* at three important Cage concerts in New York from the early 1970s through the early 1980s. His first notable performance was at The Kitchen on December 7, 1973, which John Rockwell would note as having "a sly wit and precision" (Rockwell 1973). Gillespie would later perform *Water Music* at the marathon day-long event Wall-to-Wall John Cage at Symphony Space on March 13, 1982, and again at the 10th Anniversary Concert of Symphony Space in the spring of 1983. In appreciation of his performance, the composer Philip Corner comments:

> *Dare I say, the best performance I ever saw was by Don Gillespie. He did a* wonderful *performance! Both David Tudor and Don Gillespie are very serious, but the difference to me is that Don presents a kind of very strong, almost aggressive persona — not that he's trying to do anything in particular, but very determined and very, somehow, charged — whereas while everything David does is very serious, it just seems as if he's doing a job. (Corner 1989)*

Since I have not witnessed Tudor's performance of *Water Music*, it is difficult to corroborate Corner's subjective comparison of Tudor and Gillespie, however one could also restate that Gillespie's persona is passive but focused, while Tudor's general persona is complex and mysterious. Apart from the thorny issue of subjective critical interpretation, Gillespie performs *Water Music* very much in the manner of Tudor's self-characterization of "making it very straight." For instance, when Gillespie inserted four piano preparation objects between the strings at 2.5475, his gestures were understated and efficient, and did not detract from the sounds that were produced.

Curiously, both Snyder and Gillespie are scholar-pianists, but have been rather unarticulate with discussing performance practice. Gillespie prefers to defer to the performance of Margaret Len Tan (Gillespie 1988). Tan specializes in playing the interior of the piano and is interested in the visual as well as aural aspects of piano performance. *Water Music* has been in her repertoire since the mid-1980s. She comments:

> *I think of the piece as being highly choreographed — it is what I call "pianistic choreography." I approach it as theatre, where I feel I am acting it as much as playing it. It involves a total use of the body.*

> *For instance, pouring water [at 4.4875 and 5.4525 in the score] is not as easy*
> *as it seems. The first time you have to pour fast and the second time slower. I first*
> *practiced it with a stop–watch at the kitchen sink. It probably looked very peculiar to*
> *see me practice, but you have to do that, because it's locked into a time–frame.*
>
> *By working this way I discovered that the reason Cage asks the performer to*
> *use a stop–watch, and the reason that he has occurrences at a quarter or three–quarters*
> *of a second, is because it forces you to move very rhythmically, and very precisely. (Tan*
> *1989a)*

The most memorable performace Tan recalls was at Rotterdam in December, 1988. At one point when she turned on the radio, the station announcer was talking about John Cage, who had been in Holland two weeks previous to her concert. The surprising coincidence was a delight to both Tan and the audience, and many afterward asked if she had planned it!

Tan's performance is very disciplined, exacting, and faithful to Cage's score, but she presents a very different quality of gesture in comparison with the other *Water Music* performers. Her performance persona is very willful, rigidly formal, and aggressive in focus. Her gestures thus appear more noticeable and isolated from the produced sounds. Her gestures are also rather brittle, purposefully self-expressive and out-going; whereas Tudor, Snyder, and Gillespie are all purposefully "non-expressive/theatrical" in presentation. In no way does this suggest minimizing the importance of Tan's performance. She has a powerful stage presence, and her performance of *Water Music*, and prepared piano works from the 1940s, was happily recognized by Cage himself. In appreciation of Tan's dedication to his music, Cage wrote the solo piano work *ONE* [2] for her in the summer of 1989.

The score of *Water Music* is, in itself, a part of the mise-en-scene. Cage comments:

> *The first thing that could be theatrical is what the pianist is looking at — the score.*
> *Normally nobody sees it but him, and since we're involved with seeing now, we make it*
> *large enough so that the audience can see it. (Kirby and Schechner 1965, 60)*

The published score consists of eleven pages, each measuring eleven inches vertically and seventeen inches horizontally. The first page is a general commentary on the score and first performances by David Tudor. The most midleading element in the instructions are for the three whistles — water warbler, siren, and duck — which Cage notes as being "obtainable in toy or five-and-dime stores" (Cage 1952d). Duck whistles are readily available in good sporting-goods stores. The "water warbler" whistle is not a bird call, but is a small cylinder half-filled with water, which makes a "chirping" sound when lightly blown; the "siren whistle" is a tube which, when blown, sounds like a miniature version of the old-fashioned air-raid siren. Both are readily available from stores which specialize in percussion instruments.

The actual performance score consists of ten pages, mounted as a poster measuring 34 inches horizontally and 55 inches vertically. Because the audience is able to read the score, one is provided with a sense of expectation for what is to happen. The poster size is also an implicit indication that *Water Music* should be performed as a chamber piece.

There is no narrative, melodic or harmonic pattern. There is no continuous or unifying action, unless one would consider the radio to be the "main action" of the piece. The events are discontinous and discrete, although the radio exemplifies an overlapping of discontinuous actions in simultaneity. Some events recur, such as pouring water at 4.4875 and 5.4525, or tuning the radio dial, but the only major repetition is the G-major arpeggio at 4.3925, 5.5625 and 6.3025.

Cage's *Water Music*, in addition to being engaging and delightful to read (and witness), is a prime example of the calligraphic beauty of his scores. Like many of the later scores to be discussed, the published score of *Water Music* is a reproduction of Cage's calligraphy, rather than a type-set renotation from manuscript. There are three basic notation systems employed in the score — numbers, natural language (English), and standard Western music notation. Although these notation systems are traditional, the minute juxtaposition of the three results in a very unconventional looking composition. There are 41 events notated in the score. Twenty are in linguistic notation; the remaining 21 in standard piano notation. Of the 20 linguistic notations, seven indicate use of the radio, four indicate interior or exterior piano-body sounds, four indicate use of solo water sounds, one indicates use of a solo whistle, three indicate use of whistles involving water, and one (auxiliary to all the other events) indicates shuffling a deck of playing cards. Numbers are primarily used to indicate clock time in reference to a stop-watch. Numbers are also used as shorthand in linguistic notation.

The most striking feature of the *Water Music* score is the graphic layout of notation in space equal to time. This method had already been used by Cage in previous scores as in *Music of Changes* (1951c), with a quarter note equivalent to two-and-a-half centimeters; *Imaginary Landscape No. 5* (1952a), where one graph square equals three inches of tape; or *Williams Mix* (1952f), where the score consists of same-sized images of the tape on paper (like a dress-maker's pattern). In *Water Music*, 30 horizontal inches in the score equal 40 seconds in performance. The placement of notated events in stop-watch timings thus appears in space on the page. The actual duration of events must be determined spatially and done within a time limit that will allow for the next notated event to be performed at the required time-occurrence.

There are two ways that Cage notates this method of spatial duration. The first, shown in the score excerpt in Fig. 5, shows the combination of

Fig. 5. A score excerpt from *Water Music* (1952), showing the spacial placement of events in time; © 1960 Henmar Press Inc.

standard music notation with reference to stop-watch timings. In this example, the staccato eighth and whole-notes at 4.0075 are initially performed according to the stop-watch, but actual duration is read in musical time in reference to the note-heads. The placement of the staccato eighth-notes at 4.03 appear spatially in the scale of 30 inches equal to 40 seconds as approximately one-and-a-half inches, equivalent to two-and-a-quarter seconds. The tied notes from 4.0075 to 4.0375 are also written in space equal to time — here the stop-watch timing at 4.0075 for two whole-notes gives occurrence, the note-heads indicate the tones to be sustained, and the final duration is determined in reference to the spatial layout and the redundant numerical notation of the stop-watch at 4.0375. This example also illustrates the general dynamics level employed throughout the piece, which is typically in a medium range.

The pronounced visual quality of the entire score is concretely shown in the score excerpt in Fig. 6. This example illustrates the radical use of graphic notation measured in space equal to time. Cage does not provide, as with the linguistic notations, any stop-watch indication for when the event ceases. In part, one looks forward to the G-major arpeggio at 6.3026, and then bases duration of the siren whistle on the practical consideration of initiating events accurate to the time frame. The notated siren whistle is approximately five horizontal inches, and would thus equal about six seconds. The vertical aspect of this notation may be interpreted in two ways. One way would be to

Fig. 6. A score excerpt from *Water Music* (1952), showing Cage's use of graphic notation; © 1960 Henmar Press Inc.

interpret the higher part of the line to represent a higher pitch, and the lower part to represent a lower pitch, as Cage would later notate *Aria* (1958) for a vocalist. Margaret Leng Tan provides an alternate interpretation, which makes reference to the breath being stronger when the line is higher, and a weaker breath when the line is lower.

There are no major indeterminacies with the notations used in *Water Music*. The two exceptions to this are in the actual radio stations required and the actual preparation of the piano. The score calls for specific radio station frequencies ranging from 88 to 133, which would implicitly mean that AM stations (bands from 53 to 160) would be used. Even if one accurately tunes the radio to notated stations such as 102.5, 88, or 125, the action of tuning the dial will result in an unforeseen outcome such as music, talk, or static. There is thus a blurring between intention (the notated radio station number) and nonintention (the actual sounds that occur during performance), between the fixed and the spontaneous, between art and life.

The second indeterminacy in the score is the piano preparation at 2.5475, which reads: "Prepare piano with 4 objects" (Cage 1952d). Here, one might look at Cage's tables of preparations from the prepared piano pieces from the 1940s. In the table of preparations from *Sonatas and Interludes* (1946–48), for example, Cage notes the tone, the material to be used (e.g. rubber, screw, bolt, plastic) between which strings (i.e. 1–2, 2–3, or 1–2–3), and the distance of placement measured in inches from the damper. Neither David Tudor or Don Gillespie have recalled what objects they used. When

Ellsworth Snyder performed *Water Music* on April 6, 1991, he used wooden golf tees. Margaret Leng Tan comments:

> *I chose preparations that are quick to do. The objects I use are a screw with a loose nut — it makes a lovely jangle; a half of a clothes-pin — I jam that into the strings very fast; a bolt; and a felt wedge. I chose those four because it was practical to do and because of the different sounds that result from the objects as they are inserted. (Tan 1989a)*

It is also not notated which four tones are to be prepared. This is implicitly notated further on in the score, when four tones are played at 3.2175. Underneath this music notation is the linguistic notation which reads: "(Pn. Prep. must be finished by this time)." *Water Music* has later variations in *Music Walk* (1958), *Water Walk* (1959), and *Sounds of Venice* (1959). *Music Walk* will be discussed in the following chapter.

Water Walk **and** *Sounds of Venice*

Water Walk was written in Milan and first performed by Cage on the RAI-TV quiz program *Lascia o Raddoppia* (*"Double or Nothing"*) in January, 1959 (Dunn 1962, 43; and Tomkins 1968, 130–132). For five weeks he appeared on the show answering questions about mushrooms, winning the grand prize of approximately six thousand dollars. On the quiz program, Cage also performed a prepared piano solo from *Amores* (1943), and *Sounds of Venice*, a variation of *Water Walk*. Cage later performed *Water Walk* on television in New York — on *The Henry Morgan Show* in June, 1959, and *I've Got a Secret* in January, 1960 (Dunn 1962, 43). The piece has only rarely been performed since then, and not by Cage.

> *Water Walk* is three minutes in duration. The scrupulously determinate notation requires the solo performer to execute a quick succession of disparate events according to stop-watch timings. Cage recalls the difficulty of being able to accurately perform his score:

> *. . . I . . . rehearsed very carefully, over and over and over again with people watching me and correcting me, because I had to do it in three minutes. It had many actions in it, and it demanded what you might call virtuosity. I was unwilling to perform it until I was certain that I could do it well. (Kirby and Schechner 1965, 62)*

Photographic stills taken off the television screen during the first performance suggest that he performed *Water Walk* in an exuberant manner but with a disciplined seriousness of attention (Kostelanetz 1970, illustrations 39 and 40). Judith Malina recalls seeing *Water Walk* in New York in 1960 and remembers that it was "excellent! When he did it, he gave it an actor's 'choice reading,' which made the choices themselves much more exquisite and exciting. It is the difference between good and *great* art'' (Malina 1989).

The score is in four parts — (1) a list of 34 properties, (2) a floorplan showing the placement of the instruments and objects, (3) three pages in verbal and pictographic notation of the occurrence of events in clock time, and (4) a list of written notes clarifying the other parts. All four parts are redundant in details, but in its redundancy *Water Walk* is the most completely determinate notation of Cage's theatre pieces.

The most important score parts are the floorplan and the three pages of events in time. The floorplan, illustrated in Fig. 7, is required because the various objects must be efficiently positioned to allow easy access. The floorplan thus also determines the choreography. Much of *Water Music* is played while seated, but *Water Walk* is completely performed standing up. The movement that results in *Water Walk* is primarily from side to side on stage, with occasional movement toward the back (a triangle). Both *Water Music* and *Water*

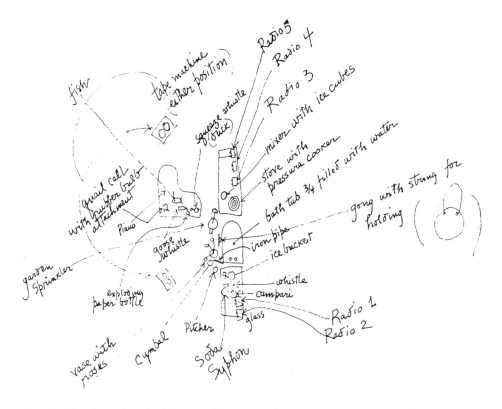

Fig. 7. The floorplan for *Water Walk* (1959), showing the placement of objects and instruments; © 1961 Henmar Press Inc. Notice that the audience, unmarked, would be facing from the right side of the figure.

Walk are designed for a frontal, proscenium style of presentation, but *Water Walk* could conceivably be performed by someone other than a trained pianist.

The three pages of timed events are the most complete notation of the score. It is primarily in linguistic notation, with also pictographic notation. It thus reads like a rebus. Each page has two lines. Each line equals thirty seconds, and each page equals one minute. The first line from the first page of this part appears in Fig. 8. Time is notated spatially in horizontally placed five-second increments, with stop-watch times indicated by numbers. Like many of the events in *Water Music*, events in *Water Walk* do not have explicitly notated durations, but only have a notation of initiation. Duration is determined by performing an event relative to being able to perform the next event.

The redundancies among all four parts may be illustrated in the first two events. The first event occurs at 0'00" and reads "Start '[fish pictogram]'." The properties list explains what kind of toy fish is to be used, the floorplan shows where it is located (on the piano bridge), and the supplementary written notes state:

> 1.   *After starting fish, place on strings of piano, low or middle register, so that movable tail fins set strings vibrating. (Cage 1959c)*

The second event is an example of pictographic notation with supplementary linguistic notation. The event is to be initiated at approximately 0'03" according to the horizontal placement of space equal to time. One is already at the piano from the previous event, and no stage movement is required. The properties list specifies a grand piano with the lid removed for easy access to the interior, and with an unhinged keyboard lid, and the damper pedal wedged or weighted to allow resonance. The supplementary written notes clarify the piano pictogram:

> 2.   *Friction: Scrape a bass string lengthwise with fingernail or coin. (Cage 1959c)*

One continues this way, reading through all four parts of the score.

There are 49 events enacted in performance. Of these events, only four have a chronological or narrative progression — making a drink. At 0'25" one puts ice into a glass; at 1'05" one pours in some Campari; at 2'00" one syphons some seltzer; and at 2'40" one takes a sip. As in *Water Music*, the majority of events in *Water Walk* appear as discrete, noncontinuous elements. Other than making the drink, the other main action is playing the specially made tape collage played from 0'10" to 2'58". There is no recognizable pattern other than a nonsymmetrical exposition of primarily disparate activities.

The most important performance (to date) of *Water Walk* by other than

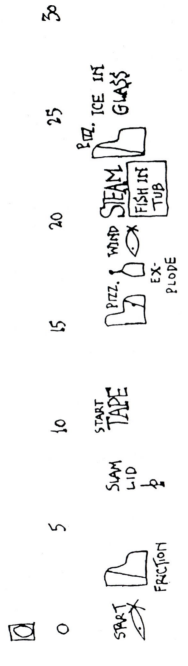

Fig. 8. An excerpt from *Water Walk* (1959), showing the first thirty seconds in the event's score-part; © 1961 Henmar Press Inc.

Cage was by Jim Burton in a videotaped performance shown at The Kitchen in New York on December 8, 1973 (Program 1973). Tom Johnson noted that Burton . . .

> . . . *pours, sprays, splashes, and squirts his way through the piece quite amusingly, though he never hams it up. As in most of the best interpretations of Cage theatre pieces, one felt that the performer was simply following a score, rather than acting a scene. (Johnson 1973)*

Water Walk has a further variation in *Sounds of Venice* which Cage performed on *Lascia o Raddoppia* the following week (Tomkins 1968, 131–2). The score was not available for further performance or publication until 1991 because of copyright problems with Cage's inclusion of the 1957 Italian pop song "Come Prima" on one of the collage tapes. The second performance, and American premiere, was by John Kennedy at Spoleto USA in May, 1991. The New York City premiere was performed by Charles Wood at Greenwich House Auditorium on April 16, 1992 (Kennedy and Wood 1992).

The *Sounds of Venice* score is similar to, but less complicated than *Water Walk*. The original score by Cage consists of a floorplan of objects, and three pages of actions in time. For publication, Don Gillespie made a list of the instruments, properties, and electronic equipment mentioned in the other parts, including a piano, slab of marble and Venetian broom, bird cage with canaries, an amplified slinky, and four tape machines playing specially made collage recordings.

The three-minute performance is notated in linguistic notation, which might account for the absence of any properties list or supplementary written notes by Cage. There are 43 events in *Sounds of Venice*. The primary difference between *Sounds of Venice* and *Water Walk* is that in *Water Walk* one is always standing up and moving about; while in *Sounds of Venice* one has the minimalist activity of sitting in a chair (from 2'03" to 2'30"), and the narrative action is getting a cigarette and putting it into one's mouth at 0'20", lighting it at 1'33", and taking a final puff and tamping it out in an ashtray at 3'00" (Cage 1959b).

Towards Theatre through Chance

There are several precedents for *Water Music*, and its later variations *Water Walk* and *Sounds of Venice*, in Cage's previous work with percussion ensemble (expanding sound resources) and dance accompaniment (interest in the visual components of performance), but the work of Antonin Artaud in particular provides a theoretical impetus for Cage's first total theatre compositions.

Artaud was a poet, actor, playwright, director, and theorist. The major influence by Artaud has been through his collection of essays published in 1938 as *Le Theatre et son Double*. Artaud's book was a major influence on Pierre Boulez, and when Cage returned from Paris in 1949 he brought Boulez's *Second Piano Sonata* along with Artaud's book. David Tudor studied Artaud's essays as preparation to play Boulez in 1950. Mary Caroline Richards, a poet and potter, realizing the importance of Artaud's thought, began to formally translate *The Theatre and its Double* in 1951. Her translation was first rejected by several publishers, and was not published in English until 1958. Richards recalls that while making the translation in 1951 and 1952 she would read it to Cage, Tudor, and Cunningham, who all responded with enthusiasm, but without any systematic discussion of Artaud's ideas. Richards recalls that Artaud was, rather, a confirmation of then-current sensibilities, a catalyst to continue what they were already doing (Richards 1989).

Artaud proposed a "theatre of cruelty" by comparing theatre to the plague, in that "The theatre like the plague is a crisis which is resolved by death or cure" (Artaud 1958, 31). He found most of European theatre to be decadent, lacking in real laughter or poetry. In Western theatre, Artaud particularly criticized the emphasis on written and spoken dialogue, noting that this "does not belong specifically to the stage, it belongs to books" (Artaud 1958, 37).

Artaud believed that, "In a word, the theatre must become a sort of experimental demonstration of the profound unity of the concrete and the abstract" (Artaud 1958, 108), and found a demonstration of this theoretical aesthetic in non-Western theatre and ritual. Here he saw a use of a complete performance language made through a "whole complex of gestures, signs, postures, and sonorities" (Artaud 1958, 44). Artaud's body-based, concretely physical mise-en-scene is reflected in Cage's early theatre compositions, but there is no aspect of a "theatre of cruelty."

The most intriguing comparison of Cage with Artaud is in the confirmation of chaos or chance being integral to the creative act. Artaud wrote that "true theatre, like poetry as well, . . . is born out of a kind of organized anarchy" (Artaud 1958, 51). "Anarchic dissociation" is the "root of all poetry" and of "real humor," a dangerous situation that is spontaneous and difficult yet ultimately heroic (Artaud 1958, 28; 42). For Artaud, it was the Four Marx Brothers's early films that most clearly exemplified this aesthetic in theatrical practice, what one might call "impulsive chance" in Mac Low's definition. While Artaud did not propose using "systematic chance," his "anarchic dissociation" is where one finds a confirmation of sensibility in Cage's work not only from Artaud, but from other historical works.

Chance music was a brief fad in the late eighteenth and very early nineteenth centuries, the most famous work being Wolfgang Mozart's

Musikalishes Würfelspiel (*"Musical Dice-game"*) K.516f. Mozart's score consists of written instructions and two tables of pre-composed measures. One takes two dice and rolls them, obtaining a number from two through twelve. One then looks on the first chart, and writes down the numbered measure indicated in the first column. One continues this procedure, according to the instructions, writing a conventionally structured waltz or minuet (Mozart 1973).

Mozart uses chance as a melodic/harmonic variation technique within a fixed, non-chance structure. The whole work is carefully controlled, with all possible tonal difficulties resolved by having all possible measures thematically related, and by having non-chance first and second ending measures between the two tables to allow a smooth and stylistically correct modulation between the first and second tables of measures. Mozart's chance is a type of parlor game that allows one to vicariously participate in the composition process. All the materials are pre-composed, and while there is no single definitive version from the myriad possibilities, the actual performer is only required to make mechanical operations (toss the dice, find the measure, and write it down).

The two most significant artists to deal with the concept of chance in the nineteenth century were Stéphane Mallarmé and August Strindberg. In *Igitur* (1869), Mallarmé writes:

> *Briefly, in an act where chance is in play, chance always accomplishes its own Idea in affirming or negating itself. Confronting its existence, negation and affirmation fail. It contains the Absurd — implies it, but in the latent state and prevents it from existing: which permits the Infinite to be.* (Mallarmé 1982, 99)

The character Igitur, in tossing the dice, participates in the paradox of existence, the burden of past, present, and future, the limitations of free-will within the cosmic reality of a chance-ordered universe. To accept chance is to negate one's personal ego and affirm the cosmos, yet curiously the very act of tossing the dice also annuls chance itself, for there is ultimately a determinate and final outcome.

A Mallarmé masterwork is *Un coup de dés* (*"A Toss of the Dice"*) (1895), and while this admittedly complex and mysterious poem is his fullest expression of chance, there is no evidence that he wrote it by chance procedures. The typography and physical arrangement of words on the page are not random, but produce various ideograms of the poem's verbal and symbolic content, such as a storm-lashed ocean, a toque with feather (Hamlet's headgear), and the Big Dipper (Cohn 1949, 11–12). The difficult syntax, and the non-linear progression of images and thoughts, rather, may be read as carefully and intentionally crafted events which imitate or mirror the act of chance. At the conclusion, Mallarmé writes: "All Thought utters Dice Thrown" and the poem does not end with a period. The reader is metaphorically left dangling in space without beginning or end. In *Un coup de dés* Mallarmé leaves us with a paradoxical vision of chance, for through the rich vocabulary and symbolic content one is left full, yet the experience of chance is itself the experience of the cosmic void. In a poem that elucidates and illuminates ultimate meaning, the final result is an austere and unavoidable silence.

The work of Mallarmé is not known to be an influence on Cage — indeed, Cage never wrote or lectured about Mallarmé — yet certainly one can see a precedent in the exploration of conceptual chance, innovative notation, and silence. The work of August Strindberg is an even less direct precedent, however one may read Strindberg as a prophet of chance in twentieth century art through his 1894 essay *"Des arts nouveaux! ou Le hasard dans la production artistique"* ("The New Arts, or The Role of Chance in Artistic Creation").

In this short essay, Strindberg writes of chance in music, painting, sculpture, and literature. In music, Strindberg notes the aeolian harp (tones produced by the wind), a musician who amuses himself "thumping away at his piano without any sequence or sense," and his own practice of randomly tuning guitar strings. Bird song is considered to be a "musical kaleidoscope," which he suggests might be duplicated by piercing the music drums of street organs at random. In sculpture, Strindberg notes making a clay model of a young lover, and in despair, pushing his hand on top of the figure's head, transforming it "into a boy of nine crying and hiding his tears with his hands" (Strindberg 1968, 101). In painting, Strindberg writes of modernistic paintings being a "chaos of colors" in which. . .

> . . . the image is presented to the spectator who has witnessed the act of procreation of the picture. And even better: the painting keeps renewing itself, changes according to the light, never wears out, is rejuvenated by the gift of life. (Strindberg 1968, 102)

The essay concludes with the example of Maeterlinck putting rhymes in the middle of his prose, which is admittedly a rather weak argument for chance in literature. However, the final sentence is prophetic of developments in the twentieth century:

> The art to come (and go, like all the others!): Imitating nature almost; above all, imitating nature's way of creating! (Strindberg 1968, 103)

Most important in the work of Strindberg and Mallarmé, is the aesthetic precedent in conceptualizing chance as the way in which nature works. It is the artist who (as in the Romantic tradition) must go to Nature herself, rather than the precedents of human works, in order to create. The true artist is thus a conduit of process, of unintentional discovery resulting in an unforeseen content devoid of closure.

Chance composition in the twentieth century begins with Marcel Duchamp's *Musical Erratum*, made in 1913 by writing 25 notes on individual cards and then drawing them out from a container one at a time in random order to determine the tones for a short song text (James 1989, 109). The song is in three parts — the first two are identified as Duchamp's sisters Yvonne and Magdaleine, and the third is identified as Marcel himself. In the original French version (see James 1989, 111 for manuscript production), the text is 25 syllables, and each syllable is to be sung on a different note. The first two parts — Yvonne and Magdaleine — are composed from the same 25 notes from F below middle-C through F two octaves above middle-C, and the third part — Marcel — is a different, though overlapping range of 25 notes from C below middle-C through C above middle-C. From all three parts, a 30-note chromatic arrangement emerges, with the first five tones appearing only in Marcel's part, and the last five tones appearing only in the other two, thus embodying symmetry. The tonal range in each of the three parts does not violate the practical limits of the conventional female or male singing voice and, hence, the chosen tones are extremely practical for actual performance. Each of the three parts use their 25 possible tones only once, which would suggest that Duchamp, after mixing up the notes in the container, drew them out one by one, and did not put back a found-tone afterwards when making a determination of the next tone. Thus, while each of the three parts share common tones, there is no sequential repetition of tones within any of the three parts.

Carol James interprets Duchamp's *Musical Erratum* as a displacement of the art song "because it violates the established method of perceiving music as melodious sequences" (James 1989, 110), and this is true when one considers that Duchamp uses tones not in a melodic but a chance-determined progression. Chance is here a decision making process for the occurrence of the tonal events, however the tonal events themselves were not initially made by chance procedures, but from a very logical, ordered, deterministic choice. *Musical Erratum* also includes several indeterminacies within the score — there is no indication of dynamics, tempo, or duration. Here, it might be said that the performers must finally make these determinations. Apart from these indeterminacies, this song is an example of what Duchamp would term "canned chance" in that there is a fixed, final score or object (Duchamp 1979, 33).

Chance procedures would later be used by Duchamp, as in *Trois Stoppages-Etalon* ("*Three Standard Stoppages*") made in 1913–14 by dropping a three-meter long string onto a canvas three times and tracing the chance-determined configurations (Naumann 1989, 29–30); and in the work of Dadaists and Surrealists, as in Tristan Tzara's poems made during the 1910s-early 1920s by cutting up newspaper articles (Tzara 1981, 39), or Jean Arp's chance collages made in 1916–19 and again in the 1930s (Hancock 1985, 47–75). Chance music was also made in this period by the Dadaist George Ribemont-Dessaignes. Victoria Nes Kirby writes of a Paris performance in 1920:

> *The piece had been composed by chance methods using a "pocket roulette wheel." Ribemont-Dessaignes made the wheel with a dial on which he marked numbers to represent semitones. Spinning the wheel and recording the numbers, he obtained his melody. He wrote the harmony in the same way. (The method for determining the length of the notes — quarter, half or whole notes, etc. — is not mentioned by Ribemont-Dessaignes, but it is quite possible that this, too, was done by chance. Unfortunately, the pocket roulette and his chance musical scores are all lost.) (Nes Kirby 1972, 106)*

(It must be noted that Tzara, Arp, and Ribemont-Dessaignes all use chance in the sense of a Duchampian "canned chance" in that there is a final, fixed result.)

Cage's use of chance in composing *Water Music* is similar to both Mozart's dice game (using charts of intuitively made pre-composed elements) and Duchamp's *Musical Erratum* (the score being in a fixed, final state, while admitting indeterminacies in the notation for individual and unique performances). The chance procedures used to make *Water Music* were from the *I Ching* (Dunn 1962, 43). Cage has commented on his use of the *I Ching* in composition:

> *My life. . .is not governed. And certainly not by the* I Ching. *I attempt to move according to circumstances. . . I find the* I Ching *useful to answer questions, and when I have questions, I use it. Then the answers, instead of coming from my likes and dislikes, come from chance operations, and that has the effect of opening me to possibilities that I hadn't considered. Chance–determined answers will open the mind to the world around. (Montague 1985, 212)*

Cage's statement, however, both illuminates and mystifies, reveals as well as conceals his use of the *I Ching*, for he typically used the *I Ching* as a method for structure and selection of events rather than using it in its original symbolic divinatory or meditative context.

The use of chance in composing *Water Music* is partly reconstructable from Cage's unpublished working notes, now housed in the New York Public Library (Cage 1952e). The notes are titled "66 W. 12" (the original title of the first performance), and consist of three parts — (1) structure, occurrence, and duration, (2) the possible events, and (3) dynamics. None of these three categories have an identifying *I Ching* hexagram number (1–64), however the notes include a short numerical structure which refers to the 64 possiblities:

1–9
9–27
27–63
64 = free sound

Clearly, the philosophical objectivity that Cage describes above in his general use of the *I Ching* and chance operations must be understood as also including a subjective, intuitive component during the actual process of chance composition.

The overall structure of *Water Music* was not made by chance procedures, but according to an intuitively made "macro-micro" organization as from the 1940s (as in the previously discussed first piece from *Two Pieces* [1946]). The structure for *Water Music* is notated in the unpublished working notes as:

> *10 × 10 = 100 × 4 secs.*
> *each unit = 4 secs[.]*
> *2 3 5 = 8 12 20*

In comparing these notes with the final score, it is clear that Cage first determined the total duration (400″ or 6′40″), and then subdivided the time of each unit (10 × 10, or 10 × 40″) into three basic rhythmic units (2, 3, and 5; or 8, 12, and 20 seconds). It is not clear from the actual score that this structure is employed. James Pritchett writes that ultimately Cage abandoned the inner structure of occurrences:

> *Instead, he devised a system by which the* I Ching *hexagrams were themselves to represent the durations directly. . . there were three possible values: 1/4 second, 1/2 second, or 1 second. The hexagram number (1 to 64) obtained for duration would be multiplied by this unit to determine the duration. Thus, when the time unit was 1/4 second, the possible durations ranged from 1/4 to 16 seconds; and when it was 1 second, 1 to 64 seconds. (Pritchett 1988, 195–197)*

Pritchett, however, does not make any demonstration of this use of the *I Ching* in the final score. (I also am unable to demonstrate this through score analysis.)

What *is* clear in the unpublished working notes and the final score of *Water Music* is the chance selection of events and dynamics during the composition process. There are three pages of intuitively composed events handwritten in pencil on commercially printed music paper, containing both standard music notation (for the piano keyboard) and brief linguistic notations for various actions. All of the notations for events are spatially brief, and could easily be cross-ruled to form a checkerboard. Included in the listed events are items such as the G-major arpeggio or duck whistle. There are also events which were not used in the final score, such as "strike match, blow out (with teeth together)," "Light a cigarette (smoke at will to?)," and "Speak: Hello!?." These unused events would have been those which were not found when tossing coins for an *I Ching* hexagram.

The dynamics chart lists possibilities ranging from pppp (very-very-

very soft) to FFFF (very-very-very loud). Here again, as with the keyboard and action events, Cage would have numbered each dynamics-level with an accompanying *I Ching* hexagram number, and then fitted the chance-found result into the previously made time structure. Thus, in the first forty seconds Cage would have initially known that there were to be three events. Knowing the occurrence in time of the three events, he would then have tossed coins to determine, according to a number found from the *I Ching*, which event and which dynamic would be used.

Further analysis is not possible because of the lack of notes that would answer more detailed and specific questions. Even on the most basic level of reconstructing Cage's probable working method in *Water Music*, the possibility of personal expression is included with the use of hexagram 64 — "free sound/free time" (Cage 1952e) — which would allow an escape from making the final composition by purely mechanical operations. Chance is used to select and structure a subjective content, yet the resultant determinations, such as playing the radio, still retain an unforeseen result.

The composition process for *Water Walk* and *Sounds of Venice* is similar to that of *Water Music*, however in these two later variations Cage used his own *Fontana Mix* score rather than the *I Ching* (Cage 1958a).

The *Fontana Mix* score is in indeterminate notation. There are ten unnumbered transparencies measuring eight-and-a-half by eleven inches, on which are randomly distributed points. The number of dots on the sheets are, respectively, 7, 12, 13, 17, 18, 19, 22, 26, 29, and 30. There are also ten sheets of paper with the same dimensions, on which are six curving lines. The six lines are differentiated by thickness and texture (three unbroken and three dotted lines; thick, medium, and thin). There are also two additional transparencies — Graph 1 is a straight line measuring 10–3/4 inches, and Graph 2 is a block-graph measuring two by ten inches, marked into 100 by 20 squares. The method of using these materials is explained in a written instruction. One takes a sheet with curving lines and places over this one of the transparencies containing points. Over this, one places Graph 2. A point that is enclosed by Graph 2 is then connected to a point outside of Graph 2 by using Graph 1. Cage then notes:

> *Measurements horizontally on the top and bottom of the graph with respect to the straight line give a "time bracket" (time within which the event may take place) (graph units = any time units).*
>
> *Measurements vertically on the graph with respect to the intersections of the curved lines and the straight line may specify actions to be made. Thus, in the case of (Fontana Mix) tape music, the thickest curved line may give sound source(s) where the latter have been categorized and related quantitatively to 20. (Cage 1958a)*

An example of what the score might look like appears in Fig. 9. In this

Fig. 9.   An example of *Fontana Mix* (1958), showing a superimposition of score parts; © 1960 Henmar Press Inc. Notice the discoloration in the center of the score, which occurs from the various layers of transparencies.

illustration, the only intersection of the Graph 1 line with a curved line within Graph 2 is the thickest unbroken line. Reading horizontally, this gives a time bracket of nine. Reading vertically, the sound (or event) would be the fifth from twenty possibilities. This example could have twelve possible superimpositions by altering Graph 1 and connecting each of the four points enclosed by Graph 2 to each of the three outside points.

Cage's unpublished worknotes for *Water Walk* do not contain the necessary information to backtrack how he made *Fontana Mix* score determinations, but some intriguing material exists nonetheless. The worknotes, written in graphpaper notebooks, basically consist of four parts: the first part is two pages of forty time brackets with one or two numbers indicating numbered events (such as "10 + 18") and some dynamics from pppp to ffff (similar to the notation of *Theatre Piece*, discussed in Chapter 5); a two-page list of actions without timings; a list of intended objects; and three pages consisting of a list of times for initiating various actions, many not included in the final, performed version and published score. An excerpt from this excised material is:

> 0'43" — *start fountain (slow faster faster fastest)*
> 　　　　*(off at 55")*
> 0'58" — *start eggs cooking*
> 1'34" — *start washing machine*
> 1'46" — *start Radio #4 + coffee maker*
> 　48" — *slam lid coffee maker + start (tape loop — water sounds?)*
> 2'13" — *rubber duck sound in tub ff*
> 2'24" — *pour coffee in tub + rubber duck again*
> 　　　　　　　(Cage 1959d)

Concerning the worksheets for *Water Walk*, Cage commented:

> *I made a list of things involving water that would be theatrical, and then I subjected it all to chance [through use of the* Fontana Mix *score] and composed it. Some of the things that were on the list didn't come up, and some things did. I did that always. (Cage 1988b)*

The actions were thus made by personal taste and intuition, and then subjected to chance procedures. Although it is at present improbable for me to make a *Fontana Mix* superimposition that would be as Cage would have used to determine a time bracket and action/s, Cage would comment on his basic approach:

> *I don't think I used all six of the lines. I used as many as I thought were necessary. And then I made lists of actions that I was willing to involve myself in. Then through the intersection of those curved lines and the straight line I could see within what amount of time I had, for instance, to put a rose in a bathtub, if that came up. If at the same time*

*playing a particular note — or not a particular note — on the piano came up, those two
things had to get done within the time allotted. (Kirby and Schechner 1965, 61–62)*

Apart from these later recollections, further speculation is futile at present.

With *Fontana Mix*, Cage created an indeterminate score to be used for
a variety of compositions. In addition to *Water Walk* and *Sounds of Venice*,
Fontana Mix was used to make a tape composition of the same title, as well as
Aria (1958) for Mezzo-Soprano, *WBAI* (1960) for radio broadcast, and *Theatre
Piece* (1960). (*Theatre Piece* will be discussed in Chapter 5).

The actual scores of *Water Walk* and *Sounds of Venice* are, like *Water
Music*, made in determinate notation. Although all three were composed by
chance procedures, they are a kind of Duchampian "canned chance" in that
there is a fixed, final score. It is only the composer, and not the performer,
who is involved in making chance determinations. Cage's solution to this
imbalance was to include the performer in the final creative process through
the use of indeterminate notation. The first indeterminate notation of a
theatre piece is the untitled event at Black Mountain College in 1952 (discussed in Chapter 5). *Music Walk* (1958), a variation of *Water Music*, and
Music Walk's immediate variation *Cartridge Music* (1960), are complex indeterminate notations similar to *Fontana Mix*, and will be discussed in the
following chapter.

3

MUSIC WALK AND *CARTRIDGE MUSIC*: VARIATIONS IN COMPLEX INDETERMINATE NOTATION

Music Walk

Music Walk was composed in Stockholm, and completed on September 24, 1958 (Cage 1958b). It was first performed by John Cage, Cornelius Cardew, and David Tudor at Galerie 22 in Duesseldorf on October 14, 1958. Cage and Tudor later performed *Music Walk* five times in the spring of 1960. In the fall of 1960, *Music Walk with Dancers* was performed seven times in Italy and Germany with Cage, Tudor, and the dancers Merce Cunningham and Carolyn Brown (Dunn 1962, 42). It was again performed by Cage and Tudor in New York as *Music Walk with Dancer* with Jill Johnston on April 4, 1962.

Music Walk is one of Cage's more complex indeterminate scores. It is for one or more pianists who play piano, the radio, and make other auxiliary sounds, while moving from area to area. Cage has not commented on his performance, but David Tudor remarks on their general approach:

> The first thing you would do is decide where you had to go, and then you would either stay where you were for that length of time or else you would move to that spot and spend the time there. You try to put things far apart so you would have little problems of getting there on time. And then usually the piece changed according to the available resources. You purposefully place things out of view of the audience such as going backstage and then playing a phonograph or making an auxiliary sound. Without dancers it was done mostly in galleries, usually with one piano. (Tudor 1989a and 1989b)

The single most memorable performance of this work is the version *Music Walk with Dancers*, performed by Cage, Tudor, Cunningham, and Brown at the Teatro La Fenice in Venice on September 24, 1960. A reviewer for *Time* would write:

> For his Venice performance, Cage prepared a typically mad melange of musical high jinks. The evening started mildly enough with Round 1, in which Cage and Pianist David Tudor sat at different pianos alternately plunking notes at up to 20-second intervals. Presently Dancer Merce Cunningham started undulating in symbolic suggestion of an embryo wriggling toward manhood. By Round 3, when Cage was thumping his piano stool with a rock, the restive audience begun to jeer. The jeers grew in Round 4, as Cage and Tudor launched into a piano duet, playing chords with

their elbows while assaulting the piano's innards with knives and pieces of tin. After Round 6, in which Cage slammed the piano top with an iron pipe and dropped bottles on the floor, an elderly music lover strode on the stage, walloped Cage's piano with his walking stick and stalked out shouting "Now I'm a musician too!"

Soon Cage and Tudor were darting about between three record players, shifting from Mozart to blues to a recorded speech by Pope John XXIII calling for world peace. By the finale, fights had broken out all over the theatre. "Get out of here!" screamed traditonalists. Replied an un–Caged modernist: "Go somewhere else if you want melody! Long live music!" Cage barked at the audience; the audience barked back at Cage. ("Yesterday's Revolution" 1960, 59)

This review is certainly limited. The patronizing tone aside, it tells little of what Cunningham did, and does not even mention Caroyln Brown. It does provide, however, some eye-witness documentation of Cage's *Music Walk* performance. Much of the *Time* review is corroborated by the composer Alvin Lucier, who was in the audience that evening. Lucier also remembers that at the beginning David Tudor walked down the aisle and dove under the piano on stage, that John Cage was playing a piano in the pit on a descending trap, and that Merce Cunningham and Carolyn Brown had cards to go to various parts of the theatre to perform. "It was a shock! It was wonderful, and was very influential in changing my attitude" (Lucier 1989).

Carolyn Brown recalls that Merce Cunningham gave her the choreography to go with *Music Walk*. She remembers doing solo ballet barre exercises, holding on to a grand piano, and performing a waltz with Merce Cunningham. She most fondly remembers that Cunningham wanted her to "fly," so she was lowered while sitting in a chair from above the stage. "It was a wonderful drama, and it was an extraordinary audience — they hooted and shrieked!" (Brown 1989).

Merce Cunningham recalls few specific details of the *Music Walk* performances, but again remembers the Fenice performance as being the most memorable. Cunningham does not recall much of his choreography, nor does he have any notes, and he does not recall having choreographed Carolyn Brown as much as she seems to indicate. He comments:

I remember very little about it actually. We each had a separate gamut of things to do, and some of the things were together and some were separate. I suspect most of them we each made up, except that some were joined. Mostly they weren't what you would call "dance steps."

Very often in those situations the theatre itself could suggest things because of the nature of it, for instance with flies where Carolyn could come down out of them; and it seems to me in one of them I did something with a chair. I think also there was one with a stairway in the back — we didn't use any curtains, any wings — and I came down it at one point and did something. I also remember at some point, I don't remember which theatre, we came and sat at the front, sitting down with our legs in the pit at the front of the stage, and we were in silhouette because there weren't any lights at the front.

*As I remember, we each had so many things, say a dozen, to do, and we could
do them in any order that we each chose to do them in, except for the ones where we did
something together. Then we would, say, make that number five between us, but other
than that we were free and separate from each other. We may even have done sequences
out of dances, but I don't remember that that well. (Cunningham 1989b)*

Cunningham does not consider *Music Walk with Dancers* to be one of his
major choreographic works, but principally his choreography was to alternate
independent solos with duet sequences. All of Cunningham's choreography
was independent also of the stage movements of Cage and Tudor. *Music Walk*
may well be considered a minor work within Cunningham's historical repertoire, but it is a rare example where musicians have occupied the stage simultaneously with the dancers, and does not reflect his usual staging style.

Cunningham also does not recall using the actual *Music Walk* score itself
from which to determine the structure and number of actions. He comments:

*John may have given us each a score which had durations in it, about how
long a given thing might be, that's very possible, and then that would be a kind of
structure within which we worked. So he may have given us the length of the piece for
that given performance, say twenty minutes or fifteen minutes or whatever it was, and
then he may even have given us further divisions within it. I don't remember further
indications than that. (Cunningham 1989b)*

John Cage's performance of *Music Walk* was apparently one of the
most memorable examples of the composer's stage presence. The *Time* review
mentions eight actions that he performed. David Tudor elaborates on the
traps mentioned by Alvin Lucier:

*At Venice John made an elaborate plan for the stage-hands, but there was no
rehearsal — it was not possible! The Fenice is a remarkable old Opera House, and there
were lots of traps, so John and I made use of these traps to theatricalize the piece. There
were two pianos. I arranged it so that on one platform the piano could go up or down.
With the other trap, it was right next to the piano, beside the keyboard. I remember John
playing that piano, his trap going down, and then him standing up, still playing
(laughs), with the trap still going down (laughs)! I was underneath the other piano
"taking a nap," and the whole thing went up in the air, and I couldn't get down
(laughs)! (Tudor 1989b)*

The unforeseen contingencies that result during performance are a hallmark
of the Cage style, but more importantly it is the score itself which is Cage's
great achievement.

The *Music Walk* score is a prime example of notation indeterminate
of its performance. The published score consists of an instruction sheet,
nine sheets with dots, and two sheets of transparencies. Each page with
dots measures 11 inches vertically and 17 inches horizontally, numbered 2
through 10 (page 1, not included, is a "blank page"). Pages 2 through 10

contain, respectively, 39, 11, 12, 23, 52, 2, 7, 19, and 19 dots in random arrangement. The first transparency measures 15–1/2 inches horizontally and 3–1/2 inches vertically. On it are five parallel horizontal lines. The second transparency measures 12–5/8 by 6–5/8 inches, on which are eight squares to be cut out. Each square contains five nonparallel lines.

In the instruction sheet, Cage writes:

> *The 10 (or that number used) pages having points (one lacking them) are to be interpreted by each performer in any order and by superimposing the plastic rectangle [containing five parallel lines] in any position (including those that would give no actions). (Cage 1958b)*

The five parallel lines, in abbreviated fashion, refer to:

1. a Use of piano strings by plucking
   b Use of piano strings by muting
   c Use of radio by altering overtone control
   d Use of radio by producing kilocycle glissando
2. a Use of keyboard (if at it)
   b String glissandi (if at back of piano)
   c Radio music (if at it)
3. a Interior piano construction noises
   b Radio static
4. a Exterior piano construction noises
   b Radio speech
5. Auxiliary sounds (including voice, piano preparations, etc.)

Cage then continues:

> *These references are to any of the lines. The total length is any time–length. Vertical relation to lines may be interpreted relatively within a given category with respect to any characteristic. (Cage 1958b)*

An example of what a superimposition would look like appears in Fig. 10.

In this example, there are only two events that result from the intersection of points with lines. This could be renotated as:

This would determine events in space equal to time by reading horizontally from left to right, although there is no score instruction for how long a page

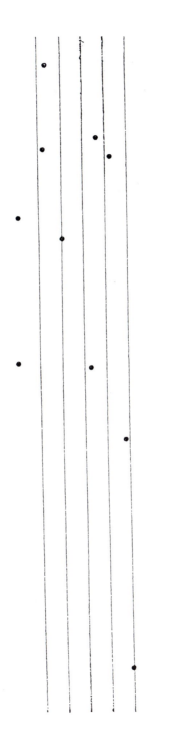

(10)

Fig. 10.   An example of basic superimposition of parts in *Music Walk* (1958), © 1960 Henmar Press Inc.

(or an entire performance) is to last. The numbering of lines is also to be decided by the individual performer. The top line could refer to the first line, the line below that to the second line, etc.; or the bottom line could refer to the first line, etc. Again, if one numbers from the top down, the bottom or fifth line refers to an auxiliary sound, which must be determined by the performer; and the next event, on line 2, could have three possible outcomes — use of the keyboard, string glissandi, or radio music. This score example is possibly how an overlay might have looked to Cage in making his own performance realizations. The first event, an auxiliary sound, was at one point interpreted by Cage as thumping a piano stool with a rock; the next event (chronologically, according to the *Time* review) refers to use of the keyboard, when Cage played clusters with his elbows. Many of the events known to have been performed by Cage were of fifth line auxiliary sounds chosen by personal taste.

The eight additional transparent squares are termed optional according to the instructions. Each consists of five nonparallel lines, to be superimposed over a dot (an event):

> They may be used at any time or not at all for the determination of: (1) number of sounds in an aggregate; (2) occurrence (earlier, later); (3) frequency; (4) duration; (5) amplitude. For these determinations, made by dropping a perpendicular from the point to the line and measuring according to any method of measurement, any superimposition and any lines may be used. (Cage 1958b)

An example of one of these transparent squares superimposed over a dot, with a perpendicular drawn to one line, appears in Fig. 11.

In this example, if one was to play a keyboard event at line 2, one could use the perpendicular by using 1/4 of an inch equal to one note. According to that measuring scale, this would mean to play five notes (using the original dimensions of the score). These five notes could then be accomplished by performing with the elbow. This is just one possible interpretation of the score for this illustration. None of the five lines on the squares are labeled, but are determined for meaning by the individual performer in answering possible questions that may arise.

The *Music Walk* score is specifically designed for "1 or more pianists" according to the instruction sheet. The choreography that results is the stage movement by the musicians enacting the events determined by making score overlays. Each musician makes his part independently, but Cage notes:

> The performers may move at any time from one playing position to another (thereby altering the references). When they are at a single playing position, it may be shared when [at] a piano by not more than 3 players (high, middle, low) or 2 (high, low). Otherwise occupancy is to be respected, producing a delay or alteration in plans. A performance lasts an agreed upon length of time. (Cage 1958b)

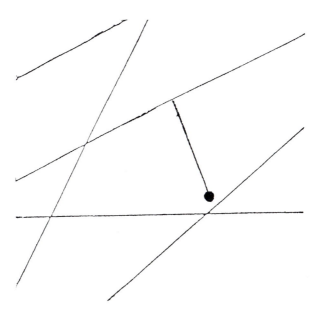

Fig. 11.   An optional square from *Music Walk* (1958), showing a dot and a perpendicular line; © 1960 Henmar Press Inc.

The choreography that results from chance determinations from score superimpositions thus might mean traffic jams. This is recognized in the instructions, and is to be avoided. In similar fashion, Cunningham avoids collisions by his dancers in his own chance choreography. In *Music Walk*, each performer is independent, but *shares* a common space and an agreed upon total duration.

The two most documentable performances of *Music Walk* are by John Cage and David Tudor. Cage's own realization of the *Music Walk* score exists among his unpublished papers. This is a set of ten cards measuring 8–1/4 by 3 inches. Each card equals one minute. The first two of Cage's *Music Walk* performance cards are reproduced in Fig. 12. Events are notated spatially, with numbers representing the initiation of an action in reference to seconds as read from a stop-watch. The vertical lines such as "piano" or "radio" indicate objects in space, stations that Cage must then be prepared to be at. The choreography involved in the performance is explicitly notated by Cage in his very first notation "in space," which clearly denotes the visual, physical movement aspect of the composition.

Cage's performance realization is rather straight-forward to read. "K" is the piano keyboard, "I" the interior and "O" the outside or exterior of the piano; "P" is to pluck a string; "M" means mute; and "R" is radio. In total,

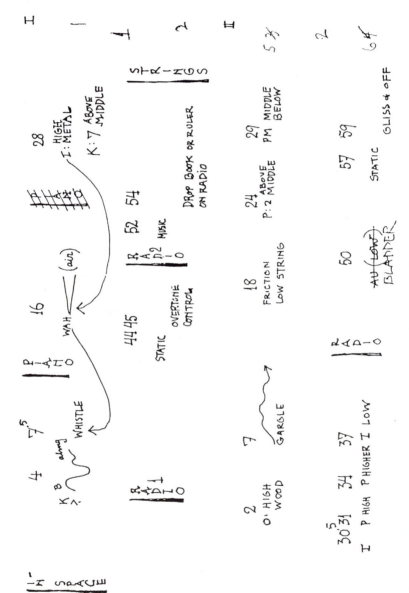

Fig. 12. John Cage's performance realization of *Music Walk* (1958), showing events for the first two minutes. Reproduced courtesy of the John Cage Estate.

Cage notated 64 events for his performance (Cage 1958c). With reference to the possibilities from the five lines in the indeterminate score, la is done 7 times, 1b 4 times, 1c 3 times, 1d 2 times; 2a 9 times, 2b 2 times, 2c 2 times; 3a 13 times, 3b 3 times; 4a 5 times, 4b one time; and 5 (auxiliary sounds) 13 times. Many of the auxiliary sounds are vocal sounds, such as phonemes at 0'04" or 1'50". David Tudor comments that Cage probably performed most of his own notated actions, but that because of the sometimes incongruent traffic jams with conflicting events, "if you don't succeed, you go on to the next notation. That was the method that we both used" (Tudor 1993). This approach also was employed in situations when a large number of events were determined for performance, but then became ultimately impractical to actually enact.

Cage probably performed *Music Walk* as scrupulously as possible according to the situation of individual performance (such was in character), but it is important to note that he varied his performances. This is explicitly notated in his notation at 1'50", which originally reads "AU (Low)." This vocal sound (notated in ink) was later crossed-out, and emended with a different auxiliary sound "Bladder," which David Tudor explains to mean a "bladder whistle," similar to a "whoopee cushion," which produces a flatulent sound (Tudor 1993). Most importantly, however, the concern for minute detail, which Cage placed upon the prospective performer of *Music Walk*, is expressed not only within the original indeterminate score, but Cage's own performance realization. Although he did not intend his own score determination to be a public notation, the care with which he made his performance version is a model from which to approach the published indeterminate score.

The other documentable performance of *Music Walk* is from David Tudor's unpublished score realization. This consists of two sheets of paper, written on both sides in pencil, measuring 3 by 8-¼ inches. Like Cage, Tudor's realization is for a ten-minute performance. An example of the first page, showing the first five minutes, is reproduced in Fig. 13.

Commenting on this realization and use in performance, Tudor states:

> *This is not necessarily the order that I played them, but I might have. The written-out realization is itself indeterminate in the sense that once you start a page [one page from Cage's score equal to 60 seconds], you finish it, then you go on to the next page, but what the next page is isn't determinate, so you can rearrange the next time you do it. Once I took all those readings, I didn't need any more information, because the piece is variable. (Tudor 1989a and 1989b)*

What is primarily notated in Tudor's realization is the occurrence of an event, a linguistic short-hand description of the action, and the dynamics level (1 soft, through 10 loud). Tudor also includes some movement cues, such as "[go

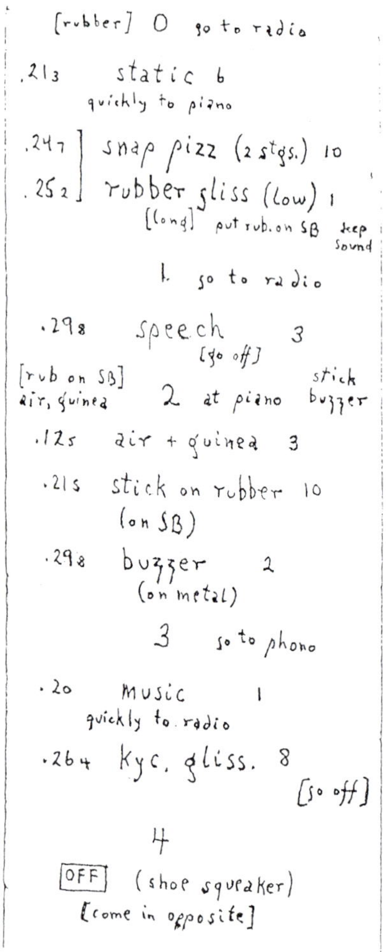

[rubber] O   go to radio

.213   static 6
           quickly to piano

.247 ⎤ snap pizz (2 stgs.) 10
.252 ⎦ rubber gliss (low) 1
           [long] put rub. on SB   keep
                                     sound

           1. go to radio

.298   speech   3
                  [go off]
[rub on SB]   stick
air, guinea   2   at piano   buzzer

.12s   air + guinea   3

.21s   stick on rubber 10
           (on SB)

.29s   buzzer   2
           (on metal)

           3   go to phono

.20   music   1
        quickly to radio

.264   kyc. gliss. 8
                         [go off]

           4

[OFF]   (shoe squeaker)
[come in opposite]

Fig. 13. The first page of David Tudor's performance realization of *Music Walk* (1958), showing events for the first five minutes. Reproduced courtesy of David Tudor.

off]" after performing at 1.298; or "[OFF]" at 4.00, Tudor's realization of the "blank page."

The meticulousness of Tudor's score determinations and self-performance instructions includes a list of twelve objects and their location. This list is (renotated):

> in left pocket – air whistle
> – guinea whistle
> in the right pocket – plectrum
> – squeaker
> in back pocket – shoe squeaker
> – goose whistle

> *at piano – thick rubber bar*
> *– thick flat plastic*
> *– metal beater*
> *– wind–up buzzer*
> *elsewhere – water warbler whistle*
> *– heavy drum stick   (Tudor 1958)*

David Tudor does not recall how he determined the time for the events, but it could be assumed that he read time spatially with the parallel-line transparency equal to 60 seconds per page. He *does* recall that the five lines were interpreted as line 1 being at the top, consequitively through line 5 at the bottom. Tudor no longer recalls how he decided which possibility to choose with each line reading — this was probably from his own personal taste. The careful attention to dynamics for each event might indicate that he used a transparency of five nonparallel lines, but Tudor does not recall this, nor are there any written notes to confirm this suggestion. Certainly part of Tudor's written realization is based on scrupulously detailed use of the score materials as Cage instructs, and part of the result is from Tudor's own personal decisions. The "blank page" in Cage's score, the fifth minute ("4") in Tudor's realization, shows this personal input. Tudor did not use the minute to remain motionless but attached a squeaker on one of his shoes, walked off, and re-entered again at the end of the minute. He states:

> *To perform the blank page you just stand quietly, but usually what you had to do was spend the time looking at what you had to do right after, because some of the things were really very lively. (Tudor 1989b)*

No doubt Tudor performed several variations based on his written realization according to different performance spaces and available equipment.

David Tudor's written realization of Cage's score is a thorough use of the inherent possibilities. There are 43 events in Tudor's realization. Of these, Tudor uses Cage's lines in the following manner: 1a is used four times, 1b and 1c do not occur, 1d is used once; 2a does not occur, 2b is used four times, 2c is used three times; 3a is used six times, 3b is used three times; 4a is used eight times, 4b is used six times; and 5 (an auxiliary sound chosen by the performer) occurs eight times with five different sounds. No performer since Tudor or Cage is known to have made such a comprehensive and imaginative use of the *Music Walk* score.

The last time that David Tudor and John Cage performed this score was with Jill Johnston as *Music Walk with Dancer* in New York on April 4, 1962. Tudor comments:

> *It didn't change at all when we did it with Jill Johnston. She was reading from her manuscripts. She was just sitting or standing on the stage somewhere. (Tudor 1989a)*

Time would review this performance by writing:

> *Occasionally reading directions from slips of paper, they [Cage and Tudor] scurried from one short-wave radio to another, twiddling dials and assaulting the audience with a drumfire of rattles, bangs, pops and nonsense syllables roared into a microphone. Occasionally they turned on an electric blender or belabored the piano. ("Composing by Knucklebone" 1962, 55)*

This review is again rather biased against Cage's work, but it includes mention of a few additional auxiliary sounds, and most importantly notes that Cage and Tudor performed the piece following their previously written-out realizations without recourse to memorization or improvisation.

A more positive view of this specific performance is recalled by the composer Philip Corner, who remembers Jill Johnston reading on a ladder, and at one point pulling a toy dog on wheels across the stage. Corner recalls that the sound had an "overlapping, seamless quality" that was generally loud but with some occasional soft-sounding moments. Corner particularly remembers the quality of movement as performed by Cage and Tudor in making their various sound events:

> *There was a lot of movement. I remember this being very lively. David Tudor and John Cage had to get up and go to other places to do things, and turn on things and do other things, so there was that whole theatrical aspect, the conjunctions in space. The movement from one point to another was very much a fast movement. Efficient. No hesitancy. It wasn't a slow drag by any means, but I wouldn't say it was hectic — it seemed like it was totally under control. They gave themselves enough time to get wherever they were going. (Corner 1989)*

Jill Johnston recalls that she made use of the score materials, but that the intersections of lines with dots were used to indicate the occurrence of an action other than those suggested in the original instructions. She characterizes her work as a "domestic, biographical performance." She wore a red dress, and recalls washing a baby bottle, suspending a Savarin coffee can from a ladder (with either water dripping into it or dripping out from it), sweeping with a broom, pulling a small child's toy across the stage ("like a quacking duck — it made a noise"), and doing a slight dance at various points. She also vaguely recalls the possibility of cooking bacon on an electric hot plate. The texts read from are no longer ascertainable, but Johnston suggests that they were probably found-text excerpts from newspapers. One item she does recall was an article taken from the *New York Times* which listed the various objects found in a vagabond's pockets when taken into police custody.

Johnston recalls that she made a scrupulous use of the score to determine the time occurrences for her various actions, but that at the beginning of the actual performance she dropped her cards, and had to be much more improvisational than either Cage or Tudor. Afterwards, she apologized to Cage for not using her cards, for which he chided her, but in a way that "didn't make me feel bad." Many of her actions produced laughter among the audience, and when asked about this reaction, Cage told her that he preferred laughter to tears (J. Johnston 1991).

 Music Walk has since been performed by others, most notably by Don Gillespie in the mid-1970s, and by Stephen Drury in the late 1980s-early 1990s, but it is a presently under-rated or over-looked score, no doubt because of the complexity of the indeterminate notation. The style of simultaneous, independent performance from complex indeterminate notation in *Music Walk* has a continuation in its variation *Cartridge Music* (1960).

Cartridge Music

Cartridge Music was composed at Stony Point, New York, during July, 1960 (Cage 1960a). It has usually been performed with contact microphones on objects (such as a table or piano bench), and various items inserted into a phonograph pick-up in place of the conventional phonograph needle. The score can also be used to create *Duet for Cymbal*, by placing a contact microphone onto the intrument; or to create *Piano Duet*, by placing a contact microphone on the soundboard of the instrument. The most common version of the *Cartridge Music* score has been the insertion of objects into the phonograph pick-up, and it is that version with which this study is concerned.

 The first performance of *Cartridge Music* was made by eight persons — including David Tudor, Benjamin Patterson, Cornelius Cardew, and Christian Wolff — in simultaneous performance with John Cage performing his *Solo for Voice 2* (Cage 1960d) at Cologne on October 6, 1960 (Dunn 1962, 34). Cage and Tudor would perform *Cartridge Music* as a simultaneous duet several times through the mid-1960s.

 The *Cartridge Music* score begins with an extremely detailed instruction sheet introducing how to use the score materials. There are twenty sheets, each numbered with a corresponding number of forms, measuring 8–3/4 inches vertically and 11–3/4 inches horizontally. There are four transparencies, which are to be superimposed on top of one of the sheets with a form or forms. Three of the transparencies also measure 8–3/4 by 11–3/4 inches. The first transparent sheet contains 19 dots randomly distributed about the sheet; the second transparency contains 10 circles randomly distributed about the sheet; and the third transparency contains a dotted curving line which meanders over the entire sheet, with a circle at one end. The irregular design of the dotted line is further reinforced by its crossing over itself at six different places. The final transparency is a rectangle measuring

10 by 2–1/2 inches: at the center is a circular clock-face measuring 1–3/4 inches in diameter, marked in conventional five-second intervals from 0 through 55.

The instruction sheet is very detailed and lucid, but the result of making score determinations is itself not fully determinate of actual performance. In brief, each performer makes his own part. First, one chooses one of the twenty numbered sheets with forms. Cage instructs:

> *Let the number of performers be at least that of the cartridges and not greater than twice the number of cartridges. (Cage 1960a)*

Thus, if there is only one performer, there would only be one cartridge (using page 1); or at most, two cartridges (using page 2). If there is more than one performer, or more than one cartridge is used, each of the performers must determine the numbering of the forms on the appropriate score page.

Over the forms sheet, one then places the four transparencies in any arrangement that places the dotted curving line in a position. . .

> *. . . so that the circle at the end. . . contains a point outside a shape and so that the dotted line intersects at least one point within one of the shapes. (If no such point exists, no action is indicated.) Then, following the dotted line from either end to the other, read the actions to be made. . . (Cage 1960a)*

The actions that can result from superimposing the first three transparencies over a sheet with forms are, in abbreviated fashion, from the following possibilities:

> 1. *Intersection of the dotted line with a point within a shape indicates a sound produced in any manner of the object inserted in the cartridge corresponding to that shape.*
> 2. *Intersection of the dotted line with a point outside a shape indicates the production of auxiliary sounds, such as placing a contact microphone on the microphone stand or a table.*
> 3. *Intersection of the dotted line with a circle within a shape indicates altering the dynamics control of the amplifier.*
> 4. *Intersection of the dotted line with a circle outside a shape indicates an alteration of tone control of the amplifier closest to the cartridge/shape.*
> 5. *When points or circles are intersected by the dotted line where the line crosses over itself, this indicates a repeated sound pattern.*
> 6. *Changing the object in a cartridge is indicated when a circle is intersected by both the boundary of a shape and the dotted line.*

Over this, one then places the clock-face transparency to measure time. Cage writes:

> *Time bracket(s) for action(s) [are] to be made given by entrance(s) and exit(s) of the dotted line with respect to the stop-watch circle. If no such entrance or exit occurs, no specific time is given. The action should then fall outside any time bracket(s)*

established. The seconds given refer to any one of the minutes of the total time
programmed which may be any agreed-upon time. (Cage 1960a)

The best documentation to show how Cage's score might look in performance is from David Tudor's realizations. Tudor showed me several different realizations that he had made. Most of them are for ten-minute performances, which he also recalls as being the duration of most of the live performances. A photocopy from the first page (from three pages) of one of Tudor's realizations of *Cartridge Music* appears in Fig. 14. At the left are the time brackets, as would have been shown from the entrance and exit of the dotted line intersecting at the appropriate positions on the stop-watch transparency. Time in *Cartridge Music,* in both Cage's score and Tudor's realization, does not include the occurrence of an event (as in all the previous theatre pieces discussed), but gives a duration *within* which an event or events may be performed. Reading on the first line, "A_o" means an auxiliary sound produced on neither cartridge 1 or 2, and "2:x" means a sound produced on cartridge 2. The second line shows "$1:x^r x^r$" which means two repeated sound patterns on cartridge 1; and "$2:\underline{T/}$" means increasing the tonal level on the amplifier for cartridge 2. In the other lines, a "V" means volume, and "$\boxed{C}$" means to change the cartridge. With these explanations of Tudor's abbreviated symbols, one can easily follow the rest of Fig. 14.

Tudor's written realization, of course, is in itself an indeterminate notation. It does not tell what objects are to be placed into the pick-ups, what the auxiliary sounds are, or how to manipulate either the cartridge or auxiliary sound objects. Tudor's realization, like Cage's score, is nonetheless very practical and efficient. An example of an overlay using Cage's score as it

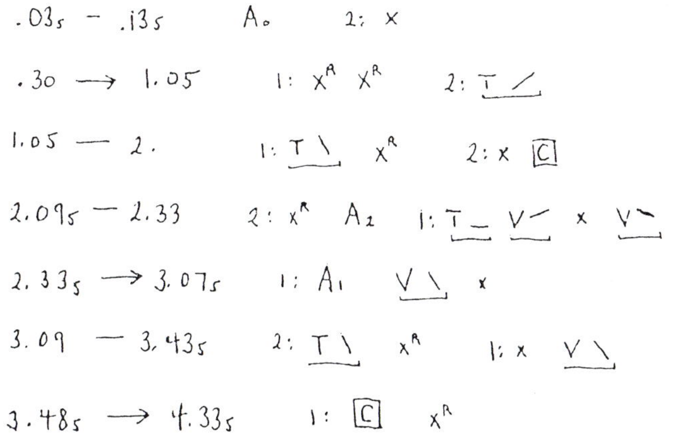

Fig. 14.   A performance realization of *Cartridge Music* (1960) by David Tudor, showing the first of three pages. Reproduced courtesy of David Tudor.

might have looked like when David Tudor made the first line in his realization appears in Fig. 15. In my score overlay, one reads beginning with the
circle on the dotted line. Cartridge 1 would be the form on the left, and
cartridge 2 would be the form on the right. Reading from the circle on the
dotted line, the first action would be an auxiliary sound produced on neither
cartridge 1 or 2, and the second action would be producing a sound on
cartridge 2. In consonance with Tudor's first line, my score overlay shows no
additional event (no other intersections of the dotted line with either a point
or a circle). What this example of Cage's score illustrates is not only that his
complex indeterminate notation is very practical and really not so complicated
once one actually begins using the materials, but that Tudor's written realization from Cage's score is a meticulous and accurate, demonstrable interpretation. This is concretely shown in my score overlay, but Cage's score is so
variable, and is so complex, that it is as much a matter of luck as study that
makes this possible to show.

Perhaps the most intriguing element not notated in Tudor's realization is what specific objects are inserted into the phonograph pick-up, or

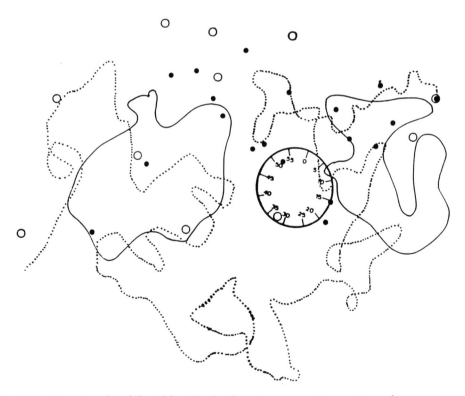

Fig. 15.   An example of *Cartridge Music*, showing a superimposition of score materials; © 1960 Henmar Press Inc.

what specific objects are attached with contact microphones to produce auxiliary sounds. Cage suggests objects such as "a coil of wire, a toothpick, a pipe-cleaner, a twig" (Cage 1960a), or "matches, slinkies, piano wires, feathers, etc." (Cage 1962a) for the cartridges; and for contact microphones to be placed on the "microphone stand, table" (Cage 1960a), or "chairs, tables, waste baskets, etc." (Cage 1962a) to produce the auxiliary sounds. When asked what objects were used, David Tudor recalled:

> *We used coils of wire of any length, and feathers. I have a collection of things that you wouldn't believe would be useful. A threaded rod, if you can get it small enough in diameter — a threaded bolt (only it's not a bolt, it's a rod) — they are very nice to perform with because they are very abrasive, they make a lot of friction. (Tudor 1989a)*

Two versions of *Cartridge Music* realizations made by Cage for his own performances with David Tudor exist among Cage's unpublished papers (Cage 1960b). These are notated in black ink, with additional penciled annotations, on the back of the *Music Walk* cards. Each of the ten *Cartridge Music* cards equal one minute of performance. The first two cards are reproduced in Fig. 16. Time brackets are notated in spatial notation with numbers in reference to seconds as read on a stop-watch. Below the time brackets are

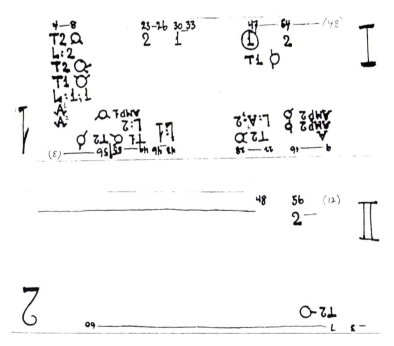

Fig. 16. John Cage's two performance realizations of *Cartridge Music* (1960), each showing events for the first two minutes. Reproduced courtesy of the John Cage Estate.

Cage's abbreviated symbols for the actions. There are 36 actions notated in the version paginated with Arabic numerals, and 43 actions notated in the version paginated with Roman numerals. Both versions use only two cartridges.

Beginning with the first card in the Arabic numeral version, between 0'09" and 0'16" one is to make a sound with auxiliary sound 1, adjust the volume on the amplifier for cartridge 2 between dial settings 1 through 5, and then readjust the dial setting on amplifier 2 to dial setting 2; between 0'12" and 0'28" one adjusts the tone (bass and treble) for cartridge 2 between dial settings 2 and 4, and makes a repeated sound ("L" meaning "loop") with auxiliary sound 4, and cartridge 2; and at 0'43" to 0'46" one makes a repeated sound pattern on cartridge 1. With this information, one can easily read the remaining notations. The Roman numeral version, read by turning the cards 180°, has only one additional notation not found in the Arabic numeral realization. This is the circled 1 at 0'47", which would mean to change the cartridge object. It is interesting that when Cage made his own score superimpositions to determine the actions for his own performance, the Arabic numeral version has no cartridge changes; and the Roman numeral version only has two additional examples of changing cartridges (cartridges 2 and then 1, between 5'27" and 5'31"). When asking David Tudor about my interpretations of Cage's realizations, he agreed with my readings, but added that when there were many score determinations within a brief period of time, "you would undertake to do as many actions as feasible to be performed" (Tudor 1993). In consonance with Tudor's own performance versions of *Cartridge Music*, Cage's realization is a very practical notation which determines the basic parameters of the score materials, but is still indeterminate as to the actual objects used to be manipulated in the cartridge or employed as auxiliary sounds. Cage and Tudor thus made a disciplined performance that included a semi-improvisational component as well.

Journalistic reviews of *Cartridge Music* performances by Cage and Tudor range from disparaging to mixed-reaction to enthusiastic, but there is nonetheless some documentation of what objects were used, as well as some indication of how visual the piece was. Raymond Ericson reviewed the American premiere, performed at the Museum of Modern Art on April 20, 1961, for the *New York Times*:

> *Attach one end of a Slinky toy . . . to a phonograph cartridge wired to an amplifier, then stroke it, bounce it, vibrate it, drag it along the floor and hear what comes out of the speakers. This was the basic formula for "Cartridge Music". . .*
>
> *Actually there were two cartridges, one suspended from a stand, one attached to a low table. Into these cartridges went a feather, bits of wire, toothpicks, pipe cleaners, nails, a tiny Japanese parasol, even a tiny American flag. The resultant boops, blasts, crackles, and thunderous booms were haralded as "a new world of sound."*
>
> *This was nonsense. Any amateur who has fumbled around with "hi-fi" equip-*

> *ment has experienced them all before. The composer and David Tudor were the stage*
> *managers — they could scarcely be called performers — for this work. (Ericson 1961)*

Aside from Ericson's negative bias in reporting, there is some documentation of objects used. The statement that Cage and Tudor can not be called performers of this work, of course, is a completely incorrect interpretation. Not everyone has the ability or patience to work from Cage's highly sophisticated score, or to make such a meticulously written realization and performance as David Tudor and John Cage.

Louis Guzzo would write a mixed-reaction review of a performance in Seattle in September, 1962:

> *"Cartridge Music" was the piece de resistance as both men pushed furniture*
> *around (even the piano bench was wired for sound), set off a coil spring linked to a*
> *microphone, rubbed small gadgets and wires, slapped almost everything in sight and*
> *operated all four tape-recorders.*
>
> *A precise description of the composition is impossible, but the listener*
> *suddenly seemed to understand what it must have been like for the first wave of*
> *marines at Iwo Jima.*
>
> *Cage and Tudor paced to and fro, scripts in hand. They looked like a couple of*
> *men who had just received an assemble-it-yourself appliance from Montgomery Ward.*
> *Nevertheless, it was fascinating, for all that. . . (Guzzo 1962)*

This review mentions several auxiliary sound objects and is particularly evocative in documenting that Cage and Tudor performed this not from improvisation or memorization, and that there was a lot of back-and-forth stage movement. What the four tapes were is not documented, but quite possibly these were the four separate tapes that comprise Cage's lecture "Where Are We Going? And What Are We Doing?," available from C. F. Peters and published in *Silence* (Cage 1961, 195–259). Guzzo's "Iwo Jima" metaphor seems to be a rather subjective exaggeration, but the "assemble-it-yourself" quality of their performance is an accurate insight into the very nature of *Cartridge Music* (or Cage's indeterminate notations in general), because that is basically what one must do with the score.

The most enthusiastic review of *Cartridge Music* is by Peter Yates, a supporter of Cage's music since the 1940s. Yates describes a performance in Los Angeles in September, 1964:

> *Cage and his companion of many performances, the pianist David Tudor, each*
> *following a different sequence of events by chance, insert slinkies, pipe cleaners,*
> *miniature flags, even a tiny birthday candle which is then lighted, into the needle slots*
> *of the cartridges and agitate them, producing noises in the loudspeakers, which*
> *accompany the performance of low-frequency sounds culled from Time Records of*
> *Cage's music. One watches the actions of the two performers as in other days one*
> *watched the actions of the clowns circulating around the three rings of the circus, and*
> *the more one relaxes into the uninhibited attention the funnier it gets. (Yates 1964, 22)*

In Yates's review one senses that (at least for those who appreciate Cage's work) this was a very enjoyable performance, although one should not be misled into thinking that Cage and Tudor were acting like clowns. Both have always been very serious performers, and it would have been completely out of character for either of them to have "guyed" the performance. The recordings played from the now-defunct Time Records issues may have included *Double Music* for percussion ensemble, composed with Lou Harrison in 1941; *Aria with Fontana Mix* (both 1958); or the 1962 recording of *Cartridge Music* itself (Gena and Brent 1982, 202–207).

The 1962 *Cartridge Music* recording issued by Time Records is a twenty-minute version that superimposes four different simultaneous duets by Cage and Tudor. About this version, Tudor comments:

> *It was quite obvious that the timings were going to give the recording problems, because with just two performances [two performers] it's not very dense, and so in order that half the recording would be silence we decided to simply impose it without any thought as to the actual density of it. It wasn't going to matter if silence did occur — that wasn't going to matter — it was just in order not to have too much of it. That's a standard technique with most pieces. (Tudor 1989a)*

The resultant recording, made from four separate duet performances, is rather dense-sounding. It is rather loud throughout, but there are also many moments when very delicate and soft sounds are heard as well. One soft sound, repeated, is reminiscent of someone sawing wood in the distance; another sound, also repeated, is very loud and is reminiscent of a chain-saw heard at close-range. It is in the nature of Cage's indeterminate notation that even in the recording one can not tell with any accuracy what documented objects are producing sounds in the cartridges or from contact microphones on auxiliary objects (Cage 1962a).

Cartridge Music has been performed by several other prominent contemporary composers. Christian Wolff, who was a performer in the premiere on October 6, 1960, has also performed this several other times. He recalls that the score is extremely practical, and that the theatrical element comes about, but not explicitly, because one has to move around. The result is that what the audience sees is a constant milling-about on the stage by the performers, and that the movement in playing or in changing cartridges or auxiliary sound objects thus does not appear to be normal or expected. Wolff also stresses that the performance depends upon the individuals involved, partly because of the individual score readings, and partly because of the unpredictability of actual performance (Wolff 1989).

Philip Corner recalls performing *Cartridge Music* in the latter 1960s, noting in particular the unpredictability of performance that results from Cage's indeterminate notation:

To me it was a very shocking idea that when you make a preparation on whatever basis, that it doesn't do anything. No only doesn't it do anything that has to do with your idea of what the preparations should be, but it doesn't do anything at all. David Tudor was suggesting that you could accept that. You could do something where your action didn't have any discernable result. I guess that's really the extreme example of the disinterested action. Corner 1989)

Alvin Lucier, associated with Cage since the 1960s, has performed *Cartridge Music* with students at Wesleyan University, at Lincoln Center in the summer of 1988, and at the Whitney Museum at Stamford, Connecticut, in December, 1988. Lucier states that it is a sparse piece when performed as a solo, and when the piece was first performed the long silences were seen as very shocking, but that audiences in the latter 1980s can now see that this is very beautiful. He also makes the practical comment that one can figure out what to do by making the score overlays during actual performance, figuring out what is indicated in the score, performing the indicated action or actions, and then making another score superimposition. Lucier notes, however, that he has always made a written-out realization of the score previous to actual performance, and this appears to be the way that *Cartridge Music* is tradition-ally done (Lucier 1989).

Cartridge Music has been most recently recorded twice by David Tudor, Takehisa Kosugi, and Michael Pugliese as the accompaniment for Merce Cunningham's dance *Changing Steps*. Originally choreographed in 1973, the dance was first paired with *Cartridge Music* in 1975, and made into a videodance in 1989 (Vaughan 1991). The *Cartridge Music* accompaniment to Cunningham's videodance is thirty minutes (Cunningham 1989a). The sound has a much more relaxed, gentle feel in comparison to the 1962 phonograph recording, and has a very human quality, as the sounds of the dancers's feet (as well as breathing in the more physical sections of the dance) unintentionally melds with the independent music. The second recording, released as an independent realization on CD, has a duration of 18'53" (Cage 1991a). The CD has an almost acoustic feel, and like the videodance record-ing, does not have the abrasive, "noisy" quality of the 1962 record.

David Tudor, Christian Wolff, Philip Corner, and Alvin Lucier all agree that *Cartridge Music* is now a technologically dated work because the phonograph pick-up that one must use held the needle by tightening a screw. Contemporary phonographs are no longer made this way; and indeed, the phonograph is quickly becoming obsolete equipment. Despite the matter of dated technology, the score and performances of *Cartridge Music* remain a significant achievement not only within Cage's theatre pieces in particular, but within his music compositions in general.

4

4'33", 0'00", SOLOS IN *SONG BOOKS*, *WGBH-TV*, AND *ONE* ³: VARIATIONS ON A DISCIPLINED ACTION

4'33"

4'33" is John Cage's most famous composition. It was composed at Black Mountain College during the summer of 1952 and first performed by David Tudor at Maverick Concert Hall, Woodstock, New York, on August 29, 1952 (Dunn 1962, 25). The title refers to the clock-time duration of the composition, which (usually) consists of four minutes and thirty-three seconds of silence. 4'33" has achieved a legendary status within not only Cage's work but twentieth century art as well. Many concert reviews from the last twenty or thirty years begin by reminding the reader that Cage is the composer of the "silent piece" as a pretext for a positive or negative bias in criticism.

The most articulate negative interpretation of 4'33" is expressed by David Tame, who sarcastically writes that Cage "no doubt took considerable pains to compose" this "masterpiece," and that it should "be viewed as nothing but a joke; cheap, unnecessary, and perhaps also, ego-centric" (Tame 1984, 105–106). Richard Taruskin echoes Tame's view, stating that 4'33" is the "ultimate aesthetic aggrandizement, an act of transcendent empyrialism" (Taruskin 1993, 34). The most provocative contemporary critical interpretation is by Caroline Jones, who attempts to make the case that 4'33" is an example of "closet-case" homosexual art sensibility in which "silence" becomes both a "shield and protest" to unacceptable political, aesthetic, and sexual practice during the "cold war" (Jones 1993).

Unfortunately, 4'33" is usually known from hearsay and is often misunderstood or simplified in terms of both the score and its performance. There are actually four different scores for 4'33", there are many different ways to perform the piece, and there are several later variations — all of which must be taken into consideration before making any critical/philosophical commentary. Cage himself considered 4'33" to be his most important work, noting that "I always think of it before I write the next piece" (Montague 1982, 11).

Contrary to Tame's sarcastic and erroneous documentation and interpretation, the idea of making a silent composition *was* in Cage's mind for several years previous to the actual making of a score in 1952. The idea of using silence for a composition was first expressed in Cage's lecture "A Composer's Confessions" at Vassar College on February 28, 1948. The text was for many years suppressed by Cage for publication (perhaps because of the conventional, linear autobiographical content), and was finally published in anticipation of his 80th birthday. Cage would later inaccurately recall that this lecture was concerned with the nine permanent emotions in tradtional Indian aesthetics — four positive (white), four negative (black), and one in the center (without color). The central emotion is tranquility, the freedom from likes and dislikes, the absence of activity:

> The marvelous thing about it is when activity comes to a stop, what is immediately seen is that the rest of the world has not stopped. There is no place without activity.... So the only difference between activity and inactivity is in the mind. (Montague 1982, 11)

Such thought is reflected in the increasingly thin texture of solo piano writing as in *A Valentine Out of Season* (1944), *Two Pieces* (1946), and *Dream* (1948), which present a stylistic continuum from personal taste and expression towards silence and egolessness. The actual lecture is less concerned with philosophical material, but his later recollection of the lecture makes clear the influence from his then-contemporary studies in Eastern philosophy and aesthetics during the latter 1940s as a theoretical justification for making a "silent piece."

Toward the conclusion of "A Composer's Confessions," Cage stresses his concern to use new materials for music composition, and writes that he would like. . .

> . . .to compose a piece of uninterrupted silence and sell it to Muzak Co. It will be 3 or 4½ minutes long — those being the standard lengths of "canned" music — and its title will be Silent Prayer. It will open with a single idea which I will attempt to make as seductive as the color and shape and fragrance of a flower. The ending will approach imperceptibility. (Cage 1992a, 15)

This first public pronouncement of making a silent piece is further revealed in a 1949 review and interview in *Time*:

> The first step in describing silence. . .is to use silence itself. Matter of fact, I thought of composing a piece like that. It would be very beautiful, and I would like to offer it to Muzak. . . ("Music" 1949, 36)

With this information, it is obvious that Cage was thinking of the silent piece as including a social critique of middle-brow musical taste, and the commodi-fication of art through "the music industry/show business." While Jones's sexual interpretation of 4'33" is intriguing, there is no documentary evidence to concretely verify that position, and as such is more accurately relegated to personal speculation.

Probably the most significant aspect of Cage's thinking in making the silent piece was not from Eastern aesthetics or social criticism, but from a theoretical insight into the practical nature of sound itself. In his 1949 essay "Forerunners of Modern Music," Cage writes:

> *Sound has four characteristics: pitch, timbre, loudness, and duration. The opposite and necessary coexistent of sound is silence. Of the four characteristics of sound, only duration involves both sound and silence. Therefore, a structure based on durations (rhythmic: phrase, time lengths) is correct (corresponds with the nature of the material), whereas harmonic structure is incorrect (derived from pitch, which has no being in silence). (Cage 1961, 63)*

He would be reluctant, however, to actually make the silent composition until seeing the White Paintings of Robert Rauschenberg. Rauschenberg's White Paintings were first publicly exhibited in Cage's untitled event at Black Mountain College during the summer of 1952 (Kotz 1990, 76; discussed in Chapter 5); but Irwin Kremen recalls meeting Cage and going to visit at his New York loft in late 1951, and seeing Rauschenberg's White Paintings at that time (Kremen 1992). Cage later commented on Rauschenberg's example to actually make the silent piece:

> *I was thinking of it, but I felt that it would not be taken seriously, and so I refrained from doing it. . . But when Bob did the empty canvases, I had the courage to take the path, come what may. (Campana 1985, 103)*

Also, sometime in 1951, he entered an anechoic chamber (a room engineered to have no echo or outside sounds) at Harvard University (Cage 1961, 13). Cage would write that he. . .

> *. . .heard two sounds, one low and one high. When I described them to the engineer in charge, he informed me that the high one was my nervous system in operation, the low one my blood in circulation. Until I die there will be sounds. And they will continue following my death. One need not fear about the future of music. (Cage 1961, 8)*

This experience revealed the fact that silence is only temporal and subjective, that there is no such thing as absolute silence. On further reflection with the silent composition and his experience in the anechoic chamber, Cage would write:

> *There are, demonstrably, sounds to be heard and forever, given ears to hear. Where these ears are in connection with a mind that has nothing to do, that mind is free to enter into the act of listening, hearing each sound just as it is, not as a phenomenon more or less approximating a preconception. (Cage 1961, 23)*

It is from Cage's own writings and published interviews that most interpretations of 4'33" are made, that is, that the piece does not consist of silence but the ambient sounds which naturally occur within the environment and among the audience. The concept of silence is admittedly open to various intellectual interpretations as either positive (as in the silent worship of the Society of Friends) or as a negation (as in Hamlet's last words which equate silence with death). In order to understand Cage's composition, however, it is the scores and performance which are central.

Cage initially wrote that the "lengths of time were determined by chance operations but could be any others" (Dunn 1962, 25). He recently explained that the composition method was in using a home-made deck of cards, on which were written durations:

> *I wrote it note by note, just like the* Music of Changes *[1951]. That's how I knew how long it was, when I added all the notes up.*
> *It was done just like a piece of music, except there were no sounds — but there were durations. It was dealing these cards — shuffling them, on which there were durations, and then dealing them — and using the Tarot to know how to use them. The card-spread was a complicated one, something big.*
> [*Question: Why did you use the Tarot rather than the* I Ching?]
> *Probably to balance the East with the West. I didn't use the [actual] Tarot cards, I was just using those ideas; and I was using the Tarot because it was Western, it was the most well-known chance thing known in the West of that oracular nature. (Cage 1990a)*

Cage no longer recalled which of the many possible Tarot card-spreads he used, but when shown a variety of examples, he selected the "horseshoe spread," in Fig. 17. This arrangement of the cards would be plausible because it is not only one of the most complicated Tarot card-spreads, but also it is spatially arranged in three groups, which would then have reference to the three movements in the final composition. On another occasion Cage would also recently recall:

> *I didn't know I was writing 4'33". I built it up very gradually and it came out to be 4'33". I just might have made a mistake in addition. (Cage 1990b, 21)*

Although the original cards with durations are no longer extant, and the actual working process is not directly documentable in exact detail, Cage clearly made 4'33" with a seriousness of intent and attention to detail during the composition process.

The purportedly first score of 4'33" has not been published and is now either lost or the current existence is presently unknown. David Tudor recalls:

> *The original was on music paper, with staffs, and it was laid out in measures like the* Music of Changes, *only there were no notes. But the time was there, notated exactly like the* Music of Changes *except that the tempo never changed, and there were no occurrences — just blank measures, no rests — and the time was easy to compute. The tempo was 60. (Tudor 1989b)*

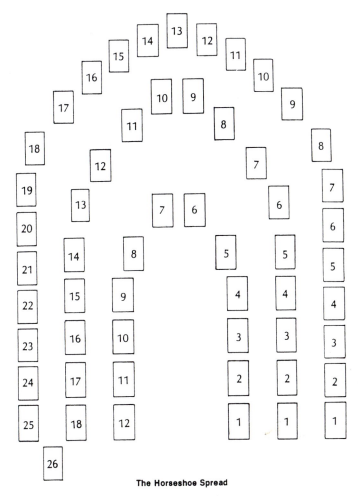

The Horseshoe Spread

Fig. 17. The probable Tarot card-spread used by John Cage in composing 4'33"
(1952) (in Kaplan 1971, 179). Reproduced courtesy of U.S. Games Systems, Inc.

In *Music of Changes* (1951) or *Seven Haiku* (1952), the duration of notes is in
space equal to time, with a quarter-note equal to two-and-a-half centimeters.
Both works have changing tempi, indicated by quarter-note metronome
timings. In 4'33" the quarter-note would probably have also equalled two-
and-a-half centimeters, with a metronome marking of 60 throughout. As an
illustration of how the original score looked, David Tudor made an illustration
for inclusion in this study, appearing as Fig. 18, with a quarter-note equal to
half-an-inch.

In the program of the first performance by David Tudor on August 29,
1952, it was listed as:

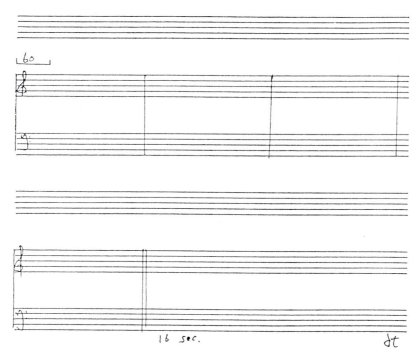

Fig. 18. David Tudor's 1989 notation example of John Cage's original score for 4'33" in 1952. Made for the author, and reproduced courtesy of David Tudor.

4 pieces . . . . *john cage*
4' 33"
30"
2'23"
1'40"

(Program 1952)

This is rather curious. If what is now known as 4'33" is actually *4 pieces,* it is then a work in four movements which add up to a total duration of nine minutes and six seconds. Irwin Kremen hypothesises that Cage sent 4'33" with a designation of the three movements underneath, and that the program typographer was confused and took it to be *"four pieces* — it is just an artifact of the people putting it together, not understanding what John wanted to do" (Kremen 1992). "4 pieces" never happened — rather, David Tudor performed four minutes and thirty-three seconds of silence in the three movements of 30", 2'23", and 1'40", denoting the beginning and ending of each movement by closing and opening the keyboard lid. Tudor also adds:

> *I used a different pedal in each movement! The idea of closing the keyboard*
> *cover was John's idea. You put it down and start the [stop-] watch, and then open it and*

stop the watch — so it is never the same. It's not going to be four minutes and thirty-three seconds, it's going to be much longer (Tudor 1989b)

The score is crucial to David Tudor's performance. He comments:

> *It's important that you read the score as you're performing it, so there are these pages you use. So you wait, and then turn the page. I know it sounds very straight, but in the end it makes a difference. (Tudor 1989b)*

Tudor has made two recent full reconstructions of the now lost first score. The first was made for his performance at the Symphony Space Wall to Wall John Cage concert on March 13, 1982. For this version Tudor used standard-sized blank typing paper, and carefully added the staffs and bar lines in pencil, notating on both sides of the sheet. The first movement was on the first two pages, the second movement on pages 3 through 9, a blank page 10, and the last movement on pages 11 through 14 (Tudor 1982). For yet another performance, in a 1990 videotape session, he again renotated the three movements on commercially printed music paper, necessitating fewer page turns (Miller and Perlis 1990).

The first performance of 4′33″ by David Tudor is still considered to be the most important realization of this composition. Calvin Tomkins describes it as follows:

> *In the Woodstock hall, which was wide open to the woods at the back, attentive listeners could hear during the first movement the sound of wind in the trees; during the second, there was a patter of raindrops on the roof; during the third, the audience took over and added its own perplexed mutterings to the other "sounds not intended" by the composer. (Tomkins 1968, 119)*

Tomkin's documentation is most accurate in describing the ambient sounds that occurred, but does not focus upon the actual performance of the composition, and is misleading if one considers 4′33″ to only be for piano. Tomkins's focus on the incidental sounds, rather than the score and its performance, is the usual interpretation of 4′33″, and this closely follows Cage's own philosophical reflections. David Tudor, however, also characterizes the piece in more mystical terms:

> *It is . . . one of the most intense listening experiences one can have. You really listen. You're hearing everything there is. Audience noises play a part in it. It is cathartic — four minutes and thirty-three seconds of meditation, in effect. (Schonberg 1960, 49)*

The gestural quality of David Tudor's performance is the most significant aspect of 4′33″ being a theatre piece, something to hear as well as to see. In addition to the previously mentioned gestures of closing the keyboard cover and starting the stop-watch, and depressing one of the three piano pedals, the *New York Times*, in reviewing the New York City premiere at Carl

Fisher Concert Hall on April 14, 1954, adds that "At the appropriate time, Mr. Tudor seated himself at the piano, placed a hand on the music rack — and waited" ("Look, No Hands! And It's Music" 1954). The understated quality of gesture has, perhaps, become even more refined in Tudor's recent videotaped performance in 1990. Here, one can see very graceful, rounded gestures in such details such as starting the watch, closing the keyboard cover, as well as Tudor's close attention between reading the score and checking the reading by looking at the stop-watch. Except for turning the pages, Tudor had his hands folded in his lap during the three movements, his back erect, his expression very serious and concentrated (Miller and Perlis 1990). Apart from the ambient sounds that occur while watching this performance on television at home, the non-intentional sounds recorded in the videotape session primarily consist of the ticking of the stop-watch.

Tudor's most recent performance was on a program of various performing artists's responses to Cage's seminal composition, held at the New York Central Park SummerStage on July 15, 1994. The highlights consisted of a talk by Irwin Kremen on the importance of Cage's score as an open-content notation of space equal to time, Margaret Leng Tan doing the prepared piano version of *Waiting* (1952), with Tudor's performance of 4'33" as the finale. There was no noticeable deviation from his previous practice. The most extraordinary aspect of this performance was the choreographic accompaniment by Merce Cunningham. Cunningham and his company of dancers each occupied a position on the stage and held a different static gestural/postural attitude for the duration of each movement. The combination of Tudor's presence with Cunningham's choreography made for a moving and concise instance of mysterious calm and reflective stasis.

The second score version of 4'33" was published in *Source*, July, 1967; and again by C. F. Peters in 1993. This version, made in proportional notation, was made by Cage as a birthday gift to Irwin Kremen in 1953. The first page reads:

4'33"
for an inst[r]ument or combination of instruments
John Cage

The second page is the dedication to Irwin Kremen; the third page gives the space-equals-time scale as "1 page = 7 inches = 56";" and the remaining six pages are the actual performance score (Cage 1953a and 1953b).

The complete first movement is reproduced in Fig. 19. The time is read horizontally between the two vertical lines. The 60 at the top is the tempo indication. Time measurement is repetitive, as at the end of the movement the time is indicated in the number of seconds (and in the later movements in minutes and seconds). In this score version, the first movement

TACET

Fig. 19. The first movement from *4'33"* (1952), made for Irwin Kremen in 1953; © 1993 Henmar Press Inc.

(30″) is one page; the second movement (2′23″) is three pages; and the last movement (1′40″) is two pages. Although it is not on music staffs, this version still incorporates the salient features of the now lost "original score:" it remains the notation of space equal to time, requires page-turning during performance, and has the same durations for the three movements as listed in the program for the first performance on August 29, 1952.

The third and fourth score versions are both in linguistic notation, and are the most known and used by performers other than (and after) David Tudor. The third score, now out of print, appears in Fig. 20. The first part is the recomposed performance score of the three movements, each indicated with a Roman numeral, with the word "Tacet" underneath. The second part is Cage's own documentation of the first performance, with recomposed durations, and notes for further performance interpretations. The third part is the dedication, typed signature, and publication date (Cage 1960c). The fourth score is a calligraphic rewriting of the third score, made by Cage in the mid-1980s, and has superseded the typed version. In the fourth version, the first page is the title, designation "For any instrument or combination of instruments," and signature; the second page is the same material of performance notes in the third version, with this addition before the last sentence from the previous (typed) version:

> After the Woodstock performance, a copy in proportional notation was made for Irwin Kremen. In it the timelengths of the movements were 30″, 2′23″, and 1′40″. (Cage ca. 1986)

The third page contains the three Roman numerals, each with a Tacet underneath.

There are several major differences between these and the first two scores. The first (unpublished and now lost) score, on music staffs, would imply using a keyboard instrument, although not necessarily the piano. The second score would be assumed for any instrument, and not necessarily a solo performance. The third and fourth scores might imply a large ensemble or orchestral performance, by the literal interpretation of the word "Tacet." Cage was always very precise with language, and is traditional in using this specific music term, which is defined by Gardner Read as:

> The term tacet. . . should be used only to indicate that a performer rests throughout an entire movement. In printed music this would be indicated:
>
> II. TACET
>
> (Read 1969, 437)

"Tacet" is used in orchestral music and is often found in percussion parts. In this context, 4′33″ might be interpreted as being indicative of Cage's involve-

I

TACET

II

TACET

III

TACET

```
NOTE:  The title of this work is the total length in minutes and
seconds of its performance.  At Woodstock, N.Y., August 29, 1952,
the title was 4' 33" and the three parts were 33", 2' 40", and 1'
20".  It was performed by David Tudor, pianist, who indicated the
beginnings of parts by closing, the endings by opening, the key-
board lid.  However, the work may be performed by an instrument-
alist or combination of instrumentalists and last any length of
time.
```

```
FOR IRWIN KREMEN                                        JOHN CAGE
```

Fig. 20.   The first published version of 4'33", now out of print.

ment with percussion music, and thus could possibly be interpreted to mean an orchestral version of 4'33".

The most confounding aspect of the third and fourth scores is Cage's performance notes. The durations of the three movements he ascribes to David Tudor's first performance do not correspond to those listed in the 1952 program. David Tudor recalls that to make another score, Cage recomposed it, resulting in different time lengths (Tudor 1989a). When asked about this disparity, Cage replied that the piece could last 23 minutes but that it would still be called 4′33″, and that the durations of the three movements could be determined by *any* chance procedures, but that the piece *is in three movements*, and that the durations *must* be found by chance (Cage 1986b).

Most performances of 4′33″ after David Tudor have been in four minutes and thirty-three seconds, but not always in three movements. Most have been imitations of David Tudor, using the piano with the third score timings but without the gestures of page turning or making any alternative chance-determined durations.

Ellsworth Snyder has performed 4′33″ several times since the 1960s. When doing it as a solo, he has always used the piano, as that is his instrument. He recalls first doing it as one extended movement. Later, he divided it into three movements as indicated in the third score, using chance procedures to determine different durations adding up to four minutes and thirty-three seconds. His next performance was using the *Source* score. For still another variation, Snyder recalls a solo performance:

> I think one time I did it with how time was passing. I did it with the watch to show the beginning and ending, but I did the movements by feeling whatever length they should be. (Snyder 1989)

He also recalls a totally impromptu ensemble performance when John Cage came to Milton College around 1970 and met with a large group of students. A student in the assembly asked if they could all perform 4′33″. Snyder fondly recalls:

> We performed it then. The piece began, and we simply let the time elapse. Then at four minutes and thirty-three seconds it ended, with nobody doing anything intentional. This was in the spring, and it was done with the doors and windows open. (Snyder 1989)

Don Gillespie recalls two very different performance versions, both from the summer of 1970. In August, 1970 at the University of North Carolina at Chapel Hill, there was a chamber ensemble performance by harpsichord, piano, flute, and clarinet. Gillespie was at the piano and led the ensemble. He recalls that the third score timings were used and that all the instrumentalists had their own score copy from which to read. Gillespie used a stop-watch and made the same closing and opening gestures as done by David Tudor. He also recalls that the other performers made gestures to show that they were engaged with their instrument, but that the wind-players did not bring the instrument up to their mouth or do anything to be too obvious or comical. The performance was done in a very serious manner, and at the conclusion the audience shouted "encore!" (Gillespie 1988).

Don Gillespie also recalls witnessing another performance, one which he was not involved in, given by the full student orchestra at the North

Carolina School of Arts at Winston-Salem during the summer of 1970. Roger Hannay was the conductor. Gillespie recalls that Hannay apparently did not approve of what happened, for the students performed *4'33"* by throwing paper airplanes and making noise (Gillespie 1988). Although it might be correctly argued that Cage's score/s are indeterminate of actual performance, there is nothing in any of the scores or in his comments about this work to suggest that this interpretation was an accurate performance.

Three performances in Germany present other subtle variations. The first example was performed at Stuttgart in June, 1979, by the The-Ge-Ano Ensemble as a trio for piano, an oboe, and a female vocalist (Urmetzer 1979). The second performance of note was by the RSO Ensemble at Berlin in December, 1982, with oboe, clarinet, and bassoon. The review mentions that the performers had their fingers poised over the instrument keys in mimically playing, and that the performance lasted three minutes and fifty-six seconds (Kneit 1982). The reviewer continues by questioning whether or not the musicians were actually playing *4'33"* since the actual duration was different from the title. This is a moot point, and one which reveals an ignorance of Cage's notes in the third and fourth score versions published by C. F. Peters. Closer to an informed criticism is the fact that the performers were mimically playing their instruments, which is antithetical to both David Tudor's performance as well as John Cage's general aesthetic approach. The final German performance of note was at Stuttgart by the Südfunkchores under the direction of Rupert Huber in November, 1991 (Pschera 1991). It is important to note that the The-Ge-Ano Ensemble included a vocalist, and that the Südfunkchores performance was a completely "vocal" version, as *4'33"* is almost always performed as a purely instrumental work.

The most obviously theatrical version of *4'33"* to date was performed by Jeffrey Kresky at William Paterson College in Wayne, New Jersey, in April, 1985. Kresky used a page-turner, which one review describes as a "red-headed girl in a purple dress" who sat on a "bright orange chair" (Avignone 1985). Another review describes the complete performance in more detail:

The piano player entered with a flourish, bowed elaborately, and was greeted with loud applause. . .

Jeffrey Kresky raised the lid of the piano and took his seat at the piano bench. Dissatisfied, he got up and lowered the lid, then raised it again, greeted each time by knowledgeable members of the audience.

Next he put a large blank sheaf of paper on the piano's music rack and propped a stopwatch next to it.

Then he sat. After a while he adjusted the stopwatch. . .

The page turner rose and turned the page. Kresky made another adjustment to the stopwatch, then wiped his hands on a handkerchief and mopped his brow. He clicked the watch again. She turned more pages.

People coughed. . .

> *Someone yawned. Out in the middle of the audience someone else began whistling softly.*
> *Kresky clicked the stopwatch again, stood, and bowed to sustained applause. The piece was over. (Groenfeldt 1985)*

Judging from this documentation, Kresky's performance of 4'33" has been the most overtly theatrical version. While it is a rare later performance to include page turning, it is far different from David Tudor. Kresky's blank pages were not a score to read from, but simply a theatrical prop, a cute distraction from any serious attention to be given to the situation. In his gestures, Kresky was being obvious, humorous, and rather egotistic; while David Tudor has always been subtle, serious, and almost transparent as a physical presence.

The understated gestural quality of David Tudor is reinterpreted in Margaret Leng Tan's performance of 4'33", given since November, 1989. Tan asked me to attend a practice session for criticism in October, 1989. She performed 4'33" using the out-of-print linguistic score issued by Peters, in the manner of David Tudor. I then told her that the problem with 4'33" is that most performers do a David Tudor imitation rather than finding their own approach. I then suggested to her one way that I would do it, by using a stop-watch and silently depressing individual keys, chords, or clusters to visually show the durations of the three movements. Tan was delighted, and together we then tried out various combinations. Tan has followed my suggestion and has found critical success with this approach, although Cage commented that he was ambivalent about her performance (Tan 1990).

Perhaps the most unique performance of 4'33", apart from David Tudor, was a videotaping session at The Kitchen in New York on March 21, 1990, for the PBS "American Masters" documentary on John Cage directed by Allan Miller. The performance consisted of a large blank piece of white posterboard affixed to the music rack of a grand piano. Miller used a stopwatch, and the piece was videotaped as one movement. In this version, the most active performer was the video-camera operator, who photographed the piano and posterboard. This performance was later excised in favor of David Tudor's videotaped performance, which appears in the final documentary (Miller and Perlis 1990).

In addition to David Tudor's videotaped performance, there are also five other mechanically recorded versions of note. The first is a phonograph recording by Gianni-Emilio Simonetti, who performs the three movements according to the timings in the linguistic score, and follows Tudor's practice of closing and opening the keyboard cover. Since there is no visual cue to denote the beginnings and endings of movements, this is done by closely miked sounds of the keyboard lid in movement (Cage ca. 1980). The second recording is by the Amadinda Percussion Group (Hungary), which consists of a recording of ambient outdoor bird-song in one movement (Cage 1989a). The third audio recording is by the pianist Wayne Marshall, who performs the three movements in the recomposed durations of 1'46", 1'25", and 1'22". When listening to Marshall's CD at high volume, one can hear some sparse ambient sounds reminiscent of a janitor collecting trash in an outer hallway, muffled traffic noise, and soft creakings (Cage 1991c).

The most recent audio recording of 4'33" is by Frank Zappa, which appears on the double-CD *A Chance Operation: The John Cage Tribute* (1993). This memorial anthology includes performances of Cage's own works as well as original compositions, by such musicians as the Kronos String Quartet, Laurie Anderson, David Tudor, Robert Ashley, Meredith Monk, Yoko Ono, and James Tenney. The producer separated single-movement selections into different yet continuous bands, with the idea that the listener can then make his/her own random choices. This idea obscures Zappa's performance of 4'33" , as it is separated into five bands. Whether this performance is in five movements, three movements, or one continuous movement is impossible to say, but the five bands have durations of 35", 1'05", 2'21", 1'02", and 50", with a total duration of 5'53". Zappa's recording includes many extraneous sounds, such as distant clinks; muffled, jumbling percussive noises (like those made with a small metal trash can); finger tapping; breathing; and in the fourth band, a short electronic humming vibrato (Cage 1993). True, Cage stated that the total duration of 4'33" could be any other duration, but the frequency of various sounds makes me wonder whether these are truly "unintended and ambient" or purposefully produced noises. The conclusion of this CD is a one-minute recording (again, unnecessarily broken up into several different, continuous bands) of street sounds found outside of Cage's New York apartment, which perhaps more than Frank Zappa's overly ornate performance, reflects Cage's actual intention of ambient, unintended sounds as the content in this seminal composition.

The final mechanical recording of note (to date) is a short holograph performed by John Cage in the early 1980s. This lasts approximately thirty seconds, in which one sees Cage sitting at the piano, closing and then raising the keyboard cover at the end (Cage ca. 1982). Cage was not known as the usual performer of 4'33". Both Cage and Tudor exemplify a very nondemonstrative style of performance, and it might be interpreted that Cage's holograph was a personal acknowledgement of Tudor's long-term collaboration.

4'33" is usually not considered to be one of Cage's theatre pieces, but the above descriptions of various performances clearly document the integral components of hearing as well as seeing in this composition. Cage himself would comment, in a rather self-disparaging manner:

What could be more theatrical than the silent piece? Somebody comes on stage and does absolutely nothing. (Shapiro 1985, 105)

The essential feature of 4'33" as something to hear as well as see is continued in its variation 0'00".

0'00"

0'00" is subtitled 4'33" (No. 2). It was composed during a concert tour of Japan with David Tudor. The first performance was the writing of the score by the composer during a concert in Tokyo on October 24, 1962. The published score appears in Fig. 21. It is a linguistically notated instruction for the performer to make a disciplined action. For the first performance of 0'00", the act of notating the score was done in front of the audience, and was the example of the disciplined action. Cage recalled that the obligation to others, referred to in the score, was a fulfillment to make a new piece (Cage 1986b). The disciplined action that someone other than Cage would first do would be reading the score (usually one writes or studies a score in private) previous to doing an action in public.

The score is in two parts. The first part is the left margination, which is both a document of the original performance as well as a notation for future performance by others. The primary performance notation is the single sentence:

> *In a situation provided with maximum amplification (no feedback), perform a disciplined action. (Cage 1962c)*

The note at the bottom is Cage's grouping of three compositions as a metaphorical illustration of Basho's famous haiku of a frog jumping into a pond, translated by Daisetz Suzuki as:

Furu ike ya!	*The old pond, ah!*
Kawazu tobikomu,	*A frog jumps in:*
Mizu no oto.	*The water's sound!*

(Suzuki 1959, 227)

According to Cage, the first line — the old pond — is *Atlas Eclipticalis* (1961) for orchestra; the second line — the frog jumping in — is *Variations IV* (1963), for any number of players producing any sounds or activities within the total performance area (this is discussed in Chapter 6); and the third line — the water's sound — is 0'00". (Cage 1986b).

The second part of the score is the indented margination, written (in private) the day after the first performance. These additional notations tell the performer *how* to do the disciplined action. As a totality, this score is a prime

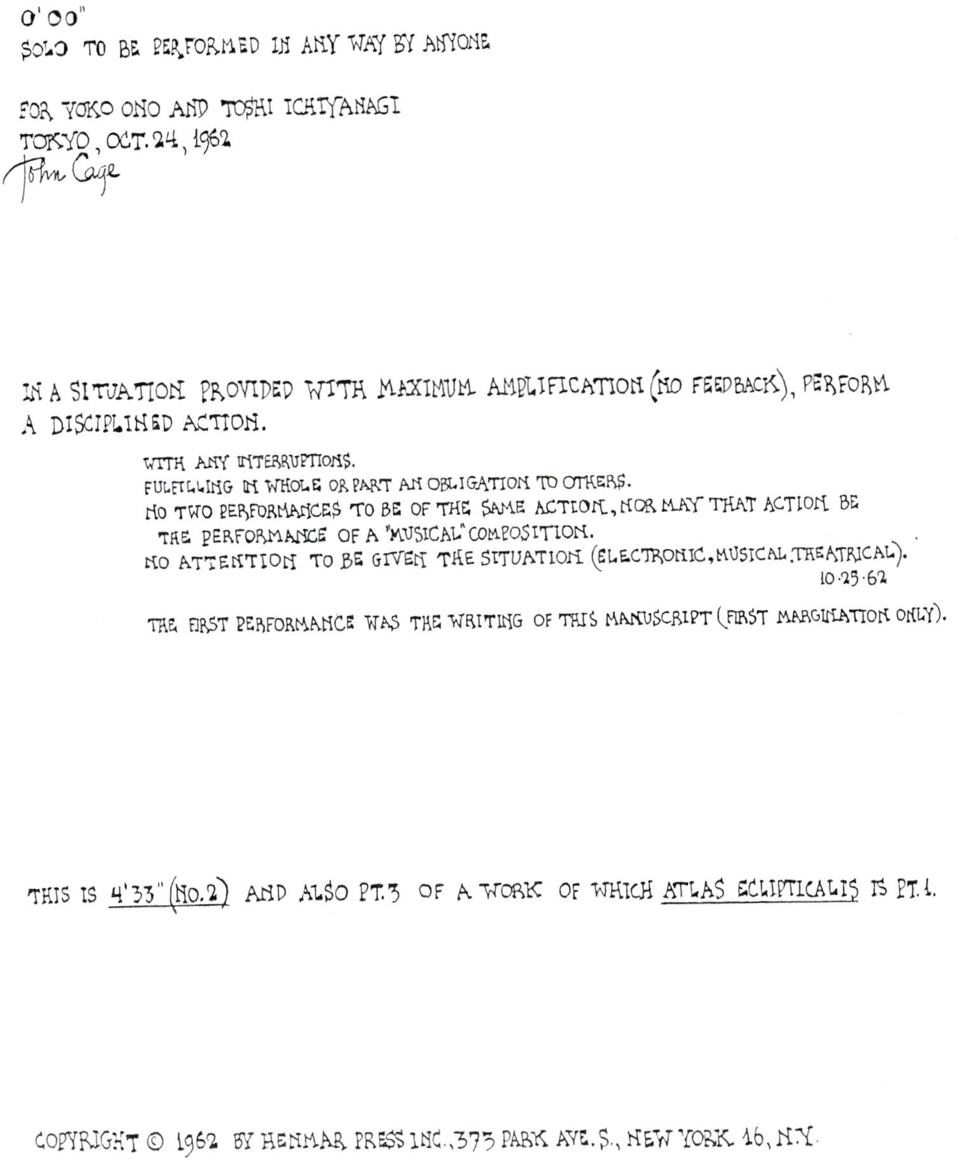

0'00"
SOLO TO BE PERFORMED IN ANY WAY BY ANYONE

FOR YOKO ONO AND TOSHI ICHIYANAGI
TOKYO, OCT. 24, 1962
John Cage

IN A SITUATION PROVIDED WITH MAXIMUM AMPLIFICATION (NO FEEDBACK), PERFORM A DISCIPLINED ACTION.

WITH ANY INTERRUPTIONS.
FULFILLING IN WHOLE OR PART AN OBLIGATION TO OTHERS.
NO TWO PERFORMANCES TO BE OF THE SAME ACTION, NOR MAY THAT ACTION BE THE PERFORMANCE OF A "MUSICAL" COMPOSITION.
NO ATTENTION TO BE GIVEN THE SITUATION (ELECTRONIC, MUSICAL, THEATRICAL).
10·25·62

THE FIRST PERFORMANCE WAS THE WRITING OF THIS MANUSCRIPT (FIRST MARGINATION ONLY).

THIS IS 4'33" (NO. 2) AND ALSO PT. 3 OF A WORK OF WHICH ATLAS ECLIPTICALIS IS PT. 1.

COPYRIGHT © 1962 BY HENMAR PRESS INC., 373 PARK AVE. S., NEW YORK 16, N.Y.

Fig. 21. The published score of *0'00"*.

illustration of how straight-forward, lucid, yet poetically evocative Cage's style of prose instructions become in making a performance piece. While language is used very concisely and precisely, the notation is paradoxically indeterminate. Cage's notation indicates that the performer is to make a disciplined, rather than a sloppy, foolish, ego-centered, or unconsidered action. It is also to be a responsible action, a social action, for whatever the disciplined action is to be, it must fulfill "in whole or part an obligation to others."

0'00" may be interpreted as being Cage's "instructions to the players," akin to Hamlet's instructions to the players in *Hamlet* Act III, scene ii. During this period, Cage was concerned with making compositions that required no rehearsal, "a technique which results in no technique" (Cage 1961, 188). The action thus will have a spontaneous quality. Cage also characterizes and clarifies a "disciplined action" as making an "experimental action":

> Relevant action is theatrical (music [imaginary separation of hearing and the other senses] does not exist), inclusive and intentionally purposeless. Theatre is continually becoming that it is becoming; each human being is at the best point for reception . . . .
>
> *In view, then, of a totality of possibilities, no knowing action is commensurate, since the character acted upon prohibits all but some eventualities. From a realist position, such action, though cautious, hopeful, and generally entered into, is unsuitable. An* experimental *action, generated by a mind as empty as it was before it became one, thus in accord with the possibility of no matter what, is, on the other hand, practical. It does not move in terms of approximations and errors, as "informed" action by its nature must, for no mental images of what would happen were set up beforehand; it sees things directly as they are: impermanently involved in an infinite play of interpenetrations. . . (Cage 1961, 14–15)*

(In this quotation, the bracket in the first paragraph appears in the original.)

Interestingly, while Cage breaks down distinctions between life and art, music and theatre, and tries to avoid dualistic thinking or value judgements, he also writes: "Composing's one thing, performing's another, listening's a third. What can they have to do with one another?" (Cage 1961, 15). The first performance of *0'00"* certainly blurs the distinctions between composition, performance, and reception as separated activities and experiences. Cage himself was the first person to say that his thought was not necessarily consistent, but while it might be misguided to play the role of an apologist, one could interpret *0'00"* as being Cage's personal exploration of a concrete multifaceted action which is (or may be) then perceived by the spectator/listener as a single event.

Cage himself is the performer best known for various interpretations of *0'00"*, and it is his own examples of disciplined, experimental, relevant actions that most accurately illustrate the style and technique implied in the published score. It is difficult now (without being to ask him) to ascertain what the actual notation was during Cage's first performance. Among his unpublished papers are three different sets of sheets relating to *0'00"*. The first is a piece written in ink on Japanese paper which reads:

To reveal:

> *0'00" For Yoko Ono and Toshi Ichiyanagi*
>
> *In a situation having maximum amplification*
> *or none (or both) act etc.*

(Cage 1962b)

The second piece is written in ink on plain paper, which includes this instruction:

> *When two or more performers are involved, they will agree beforehand on*
> *how long the performance will be. But rather than using watches, they will simply do*
> *what they have to do. When this is done, they will turn off the amplifiers + leave the*
> *performing area. (Cage 1962b)*

I would guess that this version of the score was written after the initial public performance.

What Cage probably wrote during the first performance is in pencil on both sides of a sheet of paper from a stenographic pad. Since the writing was amplified, the pencil version makes sense, because an amplified pencil makes more sound than a pen. This version appears as follows, with only slight editing, and crossed-out sections appearing in square brackets. The first page is:

0'00"   *anyone*
[Com]
Solo to be performed in any way by anyone   ?
For Yoko Ono and Toshi I.
Tokyo, Oct. 24, 1962
John Cage

Anyone knows.
Any one knows.

Copyright c

The second (reverse side) page reads:

> *In a situation [having] provided (or not) with maximum amplification, ([but*
> *no] without feedback) [or none (or bot], perform a disciplined action, [to fulfill, wholly*
> *or in such a way so that "perf." precedes "composition"; partially, an obligation to*
> *another or to oneself], having no attention to the situation.*
> No stop-watch is to be used.

(Cage 1962b)

What is most significant is that in these unpublished versions of *0'00"*, Cage's initial score/s include the possibility of using or not using (or both) electronic amplification for future performances; while his own first performance in writing the score was electronically amplified. Also to be noted is that, in comparison with *4'33"*, *0'00"* is a more obviously active and engaged performance situation that is not preconceived in either content or duration.

The semi-improvisational style of Cage making the first score is also reflected in his later performances of a "disciplined action." Ellsworth Snyder recalls Cage performing *0'00"* at the University of Illinois in 1965. Cage had vegetables which he cut up, the sounds made audible with contact microphones. He then put the cut-up vegetables into a blender, made juice, and then drank the juice, the drinking sounds amplified by a throat microphone. Snyder also recalls that Cage lit a cigarette and smoked a bit. He characterizes the performance as "gracious — it wasn't abrupt or elongated to be melodramatic" (Snyder 1989).

Alvin Lucier has written a recollection of Cage performing *0'00"* on May 5, 1965, at the Rose Art Museum at Brandeis University:

> Cage began performing 0'00" before the audience came in. He sat in his amplified squeaky chair with a World War II aircraft pilot's microphone strapped around his throat, writing letters on an amplified typewriter, and occasionally taking drinks of water. Part of the intention of this piece is to do work you have to do anyway, and John chose to answer some correspondence.
>
> Every move he made, every squeak of his chair, tap of his typewriter and gulp of water was greatly amplified and broadcast through speakers around the Museum. (Lucier 1988, 8)

David Tudor also recalls a similar performance by Cage in Berlin during the mid-1960s:

> He did 0'00" and I played Variations III, simultaneously. I believe he had a typewriter that was miked and a pencil with a contact microphone — he was doing his correspondence. (Tudor 1989a)

Cage curtailed his activities as a music performer in 1988, although he continued to give vocal performances until his death in 1992. Probably his last public performance of *0'00"* was at Lincoln Center, New York, in July, 1988. Neely Bruce recalls that Cage had a black pen-holder and a small bottle of black India ink, occasionally cleaning the *pin* on a paper towel (N. Bruce 1989). No exact durations are known for Cage's performances of *0'00"*, but estimates range from "a few" to about fifteen minutes.

There are only a few rare documentable performances by persons other than Cage. Ellsworth Snyder recalls doing *0'00"* three different ways. In the first version, he was sitting at the piano and a group of students came on stage and wrapped him from head to toe in toilet paper. Contact microphones were used so that the paper sounds could be heard. His second version was at Greenbay, Wisconsin, where a young man sat in a chair on stage wrapped from head to toe in aluminium foil. The young man sat motionless during the entire concert, which concluded with Snyder's performance of *0'00"* by putting ice cream, chocolate syrup, nuts, whipped cream, and a cherry on top of the young man's head. Snyder then ate the Sundae. He does not recall using contact microphones in this version, but that it was simply a disciplined action. The most recent time he performed *0'00"* was in a loft on Greene Street in New York in 1982, where the disciplined action was to clean each piano key with a wash-rag, starting with the lowest key and proceeding chromatically. This performance was also not miked (Snyder 1989).

Takehisa Kosugi did *0'00"* with Michael Pugliese reading *45' for a Speaker* (in Cage 1961, 146–192) at Los Angeles in September, 1987:

> *Kosugi's activity consisted of preparing and eating a bowl of ramen noodles. Bowl, cup, chopsticks, even his throat were all monitored by contact microphones so that one could hear all the intimate details of this activity. Thus, the work was anything but silent — an admirable reminder of a key element in Cage's philosophy, which is that there is no such thing as absolute silence. (Smoliar 1987)*

Kosugi's 1987 performance is the longest known realization to date.

Both Kosugi and Yoko Ono later performed their own independently made realizations of *0'00"* in the memorial *Cagemusicircus* concert at Symphony Space, New York, on November 1, 1992. Ellsworth Snyder recalls:

> *Yoko slashed a canvas and at the moment of slashing it, some red color was let loose, you know, it looked like blood, which then bled down the canvas. It didn't have any amplification as far as I know. Then she went to the piano and played some clusters, and that was it. It did not take long, perhaps two minutes. It was, I would say, rather concise.*
>
> *The other performance of 0'00" was by Kosugi. He wrote, and it was with maximum amplification. That was a pretty big, you know, coarse kind of sound; but I found it to be a very accurate realization. That was certainly longer than what Ono had done, I suppose ten minutes, or perhaps a little longer. (Snyder 1993)*

The most important recent performance interpretation of *0'00"* was by Margaret Leng Tan at the Walter Reade Theater, New York, on July 26, 1993. For ten to fifteen minutes she drew with crayons on photocopied posters showing an animal caught in a trap, with the caption "The Agony of Fur." She also affixed stamps on 25 postcards that had a photocopy of an animal, with the caption "This Fur Coat Is Still Alive." She then went out into the audience, distributing the posters and postcards, stating "I hope you will put these to good use in the winter" (Tan 1993). In this specific realization, the "obligation to others" was to animals rather than humans; and while Tan has expressed to me some reservations as to whether or not Cage would have approved of her performance content, I find this to be a very thoughtful, relevant, unique, and accurate interpretation of the score.

There are many, perhaps an almost infinite number of possible interpretations of *0'00"* which have yet to be explored and realized. Cage, however, continued to explore *4'33"* and *0'00"* through other composed variations.

Solos in Song Books

The *Song Books*, composed in 1970, contain ninety solos for vocalist and/or theatre performer. Various performances of the theatre solos will be discussed in the following chapter, and in Chapter 7. The variations of *4'33"* and *0'00"* in *Song Books* are Solos 8, 24, 28, 62 and 63; and Solos 23 and 26.

In Solo 8, the complete directive is:

> In a situation provided with maximum amplification (no feedback), perform a disciplined action.
> With any interruptions.
> Fulfilling in whole or part an obligation to others.
> No attention to be given the situation (electronic, musical, theatrical).
> (Cage 1970a, 31)

In Solo 24 the score reads:

> Engage in some other activity than you did in Solo 8 (if that was performed).
> (Cage 1970a, 88)

This form continues with Solos 28 and 62. The direction for the final *Song Books* installment in Solo 63 reads:

> Engage in some other activity that you did in Solos 8, 24, 28, and 62 (if any of these were performed). (Cage 1970a, 232)

Two performances, both of Solo 8, are documentable interpretations from this group of solos. In a performance of *Song Books* solos on March 9, 1989, at Renee Weiler Concert Hall in New York, Solo 8 was performed by Peter Perrin, who wrote a check to one of the other participants, handed it to him, and they then shook hands. This lasted approximately thirty seconds (Perrin 1989).

Solo 8 has also been performed by Phyllis Bruce in *Song Books* performances by the American Music/Theatre Group throughout the 1980s. She says that her interpretation is to read aloud something from a newspaper, or to mention a sponsor of the performance, or to mention something omitted from the published program. She performs this for about fifteen seconds (P. Bruce 1989).

The other variations of *0'00"* in *Song Books* are Solos 23 and 26. Solo 23 is subtitled *0'00" No. 2*. The score reads:

> *On a playing surface (e.g. table, chessboard) equipped with contact micro-*
> *phones (four channels preferably, speakers around the audience, highest volume*
> *without feedback)[:]*
>   *Play a game with another person (e.g. chess, dominoes) or others (e.g.*
> *scrabble, bridge). (Cage 1970a, 87)*

Solo 23 may be interpreted as being the written score, made after the fact, of *Reunion*, performed by John Cage, Marcel Duchamp, Teeny Duchamp, Gordon Mumma, David Tudor, David Behrman, and Lowell Cross at the Ryerson Theatre in Toronto on February 5, 1968 (Hulten 1993). *Reunion* consisted of Cage playing chess with Marcel and his wife Teeny, their moves on the chessboard triggering the electronic sounds being produced by the other performers.

    When asked about this performance, Cage commented:

> *Of course, it was fun to work with Marcel Duchamp! We kept on playing until*
> *we looked up, and all the audience had gone. It lasted about five hours.*
>   *I didn't talk him into doing it, I just told him that I had planned to play a*
> *game of chess which could change the music. He was fascinated!, that the moves of the*
> *pieces could change the music that we heard, so he willingly agreed.*
>   *I've never used chess the way I've used the I Ching. It comes from the*
> *principle that's in twentieth century art, namely, that you do something with the result*
> *which has nothing to do with the way you do it, which is for instance if you make a*
> *work of art and you make it by dropping things from a certain height, which is what*
> *Duchamp did with* Trois Stoppages-Etalon *[1913–14], so that the action has nothing*
> *to do with the result, except the result wouldn't occur unless you made the action. (Cage*
> *1988b)*

    Reunion was Marcel Duchamp's last major public performance, and only his second appearance as a performance-artist (his other being in *Relâche* in 1924). Cage first became aware of Duchamp's work in the 1930s, and first met him at one of Peggy Guggenheim's parties in 1942–43. Cage later composed *Music for Marcel Duchamp* for prepared piano in 1947 as the accompaniment to Duchamp's *Rotoreliefs* in Hans Richter's film *Dreams That Money Can Buy* (1948).

    Cage and Duchamp met by chance in Venice in the late 1950s or early 1960s, and Cage mentioned to Duchamp how the elder artist was working with chance procedures in the early 1910s, and that he (Cage) was doing this in the 1950s:

> *When I pointed this out to him, Marcel said "I suppose I was fifty years ahead of my*
> *time." (Roth 1973, 74)*

Cage, however, did not pursue a friendship with Duchamp until the 1960s. Duchamp had, at least publicly, given up the production of art for playing chess in the mid-1920s. Recalling their private games, Cage would relate:

He complained that I didn't seem to want to win. Actually, I was so delighted to be with
him that the notion of winning was beside the point. When we played, he would give me
a knight in advance. He was extremely intelligent, and he almost always won. (Roth
1973, 74)

The *Reunion* performance, and its later notation as Solo 23 in *Song Books*, was certainly on a personal level in Cage's mind, but it would be mistaken to regard this in purely sentimental terms. Both Duchamp and Cage have the shared attitude, as in semiotic theory, that the spectator completes any work of art. Duchamp exemplified this with his ready-mades and found-objects, such as the dog comb or little blue windows. Cage exemplied this with 4'33" and its variations. In his 1957 essay "The Creative Act," Duchamp would write:

All in all, the creative act is not performed by the artist alone; the spectator
brings the work in contact with the external world by deciphering and interpreting its
inner qualifications and thus adds his contributions to the creative act. (Duchamp
1973, 140)

Cage would similarly comment in 1965:

The structure we should think about is that of each person in the audience. In
other words, his consciousness is structuring the experience differently from anybody
else's in the audience. So the less we structure the theatrical occasion and the more it is
like unstructured daily life, the greater will be the stimulus to the structuring faculty of
each person in the audience. If we have done nothing, he will have everything to do.
(Kirby and Schechner 1965, 55)

Cage's use of language in Solo 23, in its focused yet ultimately indeterminate evocativeness, is also a reflection of Duchamp's elliptical and open-ended use of language with titles of art objects or in his frequent verbal puns. In Cage's notation, this situation becomes more complex and paradoxical the more indeterminate the score becomes.

Apart from *Reunion*, Phyllis Bruce does Solo 23 during *Song Books* performances by choosing a member of the audience and then playing Chinese Checkers, a favorite game from her childhood. She states that if the other person does not know how to play the game, "they cooperate anyway, they sort of copy what I do." Phyllis Bruce performs this solo for five to ten minutes (P. Bruce 1989).

The final *Song Books* variation of 0'00" is Solo 26, which is subtitled 0'00" *No. 2B*. The complete score reads:

Play a game of solitaire (or play both or all sides of a game ordinarily
involving two or more performers). (Cage 1970a, 91)

Research has not discovered any documentation of how this solo has been performed. It was done at least once, by the S.E.M. Ensemble in New York and Germany in 1982, but director Petr Kotik no longer remembers specific details of specific solos (Kotik 1990). Like Solo 23, Solo 26 may be interpreted as a personal composition. For many years Cage enjoyed playing chess, bridge, and scrabble. David Tudor is an excellent solitaire player, sometimes playing as a means to alleviate the tedium involved with touring. Merce Cunningham has used solitaire in choreographing *Canfield* (1969), using the 52 cards to compose movement based on the rules of the same-named game (Cunningham 1985, 115–116).

WGBH-TV

WGBH-TV (1971) is a score and television film that has been previously overlooked in Cage's ouvre, but is important as both a further variation on *0′00″* as well as a document of performance. The score consists of three separate items. The first is a hand-written letter requesting Cage to contribute something for the Celebrity Auction Sale to benefit the Reame County Opportunity Center for Retarded Children at Frankeville, Wisconsin. The second item is Cage's linguistically notated score for *WGBH-TV*, written on the back of the letter envelope originally sent from Wisconsin. The final document is Cage's letter responding to the request, noting that all three items will together constitute a manuscript (Cage 1971).

The performance score consists of some time computations for a thirty-minute telecast; a technical note that:

> *(Camera to focus without movement on work table [—] no face (just ms; hands; pen etc.); microphones [—] high amplification [—] (not contact) to pick up sound of work.)*

and the spoken statement, with pauses indicated in seconds

> *0″　　　　　　　15″*
> *"Music is being written, but isn't finished yet.*
> *30″*
> *That's why there isn't any sound." (Cage 1971)*

The film of *WGBH-TV*, available on rental from C. F. Peters, has a duration of 28′15″. Cage is photographed over his left shoulder. He is shown writing a music composition in conventional Western music notation, which appears to be a note-substitution work similar to *Cheap Imitation* (1969). The music is entirely in treble-clef, but neither Don Gillespie nor I have been able to identify what specific piece on which Cage was working. Cage speaks the statement "Music is being written. . ." five times during the film, dubbed over the visual image. Other than the sparse repeated statement, the only other sounds are of his pencil on the music paper. The most "dramatic element" within this film is Cage's smoking a cigarette while writing the music score — the ash becomes rather long, and one wonders if it will fall upon the paper — it doesn't! (Atwood 1971).

The filmed performance is, in part, a glimpse of Cage in the process of composing, but also a rather hermetic, mysterious act. We do not know precisely what it is that he is writing, but witnessing his actions becomes a tranquil, trance-like experience. Most important, perhaps, to Cage's own work as a composer and performer in this context, is his response to unpreconceived, "environmental" stimuli. The actual composition was made as a quick, general response to a request, hence it is fulfills "in whole or part an obligation to others;" and the actual performance is a very pragmatic result wherein Cage is shown doing the work he has to do (at that moment).

ONE³

ONE³ (1989) is the last of Cage's variations on *4'33"*. The score is unpublished, and has only been performed by the composer. The title is pronounced as "One, three," that is, it is the third piece in the series of solo compositions titled *ONE*. *ONE³* was performed by Cage in Japan on November 14, 1989, and again at Symphony Space, New York, on December 4, 1990. Cage recalled the original performance:

> They asked to perform the silent piece — a Japanese group was giving a concert in Nagoya — and it was a concert at the time I was given the Kyoto Prize in Kyoto. I said, I don't want to do the silent piece, because I thought that silence had changed from what it was, and I wanted to indicate that.
>
> So what I did was to come on the stage in front of the audience, and then the feedback level of the auditorium space was brought up to feedback level through the sound–system. There was no actual feed-back, but you knew that you were on the edge of feedback — which is what I think our environmental situation is now.
>
> So, after that was reached, I went into the auditorium and sat with the audience and listened to this situation, to the silence which was on the edge of feedback, and without a watch, without measuring the time as I had in 4'33" — so that was my inner-clock.
>
> In Leningrad [now, again, St. Petersburg], Sofia Gubaidulina had said that she liked my music but she didn't like the watches, and I should remember that there was an "inner-clock." So I was doing the inner-clock (laughs), and it turned out that I sat there for twelve minutes and a half, more or less (laughs); and then I went back on the stage in front of the audience and the feedback level was reduced, and that was the end of it.
>
> The complete title is:
>
> $$ONE^3 = 4'33" (0'00") + \text{\clef}$$
>
> \clef [the treble clef sign] is Gubaidulina, because it was at the Third International

Festival of Contemporary Music in Leningrad — for which this is the symbol — that I met her; and I said that this is "G," so it could be called Gubaidulina, or it could be called Gorbachev, or glasnost (laughs).

And this [the time] is 4'33". 0'00" is the obligation to other people, doing something for them. And this [the treble clef] is using an inner-clock. The thing I was doing for them was showing that the world is in a bad situation, and largely through the way we misuse technology. (Cage 1990a)

In her 1967 essay "The Aesthetics of Silence." Susan Sontag writes of the concept "silence" in terms of Claude Levi-Strauss's criteria of "raw vs. cooked," with the conclusion that since there is no absolute silence, it is a "cooked" (Sontag 1983, 181–204). While Sontag is sensitive and responsive to the *metaphor* of "silence," Levi-Strauss's dualism of raw, wild, unbounded, without human intervention versus cooked, tame, bounded, with human intervention, is the kind of logic that Cage tried to avoid throughout his mature work as a composer and theorist. Although Cage himself would agree that there is no absolute silence, it is not necessarily accurate to interpret 4'33" or its variations as being a "cooked" because there is always the possibility that at least one person, whether performing or witnessing another's performance, will experience the "raw."

ONE^3 still retains an open quality, indeed it might be considered to be a more liminal work than 4'33", or its further variations in 0'00", *Song Books*, or *WGBH-TV*, because ONE^3 is an even more subtle example on nonintention, of the need for the listener and spectator to complete the work of art, to find meaning. Cage's understanding of silence, however, changed from that of the late 1940s-early 1950s, and the early 1970s:

We are no longer certain that there will be any silence. We are no longer certain that there will be a world. It's a very serious situation, and the news is, as you know, absolutely incredible. (Cage 1990a)

5

THE UNTITLED EVENT AT BLACK MOUNTAIN COLLEGE, *THEATRE PIECE*, SOLOS IN *SONG BOOKS*, AND *DIALOGUE*: VARIATIONS ON SMALL-GROUP SIMULTANEITIES

The 1952 Untitled Event

The untitled event was a multimedia performance of several unrelated solos that included dance, film and slides, paintings, phonograph records, poetry readings, a lecture, and piano. Mary Emma Harris writes that this single performance at Black Mountain College has become the "activity that was to have the greatest impact on American art" (M. Harris 1987, 226). This touchstone of later developments, as in the Happening and the general performance art movement, has been previously documented, but no two sources contain the same recollections, and many sources omit details. The confusion in documentation also includes the matter of the score. The existence or nonexistence of a score will be discussed after presenting the basic documentation of the performance.

The first basic documentation of the untitled event was in the 1965 interview of John Cage conducted by Michael Kirby and Richard Schechner, followed by Martin Duberman's 1972 study of Black Mountain College with interviews of various performance participants and audience members. This material, together with more recent supplementary interviews, is synthesized in abridged fashion in Mary Emma Harris's 1987 book on Black Mountain. The following performance material will therefore be redundant to some readers already familiar with the 1952 untitled event, however several additional details appear which have not been previously recorded.

The event was held in the Dining Hall at the college. The duration of the performance, the time of day it was performed, and the date are all questionable from the conflicting recollections. Most informants recall it being in the evening, but M. C. Richards recalls it being in the afternoon (Richards 1989). Most recall the total duration to have been 45 minutes, but Francine du Plessix (an audience member) recorded that it lasted for two hours (Duberman 1972, 352). Carroll Williams (an audience member) recalled it being "early in the summer" (Duberman 1972, 353), but du Plessix's journal from 1952 states that it was held in August (Gray 1990, 300). David Tudor vaguely recalls playing *Water Music* in the untitled event (Tudor 1989b), and he performed a solo piano recital at the college — including *Water Music* — on August 12, 1952 (Dunn 1962, 43). The Black Mountain College calendar of events for August, 1952 lists a "concert" by John Cage to be held August 16, and while there is no corroboration, this may be the actual (or approximate) date of performance (Calendar 1952).

The audience in attendance was small and comprised faculty, students, and local people in the Black Mountain community. None of the previous accounts explicitly mention how many were in attendance, but M. C. Richards recalls:

> *There wasn't a large crowd, so there was plenty of room for these activities to take place. There were maybe 35 or 50 people there, certainly not very many. (Richards 1989)*

The audience was itself part of the theatrical nature of the event. Cage comments:

> *The seating arrangement . . . was a square composed of four triangles with the apexes of the triangles merging towards the center, but not meeting. The center was a larger space that could take movement, and the aisles between these four triangles also admitted of movement. The audience could see itself, which is of course the advantage of any theatre in the round. The larger part of the action took place outside of that square. In each of the seats was a cup, and it wasn't explained to the audience what to do with this cup — some used it as an ashtray — but the performance was concluded by a kind of ritual of pouring coffee into each cup. (Kirby and Schechner 1965, 52)*

A depiction of Cage's verbal description of the seating arrangement appears in Fig. 22. All previous accounts, however, have been vague about the floor area used by the performers around and in this audience square. A more comprehensive floorplan, drawn by M. C. Richards, appears in Fig. 23. Typed indications have been added for identification. Two arrows appear in her original drawing, and are worth noting. The arrow of going into the Dining Hall is explicit in showing the audience square to be slightly to the right of the doorway. The arrow from the audience square to the poet's ladder shows where she sat when not performing. The faint line that begins at the right and extends through the diagram shows the relative point of entry by Merce Cunningham for one of his dance solos. Although Richards does not claim that the floorplan is an accurate recollection, David Tudor in looking at this has not found any inconsistencies, nor has he been able to add any further details to her diagram.

The single most relatively complete performance description is from Cage:

> *At one end of the rectangular hall, the long end, was a movie, and at the other end were slides. I was on a ladder delivering a lecture which included silences, and there was another ladder which M. C. Richards and Charles Olson went up at different times. . . Robert Rauschenberg was playing an old–fashioned phonograph that had a*

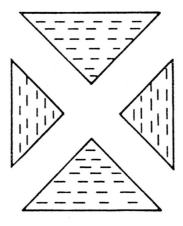

**Black Mountain
performance,
seats and stage-
space, 1952**

Fig. 22.   The seating plan for the untitled event at Black Mountain College (1952), reconstructed in 1965 (Kirby and Schechner 1965, 52). Reproduced courtesy of *TDR*/MIT Press.

> *horn. . . , and David Tudor was playing piano, and Merce Cunningham and other dancers were moving through the audience. Rauschenberg's pictures [the* White Paintings] *were suspended above the audience. . . They were suspended at various angles, a canopy of painting above the audience. I don't recall anything else except the ritual with the coffee cup. (Kirby and Schechner 1965, 52–53)*

All of the performances were independent, and not all participants were performing at the same time during any particular moment.

The motion picture that was shown was by Nicholas Cernovitch, who recalls:

> *I think it was fragments of the film I was working on. The film was black and white, and silent. The screen was to the right side of the Dining Hall entrance. (Cernovitch 1989)*

M. C. Richards recalls that the film was probably of Cornelia and her husband George, the cooks at Black Mountain College (Richards 1989). Michael Kirby, in researching the performance, notes that the film images. . .

> *. . .were projected on the ceiling: at first they showed the school cook, then the sun, and, as the image moved from the ceiling down the wall, the sun sank. (Kirby 1965, 32)*

The slides, projected on the other (left) side of the Dining Hall, were. . .

> *. . . 35 mm slides, both hand-painted on glass, and sometimes montages — or collages, using colored gelatines and other paints and pigments and materials, sandwiched between glass slides. And some photographs — abstract. . . There were the limited*

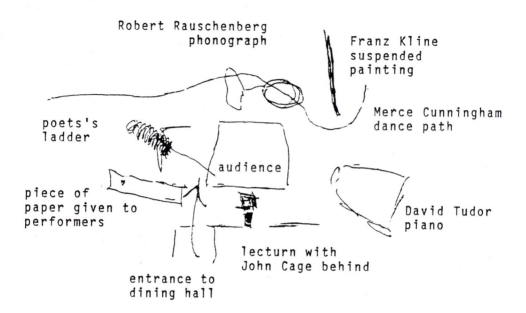

Fig. 23.   Floorplan of the untitled event at Black Mountain College (1952), drawn for the author in 1989 by M. C. Richards, showing the audience square and relative positions of the performers. Identifications have been added. Reproduced courtesy of M. C. Richards.

> *theatrical lights that the school had, jelled in different colors, and on different dimmer and on-off switch circuits. (Duberman 1972, 353)*

Cernovitch also recalls that Ilona Vonkaroly and her son projected pictures of trees (Cernovitch 1989).

Cage's part in the performance differs in various accounts. He recalls being on a ladder, which is also the recollection of Francine du Plessix (Duberman 1972, 352), however David Weinrib (Duberman 1972, 353) and M. C. Richards (1989) recall Cage standing on the floor behind a lecturn. Most informants do not recall what lecture he gave, but a summary of conflicting accounts has him reading. . .

> *. . .either his Meister Eckhart lecture, lines from Meister Eckhart, a lecture on Zen Buddhism, the Bill of Rights, or the Declaration of Independence. (M. Harris 1987, 228)*

In recent years Cage no longer remembered what lecture he performed, but in 1961 he would note that it was the "Juilliard Lecture" (Cage 1961, x; see Cage 1967, 95–111). If it was the "Juilliard Lecture," the total duration of the untitled event would then have been 45 minutes.

M. C. Richards recalls Cage's performance within the totality of independent solos:

> He was wearing a black suit, white shirt, and black tie — he was in his "ministerial garb." I remember John being there impervious to what was going on, and what it demanded of me, you know, that sensory bombardment of what's going on.
>
> When you are first exposed to that kind of theatre, it seems to me, you might mistakenly think that you are supposed to give each element the same attention that you would be giving it if it was the only thing going on. And that can be very stressful. You have to just sort of let it roll over you, and not try to make sense of the individual threads. (Richards 1989)

M. C. Richards recalls that both she and Charles Olson only ascended the poet's ladder once (respectively) to read their own poetry, at different times (Richards 1989). David Weinrib recalls Richards reading selections from Edna St. Vincent Millay (Duberman 1972, 354), but Cage, Tudor, and Richards herself all recall her reciting *her own work*.

Cage and Richards agree that Charles Olson read one of his own poems, but David Weinrib would recall that. . .

> . . . Olson had done this very nice thing where he had written a poem which was in parts, [and] it was given in parts to a section of the audience. . . [it] had to do with fragments of conversation. . . all of a sudden somebody would get up from the audience and just say this little bit. And then sit down. And then somebody else in the audience would stand up and say their bit. (Duberman 1972, 354)

David Tudor also recalls a similar activity, but in a more critical tone:

> Charles Olson didn't do anything himself, but some of his students he organized. I believe that he had in mind something subversive, which didn't happen because the actual people who were doing it didn't want to do it that way. (Tudor 1989a)

Robert Rauschenberg's 78 r.p.m. phonograph records differ in various accounts. Most informants do not recall what records he used. Francine du Plessix recalls him playing Edith Piaf recordings, while David Weinrib recalls him playing old popular records from the 1920s and 1930s (Duberman 1972, 354). There is no conflicting information on Rauschenberg's White Paintings shown suspended above the audience, but M. C. Richards also recalls a black-and-white notation painting by Franz Kline (Richards 1989). This is the painting indicated in her diagram (see for illustration M. Harris 1987, 226).

What David Tudor played is uncertain. Carroll Williams recalled Cage performing a piece using radio and duck calls (Duberman 1972, 353), but this is surely incorrect. David Weinrib recalls Tudor playing *Water Music*, which agrees with Williams's vague description. *Water Music* was performed at Black Mountain College as "Aug. 12, 1952" (Dunn 1962, 43), however Tudor recalls that that specific date was of a solo piano concert. Of his complete performance in the untitled event, David Tudor recalls:

> Well, I really don't remember, but it was likely something fragmented. I remember that I played a radio, I played a phonograph — it's quite possible I played the Water Music (laughs). There's also a possibility one of the Pastorales, but not the Music of Changes, nothing that intense. It was really more an idea of moving around place to place, so I would have done something involved with that. And, of course, playing the Water Music adds a visual element, as it [the score mounted as a poster] stands on an easel. (Tudor 1989a)

There is little information on Merce Cunningham's performance. Cunningham would recall a dog chasing him as he danced through the aisles of the audience seats, and that. . .

> . . . the music didn't support the dancing and so on. . . , nor was I to have anything to do with what anybody else was doing necessarily. . . (Duberman 1972, 356)

The floorplan by M. C. Richards indicates one entrance by Cunningham into the performance area. When drawing his path over to the wind-up phonograph, she explained that he also used the outside areas as well as the aisles for his solo (Richards 1989). Nicholas Cernovitch also recalls that Tim LaFarge was dancing (Cernovitch 1989).

One final stray detail previously undocumented is of "Tommy Jackson doing impressions in ink, printing programs with cigarette papers, which he then rolled into cigarettes" (Cernovitch 1989). No program for the event survives.

Cage has stated that each individual's "consciousness is structuring the experience from anybody else's" (Kirby and Schechner 1965, 55), which certainly is reflected in the admittedly fragmentary and sometimes conflicting recollections of the performance. This situation also includes the existence or nonexistence of a score for this work. Martin Duberman writes:

> The idea developed in conversation between Cage and David Tudor — "and our ideas were so electric at that time," Cage told me, "that once the idea hit my head — and I would like to give David Tudor equal credit for it — I immediately then implemented it." (Duberman 1972, 350)

However, neither David Tudor nor Nicholas Cernovitch recall there being a score. Tudor comments:

> I bet you it was done after the fact. Almost certainly John had a plan, but I don't recall seeing it. This has happened many times over the years with people he wants to work with. He distributes a plan that you can use or not, but it's just a piece of paper with some numbers on it. This kind of thing doesn't get documented, and it gets lost. (Tudor 1989a)

M. C. Richards and Merce Cunningham, however, recall there being a performance score. Richards states:

> As we [the performers] came in, we were given a piece of paper that had the time on it — 32" or 4'00" — for those of us who were performing, but how I knew what that time was, I can't remember. (Richards 1989)

Her recollection is significant, for while she knew that she was to recite some poetry during the untitled event, she was not given any indication of what the poems were to be, nor did she know for how long. This also correlates with Cunningham's recollection that "I improvised the whole thing" (Duberman 1972, 356), which would suggest that, like Richards, he was given written time brackets just before the actual performance.

Whether there was or was not a score, it apparently no longer exists, or the location is presently unknown. Michael Kirby writes:

> I remember him showing me the score at the time of the [1965] interview. It was framed, hanging on a wall. Perhaps it was the score to something else. It had horizontal lines that indicated when each activity would begin and end. (Kirby 1990)

Cage had commented that there was a score for the untitled event, but that it no longer exists:

> I gave the time brackets within which to work. For instance, the poets could climb ladders to read poetry within certain time periods — not all the time or any time, but within certain times. That was done in order to have one ladder and several poets. I was on another ladder. I was giving a lecture which had silences determined by chance operations. The time brackets in the entire piece were determined by chance operations. (Cage 1988b)

After Cage's death, one section of the score was discovered among his personal papers. It is for the part of the projectionist, written in pencil on an 8-1/2" by 11" piece of paper, held the long way. It is:

Projector:

Begin at 16 min.
play freely until 23 min.

Begin again at 24:30
play freely until 35:45

Begin at 38:20
play freely until 44:25

> (Cage 1952c)

The now no-longer known time brackets for the other performers were all apparently different. David Tudor recalls that his and Cage's parts were the only continuous performances throughout the entire untitled event (Tudor

1989c). M. C. Richards recalls that both she and Charles Olson each had only one time bracket within the total duration (Richards 1989). Cunningham recalls having two separate time brackets within which to perform (Cunningham 1982, 111). What apparently was made known to the performers were their unique time brackets, with no further determination of actual content, thus making the untitled event the first of Cage's theatre pieces to be scored in indeterminate notation.

The importance of the 1952 untitled event at Black Mountain College has become a part of legend, but the significance of this performance was not appreciated at the time. The composer Lou Harrison found it to be "quite boring" (M. Harris 1987, 228), while Johanna Jalowetz was heard, shortly after the performance, to mutter "Deep in the middle ages" (Duberman 1972, 353). M. C. Richards recalls that Mrs. Jalowetz's interpretation of the untitled event was that it was basically sacrilegious (religion as a reading of Cage's "ministerial" black suit and tie with white shirt), but otherwise Richards recalls that most of the audience liked it very much:

> Oh, I certainly didn't get the impression that it was a historic event, perhaps because all the elements were familiar, and at Black Mountain we had been doing light, sound, and movement workshops, and putting that all together seemed natural and not something really cultural–changing. (Richards 1989)

Nicholas Cernovitch adds: "Nobody knew we were creating history" (Cernovitch 1989).

Theatre Piece

The 1952 untitled event is now widely considered to be the first Happening, although it was not the actual performance that influenced the development of this art genre as much as it was Cage's classes given at the New School for Social Research in New York during the latter 1950s. Many of the students in Cage's composition classes — including George Brecht, Al Hansen, Dick Higgins, Allan Kaprow, and Jackson Mac Low — would become leading performance-artists. It was Kaprow's *18 Happenings in 6 Parts* (1959) that first introduced the term "Happening" to designate simultaneous multi-media performance art (Kirby 1965, 44–83).

Cage's reaction to the general Happenings movement was rather ambivalent. He appreciated Happenings as a far more valuable experience than conventional theatre but objected to the frequent use of symbolism and purposeful intention (Kirby and Schechner 1965, 68–69). An extended recollection by Cage of the New School Composition Classes, and his general teaching method, appears in Appendix 1. Apart from his direct influence as a teacher, Cage would compose *Theatre Piece* in 1960 as both a variation of the 1952 untitled event, and as an example of a Happening that has no symbolic content or purposeful intention.

The *Theatre Piece* score is one of Cage's most complex examples of indeterminate notation. It was made by chance procedures using the score of *Fontana Mix* (1958). The score of *Theatre Piece* consists of eight individual parts for one to eight performers. Each part contains eighteen unnumbered pages, a transparency of five different rulers to measure space equal to time, and a detailed instruction sheet.

There are two versions of the instruction sheet. The original instructions provided for the first performance in 1960 are preserved among David Tudor's performance notes. These original instructions, together with a detailed reconstruction of Tudor's use of the score and his first performance, appear in Appendix 3. The published instruction sheet is almost twice as long as the original and incorporates practical considerations (making cards) to realize the score, as well as stylistic notes (carrying cards about for reference) derived from the first performance.

The reproduced figures are examples from the fourth part, showing first the time ruler (Fig. 24), and then a page of actions in time (Fig. 25). Using the score materials, each performer makes an independent 30-minute program of action. *Theatre Piece* may be performed as a solo or consist of up to eight independent participants, each using a different score. In brief, each performer is to make a list of twenty nouns and/or verbs. Each word is then to be interpreted as indicating an action. In the reproduced score example in Fig. 25, there are seven actions indicated by the large numbers above the horizontal lines. The small numbers above the line, preceded by a plus or minus sign, mean to add new words to the original list, or to take out a corresponding number of words. Below each horizontal line is a column of numbers, which are to be used if the performer has any questions about how to perform a word. Each question is to be answered by first making a list of twenty possibilities. An "x" means a free choice.

Over this page one then places one of the time rulers in order to measure the time within which to perform actions. If one uses the numbers on rulers to refer to seconds, each page would then equal, respectively, 100, 120, 180, 50, or 60 seconds; or a performer may also make his own time ruler (Cage 1960e).

Each page contains two brackets (called "systems" in the instructions), which are to be performed without interruption. Once having measured the time horizontally, one must adhere to this structure. In the reproduced example of Fig. 25, the second bracket has several actions which must be performed within overlapping periods of time.

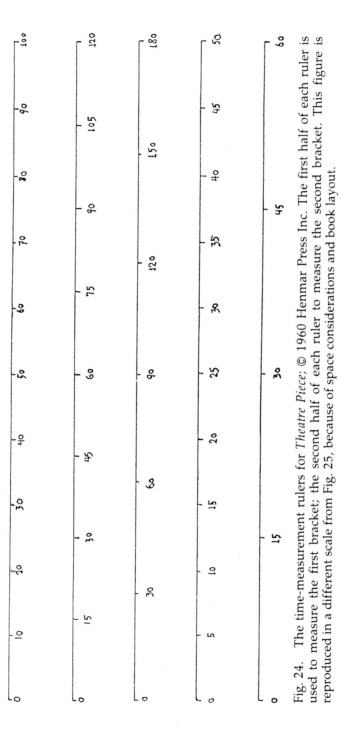

Fig. 24. The time-measurement rulers for *Theatre Piece*; © 1960 Henmar Press Inc. The first half of each ruler is used to measure the first bracket; the second half of each ruler to measure the second bracket. This figure is reproduced in a different scale from Fig. 25, because of space considerations and book layout.

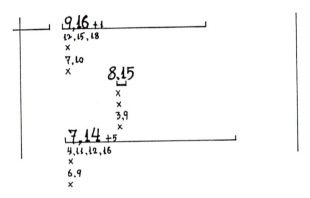

Fig. 25.   A page from *Theatre Piece*, score part IV, © 1977 Henmar Press Inc.

To give an example of how one might perform Fig. 25, let us assume that the time is measured with the 60-second ruler, and that the nouns and verbs would be:

3 — *bell*
9 — *paper*
16 — *stomp*
7 — *whistle*
14 — *hiss*
8 — *table*
15 — *splash*

Let us also assume that there are no questions to be asked with how to perform these words. One might then perform that page as follows: no action from 0'00" through 0'17"; ring the bell from 0'18" through 0'33"; no action at 0'34"; rip a piece of paper and stomp foot between 0'35" and 0'49", whistle between the lips and make a hissing sound between 0'35" and 0'53"; and knock on a table top and throw an object into a tub of water between 0'42" and 0'43". Even though this example would be of a solo, there are still several simultaneous actions which occur.

The *Theatre Piece* score may seem to be rather daunting, but it is a very concise and ultimately practical notation. Cage's comments on how one might use a more complicated page appear in Appendix 2.

Theatre Piece was first performed at the Circle In the Square in New York on March 7, 1960 (Program 1960). The performers were Merce Cunningham and Carolyn Brown (dancers), Arline Carmen (contralto), Frank Rehak (trombone), Don Butterfield (tuba), David Tudor (piano), and Nicholas Cernovitch with an assistant (lighting). John Cage also participated in the performance as a conductor indicating the passage of time.

The most detailed description of the over-all performance appeared in an anonymous review in *Time*:

> The composer himself stood in a corner with his back to the flimsy curtain. On the badminton–court-sized stage were eight performers confronting a wierd assortment of props: a grand piano, a tuba, a trombone, a cluster of plastic bags hanging by a thin wire and dripping colored water into a washtub, a swing, a string of balloons, a pair of bridge tables littered with. . . [a] champagne bottle in bucket, movie projector, alarm clock, broom, toys. After looking about to see that the performers were in their place, Cage somberly raised his left arm. "Zero!" he cried.
>
> . . .A man in sneakers and grey–flannel slacks [Cunningham] walked over to the balloons and started popping them with a pin. A contralto [Carmen] in a sickly green satin cocktail suit began singing St. Louis Blues. A dancer [Brown] in a black leotard skipped rope while the pianist [Tudor] slammed the keyboard with his elbows. "Five!" cried Cage, his arm descending like the second hand of a clock. Sneakers [Cunningham] hit the piano strings with a dead fish. Black leotard [Brown] read a newspaper while marking time to the wail of a trombone [Rehak] by flipping a garbage can with her foot. The men at the bridge tables [Cernovitch and assistant] popped the champagne bottle, threw streamers and lighted sparklers. "Fifteen!" cried Cage, and Sneakers [Cunningham] rushed forth petulantly snipping at his hair while the pianist [Tudor] polished the piano strings with a buffer and the tuba player [Butterfield] stripped to the waist, slipped on a jacket and had a drink.
>
> At 29, a black-cloaked figure [Cernovitch or assistant] stalked across the stage bearing an American flag. ("Anarchy with a Beat" 1960, 46)

While this review is far short of being a comprehensive documentation, it nonetheless provides a general description of the rather complicated simultaneous events. Another review, in the *New York Herald-Tribune*, repeats much of the same material, but in less detail (W. Flanagan 1960). Apart from recent interviews, which only provide a few other details, the other major documentation of the over-all performance is a letter written by Carolyn Brown to her parents shortly afterwards (Brown 1960). The basic floorplan of the performers and the audience is shown from her letter in Fig. 26. Like the 1952 untitled event, *Theatre Piece* was originally performed in-the-round.

There are few details to add for many of the performers. The performance of Arline Carmen is particularly lacking in documentation. The *Herald–Tribune* would note that in addition to singing *St. Louis Blues* she also "walked about and serenaded in French, [and] English" (W. Flanagan 1960). The composer Ben Johnston, in the audience, recalls Carmen performing an excerpt from *La Bohème*, and that most of what she did was operatic singing. At one point she stood in the curve of the piano-body like she was going to do something, using the preparatory gestures of classical singers, and then stood in silence. Johnston also remembers that at one point David Tudor took a rope and tied her to the piano while she was singing, all the while continuing her song without any notice of what was happening. Johnston recalls that Arline Carmen was "superb" in *Theatre Piece* (B. Johnston 1989).

Concerning Frank Rehak's performance with trombone, no other information is available. David Tudor is not sure, but suggests that Rehak and Don Butterfield. . .

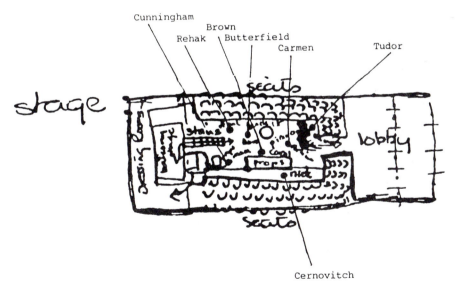

Fig. 26. Carolyn Brown's floorplan of the first performance of *Theatre Piece* on March 7, 1960. Her original drawing, which measures approximately 2½ inches horizontally and 1 inch vertically, has been blown-up for clarity. Identifications of the performers' positions have been added. Reproduced courtesy of Carolyn Brown.

. . .were probably using the score of the Concert for Piano and Orchestra *[1957–58] because they had already done it, so that was material that they had, and John worked with those guys to actually make the parts for that. (Tudor 1989c)*

The *Herald-Tribune* also notes that Butterfield played "solo fragments from what one refers to in some awe as 'the standard repertory'," and that "he struck a small cymbal that he directly suspended into the tub of water" (W. Flanagan 1960). Ben Johnston recalls that Butterfield also took the tuba apart and used the mouthpiece by itself (B. Johnston 1989). Carolyn Brown notes in the letter to her parents that Butterfield "played guitar, several tubas, changed from 'dress suit' to informal clothes, [and] drank Jack Daniels whiskey" (Brown 1960). Merce Cunningham does not recall details about what other performers did, but remembers Butterfield as "a marvelous musician" (Cunningham 1989b).

Nicholas Cernovitch is credited along with Richard Nelson as doing the lighting, but Nelson was not able to be in the actual performance because of other work that same evening (Nelson 1989). Cernovitch recalls:

John gave me a score, and I assigned various things to it such as lighting candles, flare strips, flash paper, sparklers, and small birthday candles. I tried to find various lighting sources and assign different events for the score. I followed the score, though freely. We did minimal work with electric lighting because it was a one-night rental, so there was not much time to refocus the lighting, so I decided to go the other way. There might *have been a general low-level light, which would have made the on-stage lighting effects more pronounced. (Cernovitch 1989)*

Ben Johnston recalls Cernovitch and his assistant working at the bridge tables, confirmed in the *Time* review and Carolyn Brown's floorplan. Johnston only recalls one event by Cernovitch — at one point he broke a light-bulb (B. Johnston 1989). Judith Malina, in the audience, also recalls a similar action (presummably by Cernovitch) when someone broke a glass bowl and another person came over, picked up the shards, and put them into a paper bag (Malina 1989). The *Herald-Tribune* also mentions that "assorted hands rubbed balloons, exploded paper bags, and sent toy objects into the audience" (W. Flanagan 1960).

Merce Cunningham's solo is only sparsely documentable with a few additional details. He recalls:

I remember very little about that performance. I suspect it's because we had so little time putting things together in the theatre, that all one could do was to keep one's wits together. There were a lot of things around, and there were all of us, so there was very little space to dance in.

My memory is of going in and out several times, that is, doing something, going off, or going to the back, and coming on again. It may be that we were continually in the space, but one would do something and then go back. [Referring to Carolyn Brown's floorplan, the lower left corner] I have the impression of going back here, I suppose to see what I was supposed to do next before coming out again (laughs). I have a very clear impression of that. The space to do it in was very confined. (Cunningham 1989b)

Carolyn Brown, in her letter, notes of Cunningham's performance:

> *Merce did a lovely noisy tap dance and walked on his toes with wooden shoes and did some cart wheels, and that's about all the dancing he did. (Brown 1960)*

Cunningham responded to Brown's notes by saying he used various shoes because of the space limitations, and that changing shoes was one reason for exiting and re-entering the performance space. It is significant that he used various types of shoes in *Theatre Piece* because Cunningham is a barefoot dancer and choreographer. When asked how uncharacteristic it now seems for him to do tap dancing, Cunningham laughed and replied: "I did that in my adolescence, and that took up very little room" (Cunningham 1989b). This is a decidedly minor performance in his career, but David Tudor especially recalls Cunningham slapping a dead fish on the open piano strings as a very memorable event (Tudor 1989a).

Carolyn Brown's letter to her parents is most explicit in documenting her own performance and is the most detailed record of the choreography used in *Theatre Piece*. She writes:

> *I did all kinds of crazy things:*
>
> *— opened a magnum bottle of real champagne and poured a glass and gave it to a man in the audience who was scared to take it for a minute*
>
> *— played a [William "Count"] Basie jazz record and improvised [a] jazz dance*
>
> *— put a clothesline of leotard, tights, toe shoes, [and] leg warmers into the piano and played "my piece" (Isis) with great bravura*
>
> *— opened an umbrella filled with confetti over the trombone player [Frank Rehak]*
>
> *— waltzed around giving away tiny real yellow roses*
>
> *— read lines from Dostoyevsky*
>
> *— put the huge bell of the tuba on my head and turned around slowly (that got huge applause — it was the tuba player's [Don Butterfield] idea)*
>
> *— wore a wild mask of Remy's [Remy Charlip] and played a "recorder"*
>
> *— put on a huge red button which said Sam on it (the name of our cat)*
>
> *— sat on a swing and "swang" and then cut it down*
>
> *— I did some grand battements, a glissade or two, some waltzing, some falls, some improvised jazz, some frappe and battement degage, a lot of running and skipping about. That's about the extent of my dancing. (Brown 1960)*

From Brown's self-description and Cunningham's recent recollections, both dancers were not being "dancerly" with their activities but concentrated more on theatrical gestures and using props.

The most documentable performance in *Theatre Piece* is that of David Tudor. Carolyn Brown's letter gives some indication of his very physical engagement: "David ran in and out and under and thru the piano, made tea, put on phonograph records, etc." (Brown 1960). When recently asked about what he did, Tudor could not recall any of his actions. Fortunately, he made meticulous written notes on the score pages and the assigned actions and timings for his performance. There are 46 different events, performed (with some events repeated according to chance in the score) a total of 72 times. Almost none of Tudor's events have anything to do with the piano, but include actions such as making tea, playing various phonograph records, and playing with a variety of toys and novelty store items such as a jack-in-the-box, a squeaker hammer, a flapping chicken, a shoe squeaker, and a piggy bank (Tudor 1960b). Tudor's written realization, with notes on the score pages he used, is discussed in Appendix 3.

With the actual preparation for the performance, David Tudor comments:

> *We had a rehearsal. It's not practical to have more than one. It's just like choreography — you have to find out whether what you have in mind is going to work or if somebody is going to be in your way or whether it bothers you. That's all you need to do. (Tudor 1989a)*

In performance, Tudor carried cards about with his own brief notation of the events and timings, which is the same practice as in *Music Walk* (1958) and *Cartridge Music* (1960). This style of not memorizing was in part a practical consideration because of the short preparation time. More significantly, however, it again reveals that Tudor made his performances from indeterminate scores in a very methodical, exacting, and disciplined manner, rather than there being a spontaneous and impressionistic personal improvisation.

As with all the early theatre pieces in indeterminate notation, David Tudor's written notes are a model for performing Cage's theatre pieces. Neither Tudor nor Carolyn Brown feel that most of the other original *Theatre Piece* performers made an exacting use of Cage's score. This can not be objectively proved or disproved. Cage writes in the instructions: "Each performer is who he is (e.g. performing musician, dancer, singer), but he is also performing a piece of theatrical music" (Cage 1960e). With *Theatre Piece*, Tudor was able to have the opportunity to make his most virtuosic solo performance of a theatre composition.

The final participant in the first performance was John Cage. In both the original and published versions of the instruction sheet, Cage writes: "There is no conductor or director" (Cage 1960e). Cage was not a "director" in the sense of a play director, but he did conduct the first performance. The *Time* review states that Cage "cried" out the numbers, presumably numbers in whole-minutes from one through thirty. Ben Johnston states that it is more correct to say that Cage *said* the numbers, and that he did not give the numbers at regular intervals (B. Johnston 1989). Both the *Time* review and Carolyn Brown's letter state that Cage used his arms like a clock, which would be in the manner of the conductor's part in *Concert for Piano and Orchestra* (1957–58).

Theatre Piece was next performed by seven persons, including David Tudor, at the University of Illinois on April 18, 1961, and by five persons at Oyster Bay, New York, on May 21, 1961 (Dunn 1962, 42). It was then performed in Japan in October, 1962, by David Tudor and John Cage. Tudor has preserved his written notes for the 1961 and 1962 performances. There is not much difference between his first in 1960 and the other two, except that all three used different score pages, and the Japanese performance included aromatics and dust in addition to other visual and auditory events. Cage's written notes for his 1962 performance of *Theatre Piece* apparently no longer survive, but he recalls his performance of *Theatre Piece* to be similar to his earlier solos *Water Walk* (1959) and *Sounds of Venice* (1959) (Cage 1988b). A photograph taken during the 1962 performance in Japan appears unidentified in *High Performance* (Kostelanetz 1987, 21), which shows Cage wearing his dark suit and tie with white shirt. He is walking in his socks and is holding a wooden stool in front of his face. His face is covered by what appears to be a piece of white gauze. However tantalizing these few details are, there is nothing to further document Cage's own performance of *Theatre Piece* in detail at present.

The only other major performance of *Theatre Piece* to date was at the Third Annual New York Avant-Garde Festival at Judson Hall, New York, on September 7–11, 1965, with Charlotte Moorman, Allan Kaprow, Philip Corner, James Tenney, Gary Harris, Takehisa Kosugi, and Nam June Paik. Details are even sparser than for the original performance in 1960. The *Village Voice* would note:

> The Cage piece was interesting to watch because lots of things happened. Some of the ingredients were amusing (Charlotte Moorman bowing Nam June Paik like a cello), some startling (a piano being destroyed), some were references to real life which one could have specific references to (these were all introduced by a single performer, Paik, who may have chosen them himself — a small Buddha, an electrical robot, a rosary, two bombs). Some were entertaining as ideas but dull in execution. The over-all impression was of a moderately frenzied constellation of random activities in a cramped space. (Smith 1965)

The 1965 performance was organized by James Tenney. He recalls:

> I just asked people that were already involved with the avant-garde music festival at Judson. These were all people closely involved with Charlotte Moorman. It

was a piece we hadn't seen and wanted to do. I don't remember anything I did! (Tenney 1989)

Charlotte Moorman's performance is presently not documentable with any further details. She is perhaps best known for her performance of Cage's *26'1.1499" for a String Player* (1955) during the 1960s, with the assistance of Nam June Paik. Together they theatricalized *26'1.1499"* by Moorman playing a string on Paik's naked back (using his body like a 'cello), playing the 'cello conventionally or using the body of the instrument, or using a flower stem as the bow and making auxiliary sounds such as breaking a pane of glass or firing a blank cartridge from a pistol (Battcock 1981, 142–149). Apparently much of her performance of *Theatre Piece* was similar to *26'1.1499"*.

Allan Kaprow recalls two actions that he performed in *Theatre Piece*:

> *Somebody gave me a watermelon while setting up the program. It was a hot day, so I was going to cut it up to give to others. It was suspended from a rope. I quickly sliced at it, and it fell to the ground. There was paper set underneath so it wouldn't get dirty. I had hoped that the audience would get up and help themselves.*
> *At another point I used a gasoline-powered lawn-mower and scattered pieces of paper lying on the stage. Both of those were rather aggressive actions. (Kaprow 1989)*

He also comments that he made a very strict use of the score, and that. . .

> *I thought of it as a theatrically demanding situation, something I wouldn't ordinarily do in my own work. (Kaprow 1989)*

Philip Corner only recalls one action:

> *I remember tucking-in the piano. I had a blanket, and I put it on the strings, and I tucked it in. What else I did I don't remember (laughs). (Corner 1989)*

Kaprow adds that Corner tucked-in the piano "very studiously" (Kaprow 1989). Corner no longer remembers which score part he used but recalls that while he generally followed the score, he also allowed himself some freedom:

> *I was a little looser about it than Jim Tenny. I had a watch going, and I sort of timed when I would get into an action. I wasn't precise down to the second. I'd just start doing something, estimate the time, look over at the watch every once and a while, and if it leaked over a few seconds one way or another it would be alright. Tenney seemed to have the main responsibility for keeping the time, but there was no time keeper — everyone was to keep their own time. (Corner 1989)*

No information is available about what Takehisa Kosugi did in *Theatre Piece* (Kosugi 1991).

Gary Harris recalls three actions. One was placing various small objects on a 78 r.p.m. wind-up phonograph. A photocell was focused at the spinning object, which was then converted into sound played through loudspeakers. Another action was converting sound into light. Ambient sounds were picked up by a microphone which then were converted through an audio amplifier into green and yellow lighting. The microphones were hung along the auditorium walls in a random pattern. Harris also recalls that at the conclusion of the performance he hung himself on the wall like Christ and screamed (G. Harris 1989).

Nam June Paik's performance seems to have made the greatest impression. Allan Kaprow recalls that one of Paik's actions was doing a "Kamakazi-style painting" by sticking his head in a bucket of either soap suds or paint and then painting with his hair on a long piece of paper (Kaprow 1989). Philip Corner recalls:

> *Paik was just being Paik. He was running up and down the aisle, jumping in a bucket, and maybe he sprayed himself with shaving cream. I remember he poured water over his head.*
>
> *Paik's style is so completely different from David Tudor, Paik is just the opposite. Paik is really "Mister Expressionism" — everything he does has an improvisatory quality and a very self-expressive, physical, outgoing manner. And he wasn't very precise about it. As a matter of fact, I don't think that he really made a score, or realized a score at all. I think we just said "You have 30 minutes" and he just said "Well, I'll just be myself," and he did these actions.*
>
> *The way the piece ended, actually, is one of those fortuitous things that works very well, and Paik is ingenious at that. Paik actually got the people there to become part of the performance. He was doing one of his actions down among the audience, and then (laughs) everybody else stopped. I was still sitting behind the piano, and he was still involved, and going on and on, and he suddenly was aware of the fact that he was alone. And he looked around — Jim Tenney was already off-stage — and Paik said "Where is everybody? Is it over? That's it!? Finished?. . . Jim! Jim!" (laughs). That's the way the piece ended! It was absolutely fantastic! (laughs). (Corner 1989)*

It is questionable how well the 1965 performance of *Theatre Piece* fulfilled the requirements of the score. There was a great variety of simultaneous activities, but the element of self-expressivity, and the question whether Paik followed a score or simply made an improvisation, would suggest that this was not an ideal realization, despite the fact that it was made by "an all-star cast." Allan Kaprow notes that Cage's temperment would have been offended by the aggressive quality of many of the actions, although no one got hurt. In hindsight he feels some dissatisfaction with the 1965 performace, and comments:

> *It shows how subjective we were. I tend to look back on this with a gentler view now than at the time. In retrospect, we all do what we do, and that's that. (Kaprow 1989)*

Ultimately, value judgements of the 1965 version of *Theatre Piece* can not be

decided either way, but Cage has generally been disappointed with performances of this work (Cage 1988b).

Since the 1960s, performances of *Theatre Piece* have primarily been by
college or university students. One documentable example was at Dartmouth
College in 1977. It was performed at Rollins Chapel and used the entire
interior space. Seats were arranged like in the 1952 untitled event. The
performers included student dancers, a singer, the composer Christian Wolff,
and the violin virtuoso Malcolm Goldstein. Details are vague, but Christian
Wolff at one point sat on the floor and played a flute, and Malcolm Goldstein
played the violin and a saw (Goldstein 1989; and Wolff 1989).

The virtuoso pianist Yvar Mikhashoff recalls being in a performance
done at Buffalo in June of 1977, directed by William Kirkpatrick (dancer),
with Paul Schmidt (actor), Frances-Marie Uitti ('cello), James Kasprowicz
(trombone), and Michael Pugliese (percussion):

> We all wrote a list of twenty actions, twenty things to do — eat a flower, walk
> around the stage — anything we wanted to do. Then after we did that, Bill [Kirkpatrick]
> gave us the timings by chance from the score. Then there was a second chance
> operation, if an action was to be done (a) in relation to the audience, (b) in relation to
> another person, (c) in relation to the floor, or (d) in relation to something else. They
> weren't very frequent. It must be that Bill had questions. That maybe happened twice in
> some people's score; some people's it didn't happen.
>
> In general, there were interesting things. First of all, everyone was in white —
> we decided we wanted to unify it in some way — so there was a white drop-cloth, and it
> was paint-splattered. We had one rehearsal. At one point Michael Pugliese threw a tray
> of glasses and they broke, so we decided to use polystyrene.
>
> The trombonist took apart his trombone and played. He also had a mechani-
> cal metronome, which he used to attempt to conduct. The 'cellist played excerpts from
> Beethoven. Another time she sat on the floor and ate a sandwich, which happened to
> coincide with my action "have a picnic." The food was white too — egg salad with no
> yolks, with mayonnaise, on white bread.
>
> The actor only read from Cage's writings — I think it was from Silence — and
> he had a certain number of words that he read that he determined. He also moved about
> the stage, but not very much. He was seated on a white chair, then he would get up and
> speak. It turned out from chance operations that he didn't have much to say.
>
> I had excerpts from different works. I think I played Ravel, Beethoven, and
> Satie at the piano. I also did things inside and under the piano, knocked things, sang a
> note, got up and turned around, and at one point I danced.
>
> William Kirkpatrick seemed to be going all over the stage doing dance
> movements. (Mikhashoff 1993)

The most recent documentable performance of *Theatre Piece* was by
six people on September 5, 1992 at the First Unitarian Church in Madison,
Wisconsin. The performers, aged 18 to their early 40s, were students of
Ellsworth Snyder. Snyder recalls that the main problem for the performers

was figuring out their scores. There were several sessions devoted to reading and using the notation about three weeks before the public performance. There were also three rehearsals the last week, mostly to avoid collisions, but also for Snyder to give suggestions to make the space more interesting, "to break up areas, have people spread out." It was done as a frontal performance. Snyder provides this synopsis of the six performers's actions:

> *Nancy Baillies — basically did physical action with props: a rocking chair, wafted a billowy cloth, sang a lullaby to a stuffed animal, and blew a balloon and then let it spiral in the air.*
>
> *Joseph Cunningham — played a Schubert Scherzo on the piano, repeated words from books, read a course description from the University of Wisconsin catalogue, and walked around the audience with two pictures by abstract expressionist painters and asked the audience which they liked best.*
>
> *Dan Koscielski — read from a textbook, poured water into a bucket, wobbled a large sheet of plexiglass, and threw confetti.*
>
> *Carl Maguire — wore a multi-colored costume (everyone else was in everyday clothing), made sounds with his feet (rubber soles on a cement floor), climbed the stone walls and pillars of the church, and shaved his head.*
>
> *Eavon Rolich — did slow-motion walks in the aisles and read.*
>
> *Brian Schultz — had a female manikin as a prop: danced with the manikin; at one point he simulated shaving the hair on the legs of the manikin with an electric razor, and sat and listened to a recording of an opera aria after which he vociferously applauded. (Snyder 1993)*

Solos in Song Books

The *Song Books*, composed in 1970, contain ten pieces that are variations on the notation of *Theatre Piece*. Six — Solos 6, 10, 19, 31, 76, and 77 — use numbers. Four — Solos 7, 9, 61, and 87 — are made up entirely of words and phrases. The pages measure 11 inches horizontally and 8½ inches vertically. The complete score of Solo 6 appears in Fig. 27. In the instructions to Solo 6, Cage writes:

> *The minus and plus signs may be given any significance that the performer finds useful. For instance, a minus sign many mean "beginning with" or "taking off," etc.; a plus sign may mean "going to" or "putting on" etc. Or they may refer to the degree of emphasis with which something is done. Change of type-face may also be so interpreted. Where nouns or verbs indicating expressivity are included in the list, expressivity is obligatory. Otherwise perform impassively. Total time-length and duration of individual actions are free. (Cage 1970a, 27)*

In Solo 10, the directions are to refer to Solo 6. Solo 10 includes a further notation not included in Solo 6, where the first number is below a horizontal line, which Cage notes as meaning to "overlap with preceding

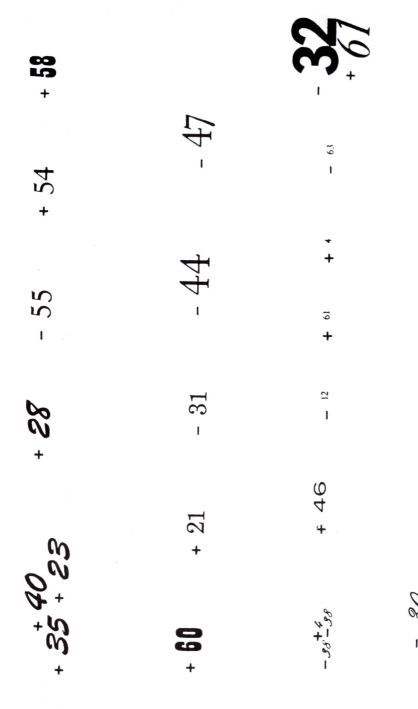

Fig. 27.   The score for Solo 6 in *Song Books* (Cage 1970, 28); © 1970 Henmar Press Inc.

activity or song." This preceding activity or song, of course, would not necessarily mean Solo 9, but any of the *Song Books* solos as done in any order during performance. Solo 19 includes the same instruction as Solo 10, but there is no overlapping with a previous solo. Solo 31 again repeats the previous instruction for Solo 19, and it is to be overlapped with a previous solo. Solos 76 and 77 are referred to the Solo 6 instructions, and neither are overlapped with previous solos.

For performances of these solos, the number of nouns and verbs is not to exceed 64. If one makes a list of fewer than 64, this number is correlated to 64 in the supplementary tables included in the *Song Books Instructions* (Cage 1970b). Thus, if one has only made a list of four words, these would be related to 64 as:

1–16 = 1
17–32 = 2
33–48 = 3
49–64 = 4

Except for the complete performance of *Song Books* in 1982 by the S.E.M. Ensemble, these solos are typically avoided. Documentation is lacking for any realizations of Solos 6, 10, 19, 31, 76, and 77.

Solos 7, 9, 61, and 87 are a variation of the preceding six solos. These four solos are notated with different series of nouns, verbs, and phrases in English and/or French, each preceded by a plus or minus sign. These words are to be interpreted according to the general directions for Solo 6, with the exception that the performer does not have to make a list of nouns and/or verbs. These solos are much more determinate in content. The duration of individual actions is free, but all of these solos are performed within a prescribed time — Solo 7 is to be performed no longer than 2′14″, Solo 9 no longer than 4′32″, Solo 61 no longer than 9′28″, and Solo 87 no longer than 9′24″.

Solos 7, 9, 61, and 87 are performed by the American Music/Theatre Group in their version of *Song Books*. For illustrative purpose, only one solo will be discussed here. David Barron performs Solo 7 by making a personally selected choice of activities. The score of Solo 7 is reproduced in Fig. 28 as an example of Cage's notation in this group of variations. David Barron enters walking (from his previous solo, Solo 54) and vocally imitates the sound of wind. He walks down in front of the first row of the audience, and then talks with an audience member. He excludes " – '*the heat of this breath*' " and next performs " + *scratch*" by scratching behind his ear like an animal. He then looks at something and sits down in a chair with his hands folded in his lap, as an interpretation of inactivity. Barron then concludes this solo by reading

John Cage's Theatre Pieces

— sound of the wind   + talk   — "the heat of this breath"   + scratch   + *obvious inactivity*   + hat
+ walking   + obvious inactivity

+ sound of the wind + look at something through something else

— talk — reading + using toothpicks and kleenex (*or other materials*); *build an object ressembling a wigwam*

Fig. 28.   The score for Solo 7 in *Song Books* (Cage 1970, 30); © 1970 Henmar Press Inc.

something from the Bible (Barron 1990). For performance interpretations of Solos 9, 61, and 87, see Appendix 4.

Dialogue

Many of John Cage's physical performances, previously discussed, have been either solos (as in *Water Walk*) or simultaneous duets with David Tudor (as in *Music Walk*). The longest of Cage's collaborations, however, was with Merce Cunningham, and it is in this context that Cage was at his most physical in the genre of action pieces. Cage and Cunningham were simultaneous movement performers in the European performances of *Music Walk with Dancers* in 1960. It was not until the mid-1960s, however, that Cage became an on-stage presence in Cunningham's compositions. In the television film of Cunningham's *Story*, in performance in Finland on September 18, 1964, Cage at one point enters at the back left side of the stage and slowly walks across to the right and off, pushing an inverted music stand in the manner of a janitor's push-broom, for about one minute. At another point he again enters with a tape measure, and measures the back of the stage, again for about one minute (Cunningham 1964).

The most frequently performed Cage and Cunningham physical piece is *Dialogue*, performed (according to the records in the Cunningham Archive) approximately twenty-one times from 1970 through 1985. Merce Cunningham recalls:

> John said, "Well, we should each do what we do," and he said "Then, in the middle of it I'll ask you a question — that's the dialogue." Well, he forgot to ask the questions (laughs)! I don't think we ever got to the point in any of them of having any real dialogue (laughs)! The "dialogue" was simply two people doing what they were doing.
>
> Very often he used written things in a way with the contact microphones, so that while he was writing the sound of the writing came through. Sometimes he would read, say, Empty Words, something like that. In some of them he had some masks that he would put on — he had two or three animal masks. It often started with him on stage left, and I would be on stage right.
>
> We both would independently figure out how long — say for five minutes or fifteen minutes or three minutes or something like that — to do so many things in an hour. We would start our watches together.
>
> I made lists always, because otherwise I wouldn't remember what I was supposed to do, so I had to have some kind of stand on which I had the piece of paper and my watch. I would do a dance, then come back and see what the next thing was.
>
> In several of them I made a piece, Fifty Loops, which was a solo thing for me which was originally made for television [in 1971], where I did a series of poses, really, which are almost static, almost in one position; and I made them so I could do them over a long, long period of time or do them quicker or shorter and shorter. So I made a

video of myself doing this, and I think it lasted an hour. I did it three times, and the first time it's shot full-figure, from the back, and it's very slow — I hold everything a long time. The second time it's shot from either the knees or the torso, I'm not sure; and the third time it moves in, and it's shot from the shoulders. And each time, I changed the tempo of the sequences, so the first one is terribly slow, the second one is less slow, and the third one is quite fast. I had a chair in Loops *— I use a chair very often (laughs). I think also in one of them I had a ladder. It seems to me it more or less lasted the whole hour of the* Dialogue *— it was on a monitor in the back — and I did other things also during the "dialogue," but we didn't do anything to do with each other in that conventional sense. (Cunningham 1989b)*

Carolyn Brown recalls that Cunningham and Cage were interesting in *Dialogue* because "Merce is at home with the body, while John is [was] not" (Brown 1989). David Tudor characterizes Cage's performance of *Dialogue* as being very much like the 1962 performance of *Theatre Piece* in Japan, only that. . .

. . .in Dialogue, *the sparseness of it made the actions stand out, made it theatrical; while in* Theatre Piece *he thought of it as the greatest amount of multiplicity. John always incorporated into it theatrical actions, and it is a direct result of his thinking about theatre. To make something apparent, you have to work at it. (Tudor 1989b)*

Unfortunately there is little concrete documentation on this seminal example of the Cage/Cunningham collaboration. Cunningham states that he no longer has any of his written action lists (Cunningham 1989b). Very few of the *Dialogue* performances were reviewed, but apparently each performance was different. An early *Dialogue*, at the Detroit Institute of the Arts on February 24, 1972, is reviewed with a few details:

Cage was silent when Cunningham spoke or danced; when Cage read, Cunningham stood motionless at his lectern. . .
      Cunningham, who wore simple red and white ballet exercise clothes, moved with superlative grace across the surface of the huge Oriental rug in the North Court; Cage, in blue denims, smoking cigarette after cigarette, sat at one side reading bits of minutely detailed short stories [as found in Indeterminacy]. *(Abraham 1972)*

The Walker Art Center performance of October 15, 1978, is reviewed with details that are similar to Cunningham's general recollection. This *Dialogue* was. . .

. . .a low-key affair ruled largely by the inventiveness and wit of the two performers. Cunningham frequently disappeared into the storage area behind the back wall of the Walker auditorium, returning moments later in a new costume. Once he appeared with a music stand, which he carried as he slowly traversed the stage. Later he emerged completely hidden by a black plastic tarp and crawled across the stage like an enormous beetle. Cage, meanwhile, stayed behind the wall most of the time; his accompaniment consisted mainly of spoken syllables from his composition Empty Words *and a*

fascinating array of sounds produced by scraping, dragging or thumping various objects he found stashed there. (Close 1978)

Dialogue is also reviewed with performances at Liverpool on June 26, and London on July 8 and 18, 1980, again reiterating the general details noted above, with particular focus upon Merce Cunningham's stage presence.

Six different scores for *Dialogue* are preserved among Cage's unpublished manuscripts. None are dated, so it is impossible to establish any chronological order. The most minimal *Dialogue* score is contained in a file of miscellaneous material labeled "Pre-1976" by Cage, and is now housed in the John Cage Archive at Northwestern University. The two-page handwritten score contains two floorplans, and a single paragraph relating simple actions involving a glove, a piece of blue cloth, a chair, two glasses of water, and smoking a cigarette (Cage ca. 1970).

The five other *Dialogue* scores are found in Cage's own manuscript collection. These originally were in a manila envelope which he labeled "ca. 1978." All but one have an accompanying series of ticked-off computer generated *I Ching* hexagrams used to make the composition. Unfortunately the manuscripts do not contain enough further information to document how the individual hexagrams then determined the notated contents. The scores are basically lists of physical actions involving the simple manipulation of various objects — presumably found on the premises before the actual performance — as well as references to short text excerpts from *Empty Words* (and in one example from also *Silence, A Year from Monday*, and *M*). All the *Dialogue* scores reveal Cage's explicit concern for having a floorplan (as in his earlier pieces *Water Walk*, *Sounds of Venice*, and *Variations IV*); the use of chance procedures to structure and select events; and indeterminacy with notating the objects employed, the occurrence of vocal events, and the actual duration of an action. For illustrative and documentary purposes, the complete score for one of Cage's *Dialogue* performances is reproduced in Appendix 5.

John Cage was never articulate about *Dialogue*, either his or Merce Cunningham's performances, and I believe that he dismissed these works in our discussions because he felt them to be rather marginal within his ouvre. However, it is the most richly intimate example of their mature independent collaboration, and presents Cage's most sustained engagement as a physical action performer in a *Theatre Piece*-type composition.

With *Theatre Piece* and its later variations, Cage presents a paradoxical situation between notation and its performance. The notation is indeterminate, and thus allows the individual performer to make personal decisions, determinations with how and what to do. Cage, however, made a crucial distinction between improvisation and indeterminately notated events:

The difference is that. . . improvisation frequently depends not on the work you have to do [i.e. the score one is to perform], but depends more on your likes and dislikes. It doesn't lead you into a new experience, but into something with which you're already familiar, whereas if you have work to do which is suggested but not determined by a notation, if it's indeterminate this simply means that you are to supply the determination of certain things that the composer has not determined. (Darter 1982, 21)

Cage also expressed this often misunderstood aesthetic in more succinct terms:

PERMISSION GRANTED. BUT NOT TO DO WHATEVER YOU WANT.
(Cage 1967, 28)

6

THE MUSICIRCUS: VARIATIONS ON LARGE-GROUP SIMULTANEITIES

The musicircus is a multi-media event of simultaneous and independent performances, often presented in non-traditional performance spaces, with a large number of participants, and lasting for several hours. The first performance designated as a musicircus was in 1967, however the development of this genre may be said to begin with the untitled event at Black Mountain College in 1952 and *Theatre Piece* in 1960. The musicircus continues the evolution of indeterminacy to its most extreme form, until in several instances the score is absent. As a composer in this context, Cage is at his most removed from the creative process, placing instead each performer and each audience member at the center. As Cage succinctly explains, "If we have done nothing, he then will have everything to do" (Kirby and Schechner 1965, 55).

The musicircus genre begins within the series of eight *Variations* composed between 1958 and 1967. *Variations I* (1958) and *Variations II* (1960) are indeterminate notations similar to the optional transparent squares of five non-parallel lines in *Music Walk* (1958): perpendiculars are drawn to points and then measured to determine frequency, overtone structure, amplitude, occurrence, and duration. Both *Variations I* and *Variations II* are designated for any number of players and any kind of instruments or sound producing means. *Variations I* and *Variations II* were first performed as piano solos by David Tudor at Cologne on June 15, 1960, and the New School for Social Research, New York, on March 24, 1961 (Dunn 1962, 29). As these compositions are music, rather than theatre, both are peripheral to this study. *Variations III* (1963) and *Variations VIII* (1967) will be discussed in the context of John Cage as a performer, in Chapter 9.

Variations IV (1963) is "For any number of players, any sounds or combinations of sounds produced by any means, with or without other activities" (Cage 1963c). The score consists of a transparency containing nine dots and three circles, and a short written instruction. Not provided is a map or floorplan of the performance area. Cage lists five basic types of performance spaces: 1. a theatre (with either one floor or with balcony or balconies), 2. a building with one or more floors, 3. an apartment or suite, 4. a closed space (i.e. "a cave"), or 5. an outdoor space. The performer or performers take their floorplan and place cut-outs of the transparency forms on it in the following manner: one circle is placed anywhere on the plan, and the other circle and seven points are allowed to fall either on the plan or outside it. The third circle on the transparency is not used. Lines are then drawn from the placed circle to each of the points. The second circle "is only operative when one of the lines so produced (one or more) intersects or is tangent to it" (Cage 1963c). Different positions of the circles and points may be made before and/or during actual performance.

The resultant superimposition gives a spatial indication of where sounds arise. Cage notes that sounds may be produced both inside and outside the total performance space, and that this may include opening a window or door as a sound producing activity. Time and space are not required to be measured. If a line intersects two or more points, sound in movement is indicated. The score instructions concisely conclude:

> *When performed with another activity which has a given time-length (or on a program where a given amount of time is available) let the performance of this take the shorter amount.*
>
> *A performer need not confine himself to a performance of this piece. At any time he may do something else. And others, performing something else at the same time and place, when free to do so, enter into the performance of this. (Cage 1963c)*

An example of how a superimposition of score parts with a floorplan might look appears in Fig. 29. The floorplan represents an apartment kitchen. In this example the second circle is not operative, and there is no indication of sound in movement. The points have been numbered, although there is no indication in the score that this need be done, nor should one necessarily begin with a point and perform sounds in a clockwise or counter-clockwise sequence. In this example, point 1 would mean a chair sound, point 2 mean opening window A to hear outside sounds, point 3 would mean kitchen sink sounds, point 4 would mean either kitchen cabinet sounds or another performance of point 3, point 5 would mean playing empty bottles and cans saved for redemption at the store, point 6 would mean sounds made in the adjoining bathroom beyond door C, and point 7 would mean opening door A to allow outside sounds from the hallway to enter the room. This rather simple example is based on my kitchen, and is only provided because no examples of floorplan score superimpositions are available from public performances.

Variations IV has rarely been performed, probably because of the extreme indeterminacy of notation and compositional nonintention of actual result. It was first performed by John Cage and David Tudor at the Feigen/ Palmer Gallery in Los Angeles on January 12, 1964 (Cage 1964). The performance lasted six hours ("Cage: Variations IV, Vol. 2" 1969). Peter Yates describes witnesssing this performance . . .

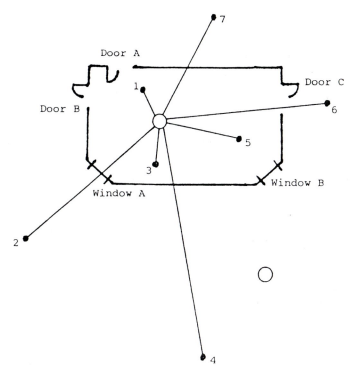

Fig. 29. Floorplan of the author's kitchen, showing the superimposition of score materials for *Variations IV*; © 1963 by Henmar Press Inc.

> *. . . for three hours . . . , each operating a portable phonograph, tape players, and radio through speakers located at various points in the building, the musical selections and sounds at random, while listeners moved about. (Yates 1967, 335)*

This performance is most accurately documented in the two-volume commercial release by Everest Records in the mid- to latter-1960s. Each record contains a total of 45 minutes worth of various excerpts from the total duration of the live performance. One misses, of course, the visual element of the gallery space, but one hears a collage of various sounds, including baby cries, American folksong, Tchaikovsky, church bells, electronic sounds, recorded laughter, speech in French and English, and the live crowd sounds (Cage 1964). Audience members were also provided with a brief set of score instructions and a paper sheet containing the forms to superimpose over the floorplan as the program. It is not known if any of the audience members made their own score realizations and performance, although this possibility was allowed.

A far different, and more visual approach to *Variations IV* was presented by the ONCE Group in Ann Arbor, Michigan, during the mid-1960s. Peter Yates describes the ONCE performance:

> *On a small platform an interview was being mimed (an American composer interviewing another American composer), while a tape of the actual interview, taken from a broadcast, played through an inconspicuous loudspeaker. The interviewee blasted several of his more popular contemporaries, saying many things about musical conditions and personalities as true as embarrassing, while the mimed "feedback" turned it all to parodic comedy, the audience laughing at truth and parody together. Meanwhile a girl was being tied to the top of a metal pole. Firecrackers were exploding, an automobile running outside an open door. A man appeared, bemused and carrying a baton, as if expecting an orchestra. A girl approached him with a scarf, wound it around his neck, returned to exchange his glasses for dark glasses, to outfit him with a piano accordian, finally to replace his baton with a blind man's white, red-tipped cane. The image of the reduced conductor was led up the aisle, bleating his accordian. (Yates 1967, 335–336)*

Variations IV was more recently performed by the S.E.M. Ensemble at the Paula Cooper Gallery, New York, on June 16, 1989. Director Petr Kotik programmed Cage's work in a retrospective concert of music from the 1960s because the score is so rarely performed and is one of the seminal experimental compositions of the period. Kotik is uninformative with how he personally used the score, but states that each of the five participants independently made their own part, and then treated the actual content as being an improvisation (Kotik 1990).

The S.E.M. performance lasted thirty minutes, which was the duration agreed upon by the five participants. The musicians employed traditional wind instruments (flute, trombone, and trumpet), pre-recorded and electronic sounds, a radio, and the existing gallery doors (the street entrance, closet, and elevator). A floorplan of the performance area appears in Fig. 30. All five performers were situated in the back area of the gallery, unseen by the audience for the first five minutes. They then entered into the audience area. The basic areas used by the individual performers are notated in Fig. 30 with a circled number. There were occasional instances of sound in movement, by either walking very loudly on the wooden floor, or slowly walking while playing a wind instrument. The performance concluded with all the participants in different areas of the gallery.

The dislocation from score to performance is complete in *Variations V*, notated during September–October, 1965, after the first performance at Lincoln Center, New York, on July 23, 1965. The unscored collaboration included choreography by Merce Cunningham with himself, Carolyn Brown, Barbara Lloyd, Sandra Neels, Albert Reid, Peter Saul, and Gus Solomons, Jr.; electronic devices by Robert Moog; films by Stan VanDerBeek and distorted television images by Nam June Paik; lighting by Beverly Emmons; the musicians John Cage, David Tudor, Malcolm Goldstein, Frederick Lieberman,

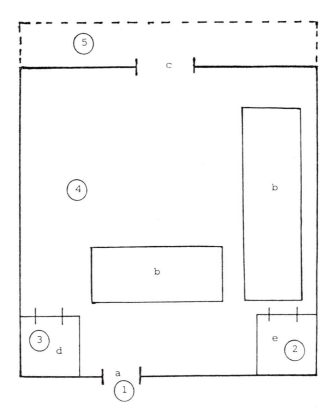

Fig. 30.   Floorplan of the Paula Cooper Gallery, New York, as used by the SEM Ensemble for a performance of *Variations IV* (1963) on June 16, 1989. The symbols refer to: a is the street entrance; b shows the seated audience; c is the entrance doorway of the musicians; d is an elevator; and e is a closet. The positions of the five performers at the conclusion of the performance are shown by the numbers 1–5.

and James Tenney; and Billy Klüver as technical consultant. Cage made tape recordings, and Max Mathews designed a mixer to control the volume, tone, and distribution of sound among six loudspeakers (Cage 1965b).

Billy Klüver writes a description of the performance:

> The sound sources for Variations V *were short-wave radios and tapes of such things as a recording of an ordinary kitchen drain, a sound John particularly liked, according to David.*
>
> *At Bell Labs we put together ten photocells which triggered switches that could turn on and off the audio. They were placed around the edge of the stage. When the dancers passed in front of them, sounds were switched on and off. Robert Moog had also contributed ten capacitive antennas which were activated when the dancers passed close to them.*
>
> *The equipment was set up at the back of the stage behind the dancers, and*

everyone worked there during the performance. On the wall behind us was projected
film material from Stan VanDerBeek and Nam June Paik. (Klüver 1988, 7–8)

A fifty-minute black-and-white sound film of *Variations V* was produced in 1966 by Studio Hamburg in Germany, and is available from the
Merce Cunningham Dance Foundation. Apart from such filmic devices as
close-ups, dissolves, and cut-aways, the major difference between the film
and the live-performance is that the musicians are positioned in the front of
the dance area rather than at the back. The choreography includes several
non-dance activities such as Merce Cunningham potting a plant and Carolyn
Brown repotting it, and Cunningham riding a bicycle around the electronic
poles. The projected images include a short sequence from the film *Born
Yesterday* (1950) with Judy Holliday and Broderick Crawford, some excerpts
from commercials for coffee or Pan Am, and a short sequence from the early
1960s made-for-television cartoon *The King and Odie*. The music is mostly
radio or electronic sounds, with occasional snipets from the classical piano
repertoire (Arnbom 1966).

Cage's score after-the-fact of performance contains a list of the participants, and brief written notes and reflections. Typical examples include:

Performance without score or parts.

Perform at control panels in the role
of research worker.

Intermittent.

Accept leakage, feedback, etc.

Irrelevance.

As dance ends, turn off amplifiers (if,
due to leakage, necessary).

Non-focused.

Escape Stagnation. (Cage 1965b)

The score is thus a practical and aesthetic document for disciplined improvisation and collaboration rather than being (as is usual) a prescriptive notation
indicative of future performance. It is also not a description of the actual
performance, but is evocative and formal in its use of language. *Variations V* is
as unrepeatable as the 1952 untitled event and is unlikely to be revived by
others.

Another work done in the same year is *Rozart Mix*, first performed at
the Rose Art Museum at Brandeis University on May 10, 1965 (Lucier 1988,
14). The published score consists of the back-and-forth written communication between John Cage and Alvin Lucier in preparing a program. Cage was
too busy to fully compose a new work, but suggested an electronic piece for
twelve tape recorders playing tape loops. In one of the letters written to

Lucier, Cage wrote about the preparation of the tapes, including pictographs for splicing technique:

> *Record just anything (lots of speech, some music, not much in way of continuous noises) then cut quite small (not longer than 4 or 5 inches, down to fragments — tiny). Then splice together ignorantly sometimes not or*
>
> ⇌ *but* \ / / \
>
> *etc. Make only a few shortest viable length; make some very long — all lengths in betw. perhaps determining length by chance. (Cage 1965a)*

Of the first performance, Alvin Lucier writes:

> *Tom Garver, assistant curator of the Museum, had rounded up the twelve tape recorders. We placed boxes of loops in convenient places and set up a table for repairing them. Several Brandeis graduate students had willingly agreed to participate. The performance consisted simply of choosing loops, threading them on the recorders, and extending them around the mike stands. A few of us removed our shoes and socks so that we could wade across the water, extending longer loops across the pool [in the Museum].*
>
> *As we were going about our simple tasks of threading, replacing and occasionally repairing our loops, we could sometimes recognize loops that we had made, but more often than not, the mix of sounds in the Museum was overwhelming. In those parts of loops which were spliced with tiny fragments of tape, no sound was identifiable. Those made up of longer segments . . . gave the impression of collage. John had no wanted a real beginning or ending to* Rozart Mix, *so we continued playing until most of the audience had left the Museum. (Lucier 1988, 14–15)*

Rozart Mix was more recently performed simultaneously with *Song Books* at the Pierre Hotel in New York on May 25, 1989. The performers surrounded the audience, as shown in Fig. 31. For the 1989 performance, Alvin Lucier organized 24 persons (primarily students from Wesleyan University) to play the twelve tape machines. (I was also a participant.) Lucier and assistants made tapes spliced in the style of the 1965 version, and there were also many short tapes provided by celebrities such as David Bowie, John Cale, Yoko Ono, and Susan Sontag. Lucier assigned two persons to each tape machine — one to thread the tape, the other to pull it relatively tight around a microphone stand and make sure that the tape was not tangled. He did not have the participants read Cage's published score, but gave an oral instruction. After threading and playing a tape, we were then told to replace it with a new one "after a while." Lucier added very strongly that we were not to do anything extra, but just to do the task as simply and efficiently as possible. The activity was not to be made purposefully "theatrical" through a manner of performing our tasks in an obvious way.

The tape loops ranged from about two to fifty feet long. Because of the limited space, sometimes various tape machines had loops criss-crossing. Performers were also told that a mike stand could be positioned on the floor

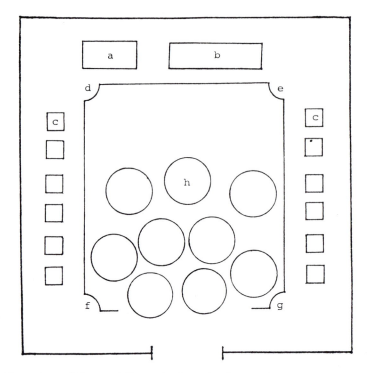

Fig. 31.   Floorplan of *Rozart Mix* with *Song Books*, performed at the Pierre Hotel, New York, on May 25, 1989. The symbols refer to: a is the table with sound-mixing equipment; b is the table with *Rozart Mix* tapes, supervised by Alvin Lucier with assistants; c shows the twelve *Rozart Mix* tape machines and microphone stands; d is David Barron; e is Neely Bruce; f is Toby Twining; g is Phyllis Bruce (the four *Song Books* performers); and h shows the tables of the guests having dinner. The empty area of the floor was used for dancing at intermittent moments during the performance, and after the conclusion.

amongst the tables of the audience (who were eating dinner), but this was rarely done.

The performance began around 6:30. The sound was very dense, and often one could not distinguish any individual tapes from the ensuing mix. Lucier was disappointed with the quality of the celebrity tapes, for these usually consisted of identifiable spoken statements rather than having the sound-collage quality of the original *Rozart Mix* tapes. Sample celebrity tapes included anecdotes, counting numbers, or making abstract vocal sounds (i.e. speaking in phonemes). One tape, played for over ten minutes, was of someone singing "Happy Birthday To You" over and over.

As the performance progressed, many of the participants became bored and inattentive. Several had to leave at 9:00 to go back to Connecticut that evening. For the last hour there were only two or three of us playing four or five tape machines. I tried to get those of us who remained to make it as complex and as dense-sounding as possible. Eventually Lucier told us to stop shortly after 10:00.

Variations VI was composed in March, 1966 (Cage 1966). The score is, like the earlier works in this series, an example of complex indeterminate notation which is prescriptive for a performance of loudspeakers and sound sources distributed in space.

The score of *Variations VI* contains four sheets measuring 11 by 17 inches. The first sheet is the instructions; the second sheet is a horizontal line centered vertically on the page, measuring twelve inches; and the third and fourth sheets are transparencies containing 12 straight lines, 38 triangles, 57 bisected lines, and 114 half-circles with diameters (Cage 1966). One cuts out the transparency shapes, and uses as many required for a practical and specific performance. The triangles represent the number of loudspeakers, the half-circles represent sound sources, the bisected lines represent the available components (such as "amplifiers, pre-amplifiers, modulators and filters"), and the straight lines represent the total number of practical sound systems.

For the purpose of illustration, Fig. 32 represents the use of score materials (renotated for convenience) for my home stereo system. There are two loudspeakers (two triangles labeled A and B); four sound sources (half-circles numbered to represent 1. cassette tape, 2. CD player, 3. record player, and 4. radio); one amplifier (one bisected line); and two short straight lines (according to the instructions, one adds one extra line to the total number of sound systems, which in this example is one). The performer drops the required number of transparency cut-outs on the sheet with the long vertical line. The symbols that are between the two short transparency straight lines are then to be used for a moment in performance. In this example, it would be playing a phonograph record on speaker B.

Cage notes that:

> The orientation of the converging straight lines with respect to the non-transparent (vertical) line may suggest distribution of sound in space. (Cage 1966)

In Fig. 32 I would interpret the instruction to mean that the sound would be relatively far away from the central point of reception. The straight line on the half-circles, and the long line on the triangles and bisected lines mean: if the rest of the figure is relatively to the left of the long vertical line (as in loudspeaker B) this refers to "indicating continually unvaried (or unaltered) operation;" and when the rest of the figure is relatively to the right, this indicates "continuously varied (or altered) operation" (Cage 1966). In my illustration, this would mean to play different phonograph records. Cage also

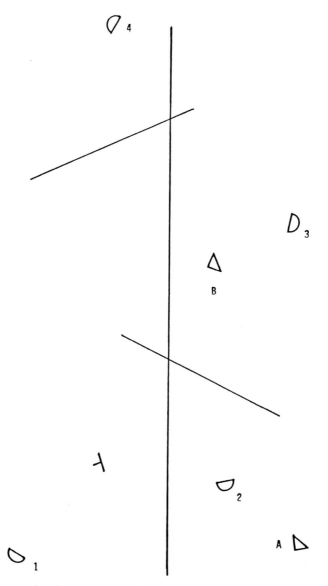

Fig. 32.   An example of superimposed score materials for *Variations VI* (1966), made by the author in 1992; © 1966 Henmar Press Inc.

notes that the "power of the amplifier be less or equal to a loud-speaker's capacity to receive," which would mean a generally loud level of volume. The score is particularly non-self-expressive, for Cage instructs:

> *Let the notations refer to what is to be done, not to what is heard or to be heard. (Cage 1966)*

Variations VI was first performed in the Sculpture Court of the Art Gallery of Toronto on May 13, 1966, and included electronic circuitry, microphones, radio, tape, and a television set (Kraglund 1966). Unfortunately, this work has very little documentation. David Tudor has no notes for any of the later *Variations*, but has recently commented:

> Variations VI *was one of the most enjoyable pieces to perform. It's interesting because if you're in a controlled situation it's very, very beautiful, it turned out to be very theatrical.*
>
> *Both* Variations VI *and* Variations VII *are very theatrical. I don't believe there is any mention in the published score about the necessity of how much material there is, but the idea is, as with most of John's work, multiplicity, and I've always enjoyed it.*
>
> *I taught one semester of performance practice to students at the Mills College Electronics Center, so I put on a performance of* Variations VI *that worked very nicely. It just simply absorbed every piece of equipment that was available, and then we had standing coat racks, all draped with every cable that was available, so it was like a maze with all these people wandering in and out doing — what-not. It becomes very theatrical, I mean, a real piece to watch.*
>
> *The nicest performance, I thought, was the one John and I did at Washington at the Pan American Center. We had quite a large hall, and a lot of equipment, most of which we brought ourselves. We decided to make a real concert performance, so we had an intermission (laughs).*
>
> *We decided where to have the intermission just arbitrarily, and it was very nice because you turned off all the equipment, and then there was a friend that could come who brought some Tequila to make Margaritas, and then we would reassemble the audience. I thought it was a very nice way to do it. (Tudor 1989a)*

John Cage, however, did not recall performances of *Variations VI* with the same fondness:

> *I finally decided that we weren't doing it correctly, and I pointed this out to David, and he said well the only way we can do this correctly is to keep on doing it (laughs) incorrectly to discover what is wrong in our performances. I was not very happy with our performances, but he was pleased. They didn't seem to me to be any more complicated than with one sound system. The performances lasted two or three hours. (Cage 1990a)*

The most documentable performance of *Variations VI* was at the YMHA on 92nd Street in New York on February 25, 1967. It was called *TV Dinner: Homage to E. A. T. (Food for Thought)*. E. A. T. (Experiments in Art and Technology) was founded in 1966 to foster interaction and collaborative experimention between artists and engineers (Klüver, Martin, and Rose 1972, passim). Cage does not recall who called it *Homage to E. A. T.*, but that the title was not his idea. When asked about any details of what happened, he did not provide any, but became very angry, saying that the engineers were inept and that it did not come off as planned (Cage 1990a).

The performance began with Merce Cunningham dancing behind a swinging strobe-light. Films by Len Lye and Stan VanDerBeek were projected on the auditorium walls. The curtain then rose to show about twelve people sitting at a table (G. Harris 1989). Billy Klüver, a participant, would later write:

> ...*we ate an elegant meal on stage as we talked. Everything was wired with contact mikes — forks, knives, plates, glasses. Fred Waldhauer sat at the end of the table and worked his matrix switching system that could switch any mike to any channel, one mike to many channels, or many mikes to one channel, etc., thus moving the sounds among different speakers. Stan VanDerBeek used television projectors to show close ups of the diners on the walls of the auditorium. (Klüver 1988, 11–12)*

Nicholas Cernovitch also made on-stage lighting effects as the dinner progressed (Cernovitch 1989). Gary Harris, another participant, recalls covering the walls with white paper to accomodate the projections, and working the curtain. The performance lasted over three hours (G. Harris 1989).

Another performance that used the theme of a dinner was *Newport Mix* (1967). There is no score, and little documentation. Cage would later recall:

> *That was a dinner on the river at Cincinnati. It was a restaurant called Newport, or a town opposite on the Kentucky side. And people were invited to come, but they couldn't get in unless they made a loop, so it was really the* Rozart Mix *for people who were invited. And if they couldn't make loops, they were made for them at the door, and they could produce the sounds that were then used as loops throughout the dinner party. Most of the people didn't make loops. I was at the University of Cincinnati, and there were a number of composers there who helped me generally in projects. They had to make them. I didn't make the loops.*
>
> *[Questions: How long did it last?]*
>   *Through the dinner, at least (laughs). (Cage 1990a)*

Variations VII (1966) has no score, but is similar to *Variations VI*. Cage recalls: "I don't think I made a score of *Variations VII*. The difference is receiving sounds in a plurality from distances, picking up sounds from other places than where you were" (Cage 1990a). It was first performed by John Cage, David Tudor, and two assistants, for two evenings during the *9 Evenings* at the 69th Regiment Armory, New York, in October, 1966. *Variations VII* employed 95 sound sources: 30 stage lights with 30 photocells, a television screen, 6 contact microphones, 20 radio receivers, 10 telephone lines, 10 electronic sounds, 12 machinery sounds (including juicers, blender, washing machine, and contact mike on soda bottle), 2 Geiger Counters, a television screen, and 4 body sounds (heart, brain, lungs, and stomach). All of this available material was routed through 17 sound outputs (*Variations VII* notes 1966; and Klüver 1988, 8–9).

Billy Klüver, a technical assistant and collaborator, would later write:

> *This led one engineer to write in his notes: "Motive: all sound sources in the world." New York Telephone installed ten telephone receivers in a steam trunk near the performance area, which was padlocked to cut down on the telephone bill. Cage arranged to call and leave the lines open during the performance to Lüchows Restaurant, the Aviary at the Zoo, the 14th Street Con Ed power station, the ASPCA, the New York Times press room, a bus depot, etc. A magnetic pickup fed these sounds into the system.*
>
> *The photocells were mounted in the performance area so that the performers moving on the platform [the control area] triggered the sound sources. The lights used for the photocell system threw shadows of the performers on large white screens in back of the performance area. The audience was encouraged to leave their seats during the performance and many stood close to the performers, others walked around the Armory, or lay down on the floor to listen to the sound reverberating through the hall. (Klüver 1988, 10–11)*

Reviews were mixed. Grace Glueck, writing for the *New York Times*, would sarcastically patronize the entire series of multi-media performances (including works by Deborah Hay, Yvonne Rainer, Robert Rauschenberg, and David Tudor) as "Disharmony at the Armory" (Glueck 1966). Jonas Mekas favorably interpreted Cage's piece as an optimistic view of everyday life as art:

> *Peter Kubelka says Madison Square Garden is the most beautiful auditorium in the world. In a sense it is ... that's why it was so great during the John Cage performance all those hundreds of people got up and moved across the floor area to where the musicians were working — and for a moment it looked and sounded like I was in Grand Central. (Mekas 1966)*

John Brockman, writing for the *Village Voice*, would note that . . .

> *. . . John Cage . . . showed his masterful authority and theatricality with the most successful piece of the festival. (Brockman 1966)*

Cage, however, did not recall the Armory performances of *Variations VII* with any nostalgia:

> *That was another case where the engineers couldn't make things work properly. When they saw the telephone off the hook, which I had carefully arranged so I could get the sound from different places around the city, they put the things back on, and there was no way for me to re-establish the connection. It makes me angry to just think about it. (Cage 1990a)*

One other documentable performance of *Variations VII* was performed as a solo on February 22, 1967, at Muhlenberg College in Allentown, Pennsylvania. Cage made this version by "combing the air around New York City for radio transmissions and recording the hums and squawks that 'hams' [ham-radio enthusiasts] know so well" (R. Flanagan 1967). Shortly after the Muhlenberg College performance, composer-in-residence and faculty member Ludwig Lenel recalls asking Cage "What do you think about rock music?," and Cage replied, "I like it — because it's loud!" (Lenel 1977).

The metaphor of rock music is especially telling. It was during the mid-1960s that major groups such as The Beatles and The Rolling Stones were playing not in clubs or theatres but in large sports stadiums or other non- traditional concert spaces that could accommodate several thousands of people.

Cage had been developing in a similar direction with the later *Variations*, but more than rock music, it was the work of Charles Ives that influenced Cage towards making the first performance designated as a musicircus. Charles Ives (1874–1954) was an insurance executive and musician. Ives wrote several compositions that presented sound-collages of juxtaposed rhythms, key signatures or tonal centers, melodies, harmonies, and dynamics. Ives also used familiar material in his sound textures, such as the inclusion of "The Telephone Song (Hello, Ma' Baby)" in *Central Park in the Dark* (1906) or "Shall We Gather at the River?" in the third movement of the *Fourth Sonata for Violin and Piano* (1902–1915). His last composition, begun around 1912 and left unfinished in 1932, is the *Universe Symphony*, which was to have groups of musicians playing unrelated and simultaneous musics in a wide geographical area (Ives 1972, 106–108).

Cage was not initially attracted to Ives's music when he first became aware of it in the 1930s, but in the mid-1960s he wrote two short statements in critical praise of Ives's achievements and foresight. Cage particularly commended Ives for his early use of simultaneity, the importance of separating sounds in space, for writing non-referential passages, a sensitivity to inactivity and silence, and for score indications for the performer to perform according to individual choice (Cage 1967, 37–42). Both Ives and Cage also share a love of the thought and personal example of Henry David Thoreau.

The first performance called a musicircus was *Musicircus*, presented at the Stock Pavilion at Urbana-Champaign, Illinois, on November 17, 1967, from 8:00 p.m. to 1:00 a.m. (Zumstein 1967). It was, in part, an expression of a Thoreau-influenced example of anarchy, the individual, and society (Husarik 1983, 5), as well as a Cagean version of Ives's *Universe Symphony*. Cage did not make a score, but simply invited the various performers to participate. Approximately 5000 people were in attendance. Bruce Zumstein would note:

> *It was a highly heterogeneous audience. Little boys caught freely flying balloons and carried them off. Their parents sat in the stands. . .*
> *University students walked through the performance. . .*
> *Persons dressed in bedsheets tried to avoid drafts from the open stock doors, and girls on dates climbed on boys' shoulders to see who was there and doing what.*
> (Zumstein 1967)

The most concise performance description is by Cage, who would later write:

> *There were: the composer Salvatore Martirano, who, like the others, used a group of performers and gave a program of his own; Jocy de Oliveira (Carvalho), who gave a piano recital including Ben Johnston's* Knocking Piece, *music by Morton Feldman, etc.; Lejaren Hiller; Herbert Brün; James Cuomo and his band; another jazz band; David Tudor and Gordon Mumma; Norma Marder giving a voice recital sometimes accompanying a dancer, Ruth Emerson; the mime Claude Kipnis, who responded with a whole sound environment; . . . In the center of the floor was a metallic construction [by Barney Childs] upon which the audience could make sounds. . . No directions were given anyone. I connected contract mikes to the light switchboard, changing the lights and, at the same time, producing sounds of the switches. At either end of the Pavilion but beyond screens, were places to buy apple cider and doughnuts, popcorn, etc. (A reference to Ives.) Ronald Nameth arranged the play of films and slides. And also obtained dark light and large balloons. . . The various musics each had a stage or platform near the bleachers so that the floor was free for use by the audience. The general sound was of a high volume, though not everything was amplified. Loudspeakers were high up around the perimeter. The general shape of the building is rectangular but with rounded ends. (Kostelanetz 1980a, 194)*

Other details of the event include David Tudor playing the air vents (Tudor 1989c); a blackboard with black-light chalk for visitors to make their own black-light drawings; solos by dancers from the Merce Cunningham Dance Company performing individual routines that "appeared as silhouettes on screens across the pavilion" and that occasionally "children would dart back and forth chasing these shadows" (Husarik 1983, 4–5).

The 1967 *Musicircus* is a culmination of Cage's use of unrelated simultaneities, of non-intentional and multiple focus, of multi-media presentation, and of an increasing reliance on indeterminacy, to the point where no score exists. Several different musicircus-type performances have been organized by Cage through the remainder of his career.

The most elaborate, large-scale musicircus is *HPSCHD*, performed on May 16, 1969, at Assembly Hall at the University of Illinois, Urbana-Champaign. For two years Cage collaborated with Lejaren Hiller in the chance composition of seven harpsichord solos, using computer print-outs of *I Ching* hexagrams. Each harpsichord solo is twenty minutes in duration, to be repeated at intervals during the total performance.

Solo I was performed by David Tudor, who played a score made from a chance-determined 12-tone gamut; Solo II was performed by Antoinette Vischer (to whom the piece is also dedicated), who played realizations of Wolfgang Mozart's *Musikalisches Würfelspiel* ("Musical Dicegame"); Solo III was performed by William Brooks, who played measures from six Mozart keyboard compositions structured by chance according to Mozart's Dicegame; Solo IV was performed by Ronald Peters, whose score was similar to Solo III but with independently determined bass and treble parts; Solo V was performed by Yuji Takehashi, whose score consisted of works by Beethoven, Chopin, Schumann, Gottschalk, Busoni, Cage, and Hiller, chance-structured as in Solo III; Solo VI was performed by Neely Bruce, whose score used the material of Solo V in the structural manner of Solo IV; and Solo VII was performed by Philip Corner, whose score consisted of a one-page written instruction to practice or perform any compositions by Mozart (Husarik 1983, 7–10).

Each of the seven harpsichordists sat on raised platforms, with each instrument amplified. Fifty-two tapes of electronic waveforms and microtonal pitches from 5 to 56 tones to the octave were made by Cage and Hiller using *I Ching* computerized determinations (Husarik 1983, 10). Just prior to the performance, Cage explained: "This breaks the scale into such small components that at times the listener cannot detect tone differences" (Kuhn 1969).

The basic sound of the live performance is documented in a recording, released in 1969 by Nonesuch Records, of a 21-minute version played by Antoinette Vischer, Neely Bruce, and David Tudor, with the chance-determined electronic tapes. The sound is rather gentle, tinkling, like a multitude of antique music boxes playing at once. The record also includes a computer print-out of 5-second intervals allowing the home-listener to adjust the volume and timbre (Cage and Hiller 1969).

Missing from the recording, of course, is the highly visual content of the live performance. The building was circular, with both a 340-foot circular circumference screen as well as 11-by 40-foot screens, onto which were projected 40 films and 6800 slides (Haas 1969; and Husarik 1983, 12). Films included documentaries on Stonehenge, George Méliès's *A Trip to the Moon* (1903), films from NASA, and recent experimental and computer-generated animation (Husarik 1983, 14). The slides mostly comprised images provided by NASA, the Mount Wilson Observatory, and the Adler Planetarium; 1600 hand-painted slides, made through computerized *I Ching* determinations, were also shown (Husarik 1983, 12). The visual theme of *HPSCHD*, references to outer-space, evolved in Cage's mind from working with the *I Ching* with the aid of the computer: "We then thought of the microscope [e.g. microtones] and the telescope as instruments that also break things down into smaller parts and used this as the theme for the pictures" (Kuhn 1969). A floorplan, made by Frances Ott Allen, an audience member, appears in Fig. 33.

The performance was also visual in the movement of the audience through the building, and in ambient lighting effects that occurred during the film and slide projections. Stephen Husarik writes:

> Some participants wandered from station to station, while others simply milled about. To one side posters were being silk-screened, and also paper smocks and T-shirts (even long underwear) with zodiak images. In the central arena many people were lying down, looking at the visual spectacle above them. Conversation was

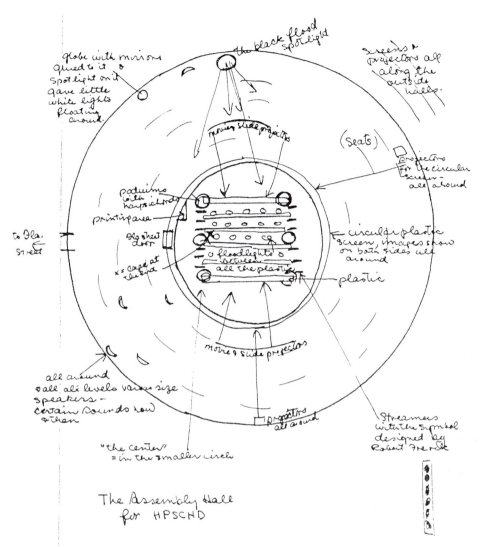

Fig. 33.   Frances Ott Allen's floorplan of *HPSCHD* at the University of Illinois, Urbana-Champaign, on May 16, 1969. Reproduced courtesy of Frances Ott Allen.

relatively muted, though the voices of participants could be clearly heard above the music whenever it seemed necessary for them to be heard.

    Cage instructed a technician to change the lighting whenever it suited him. Now and then blacklights came on and set the HPSCHD banners [around the hall] and smocks to glow. [Ronald] Nameth decided that the light from the projectors was not sufficient to illuminate the interior and so went to the control panel and slowly turned on a soft blue light that came from the center of the domed ceiling and spread itself down all the aisles. (Husarik 1983, 15–16)

The performance of *HPSCHD* was for four-and-a-half hours, beginning at 7:30 p.m. It was received very favorably by those in attendance (Husarik 1983, 17–19; Haas 1969; Willis 1969; and Kostelanetz 1969). For a comprehensive first-hand experience of the complete performance by an audience member, see Appendix 6.

There were also two other, less elaborate examples of a musicircus in 1969 — *Demonstration of the Sounds of the Enviroment*, and *33 and 1/3*. Neither work was ever notated. Cage recalled both performances:

> Demonstration of the Sounds of the Environment — *I think that was done at a University in Wisconsin. I talked to the audience, and then made with them a chance-determined tour — we made it in the theatre, you see — by foot of the campus. We used the* I Ching. *You'd have a map, and you make a grid, and if the grid is 64 by 64, then you know where you're going if you ask two questions of the* I Ching.
>
> *[Question: Would you ask for the number of places to visit?]*
>
> *No, I don't think I did.*
>
> *[Question: Then how did you determine how many?]*
>
> *Oh, it was practical. It was taking a whole audience on a walk through the university grounds, so we didn't want it to take too long because they weren't there for any length of time, it was just to be for this hour-and-a-half, so to speak.*
>
> *And then, we simply walked in a line through the campus, and we didn't say anything. We listened to as many sounds as we could. After we had two or three places to go, we just returned to the Hall.*
>
> *So, it was a way of getting them to listen, and spend an hour-and-a-half. And when we got back there was some talk about the sounds we'd heard.*
>
> *33–1/3 — That's where the people play the records. When you came into the Hall there were piles of records [300] in front of record players — I think there were twelve — and they were 33–1/3 [r.p.m.]. And there's no one playing them, so that the audience is obligated, if they want any sound, to play them. I just got a large number of records, so that there'd be piles of records in front of each play-back. If they couldn't do it, there were assistants to help them.*
>
> *It was done first at the University of California at Davis, in a thing called* Mewantemooseicday. *"Me-Wantem" is a reference to Thoreau, because he asked his Indian guide what he wanted for breakfast, and his answer was "Me wantem fat" (laughs). So this was* Mewantemooseicday *(laughs) because it was a day full of music. 33–1/3 was in the evening.*
>
> *[Question: Do you remember how long it lasted?]*
>
> *No, because there were things going on simultaneously in other places, so I couldn't watch over everything.* (Cage 1990a)

Both *Demonstration of the Sounds of the Environment* and *33–1/3* are the two most concrete examples of Cage's work where not only each audience member's observations structure the performance, but where each person is also an active performer whose very actions make the piece.

The first European performance of a musicircus was *Musicircus* at Les

Halles in Paris on October 27, 1970, attended by 5000 people. Performances included Terry Riley's *In C*, several pop groups, a solo 'cellist, an accordianist, a boys' choir singing Renaissance madrigals, a brass band, a jazz trio, wrestling, a Lebanese belly dancer, and a trapeze act (P. Schneider 1970; and " 'Musicircus' Has It All Mixed In" 1970). Several audience members also made their own performance, banging on tin cans, and chanting "Liberez Geismar" in honor of a recently jailed student from the May, 1968 riots (" 'Musicircus' Has It All Mixed In" 1970). Pierre Schneider would write that the Paris *Musicircus* was a cross between Zen (inner tranquility "at the heart of tempest so silence lies at the center of sound storms") and of Mao ("contempt toward the proletariat of the sound world: noise") (P. Schneider 1970).

Cage's major musicircus of the 1970s was *Renga with Apartment House 1776*, jointly commissioned by the orchestras of Boston, Chicago, Cleveland, Los Angeles, New York, and Philadelphia in commemoration of the bicentennial of the United States in 1976. *Renga* contains a conductor's score and 78 parts made from drawings in Henry David Thoreau's *Journals*, superimposed upon a horizontal time-plot. The score of *Renga* is in the same type of notation system used in *Score and 23 Parts* (1974), which is discussed in Chapter 9 in the context of Cage as a performer. *Apartment House 1776* is for 24 musicians — four quartets, four instrumental soloists (snare drum, fife or piccolo, violin, and keyboard), and four vocalists, representing the Protestant, Sephardic, Native American, and Negro song traditions. The instrumental music in *Apartment House 1776* is based on eighteenth century dance and miltary tunes, anthems and congregational music, and music from the Moravian Church. Cage's floorplan for the performers appears in Fig. 34.

The four vocalists with each of the six orchestras were Helen Schneyer (the Protestants), Nico Castel (the Sephardim), Swift Eagle (the Native Americans), and Jeanne Lee (the Negro slaves) (Program 1976). Performances were greeted with mixed, and often polarized, reactions. Andrew Porter would review the New York performance, conducted by Pierre Boulez, as something that . . .

> . . . *became tedious. The texture was unvaried. All the points had long since been made. Although each component moved at a different pace, the superimposition of all those paces made the general progress seem a trudge — a slow-moving parade, despite the individual capering and animation of those taking part. The ear seized for relief: Chief Swift Eagle . . . started smacking his stomach, broke into peals of hearty laughter, began to play a wooden flute, [and then] was quickly drowned by fife-and-drum signals from the other side of the platform. Boulez presided over it with imperturbable aplomb.* (Porter 1976)

Richard Dyer would write of the performance of the Boston Symphony Orchestra conducted by Seiji Ozawa:

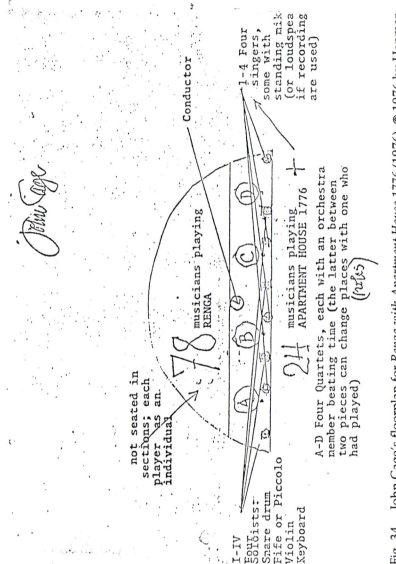

Fig. 34. John Cage's floorplan for *Renga with Apartment House 1776* (1976), © 1976 by Henmar Press Inc. Notice that Cage's right-margined typed identification ran off the page, and should read "... standing mikes (or loudspeakers if recordings are used)."

The overlapping textures were fascinating to hear, but the continuing coher-
ences of the whole were as elusive as they were probably meant to be. What these old-
fashioned ears kept settling on were the individual bits of traditional music continuity
— on the articulate fife-playing of Lois Shaefer, on the drum bits drilled out by Arthur
Press, and especially on the vocal work, particularly the caramel-toned laments of
Jeanne Lee and the corrugated fervency in the voice of Helen Schneyer. (Dyer 1976)

I recall hearing a live recording of the Boston Symphony's performance of *Renga with Apartment House 1776* broadcast on National Public
Radio during late 1976 or early 1977. It seemed reminiscent of *Variations IV*,
but in an orchestral and vocal version. The performance was approximately
thirty minutes, followed by five minutes of very excited applause and very
strident "BOOS!" from the audience. Alison Knowles recalls a similarly
divided audience at the New York performance, where many people rather
noisily walked out, and that she, Jackson Mac Low, and Dick Higgins stood
up and silently held hands as a demonstration of support and solidarity with
Cage's work (Knowles 1989).

A 1991 recording of *Apartment House 1776* (without *Renga*) was issued
in 1994. The four vocalists were Walter Buckingham (Protestant), Darrell
Dunn (Native American), Semenya McCord (African American), and Chiam
Parchi (Sephardi), with chamber orchestra from the New England Conservatory. Hearing *Apartment House 1776* by itself, I find, becomes a very different
experience from the 1976 performance. The four vocalists and chamber
instrumentalists are much more isolated components in this musicircus situation. While there still remains a multiplicity of simultaneous material, one can
better hear the individual components and qualities of performance. The
predominance of hymn tunes used for the instrumental portions lends an
almost neo-baroque ambience throughout, punctuated at time by fragments
of antique military percussion. The vocal work is gentle yet impassioned, and
gives credence to the myth of American society as a "melting pot" that can
peacefully accept multi-cultural values and life-styles (Cage 1994a).

More recent musicircus performances do not have any score. *Il Treno
di John Cage — Alla ricera del silenzio perduto* was a five-hour train trip during
the music festical at Bologna on the 26th–28th of June, 1978. Microphones
were underneath and inside the cars, and people were free to move about
from car to car. In the various cars were a pianist, a folksong group, a wind
ensemble, a television set, and at one point people began to dance at a train
station (Block 1980, 125).

House Full of Music was performed at the Übersee Museum in Bre-
men, Germany, May 1–11, 1982. Cage's unpublished notes appear to be
incomplete, but contain a floorplan of the three floors of the building, a note
for making 64 different microphone positions, and notes for six categories of
musical performers — 1. Children 6–9 years old (beginners and primary

course pupils), 2. various instrumental groups playing historical music from the Renaissance to the present, 3. chamber music in various styles, 4. solo and duet pieces, 5. orchestral works, and 6. jazz, pop, and folklore pieces. *House of Music* was performed from 8:30 to 11:00 p.m., and contained mostly traditional German music, including folk tunes, and compositions by Bach, Beethoven, Brahms, Hayden, and Mozart (Cage 1982a).

A similar work to this is *Music Circus for Children of Torino*, performed at Turin, Italy, on May 19, 1984. According to Cage's unpublished notes, this was performed by 41 children aged five to eleven years old, who sang songs such as "Jingle Bells," "Frere Jacques," "L' ABC," and Italian folk- and school-songs (Cage 1984).

During the 1980s the musicircus became not so much a festival of global music, but a playful retrospective of Cage's own historical output in music composition. Solo and simultaneous performances of Cage's works, performed at the Almeida Festival in London on May 28–30, 1982, were filmed and edited together as *John Cage: A Music Circus* (Greenaway 1982). Film director Peter Greenaway does not concentrate on any single extended moment during the various performances, and cross-cuts with interviews and film asides. As a result, the film is only a very fragmented documentation of the live-performance experience. It is, however, with the exception of the film of *Variations V*, the best currently available audio-visual record of a typical musicircus.

The most important large-scale musicircus of the 1980s was *Musicircus* on September 12, 1987, at the Embassy Theatre in Los Angeles. This was the finale of a week-long celebration given as a kind of "home-coming" in honor of the composer's 75th birthday. The 1987 *Musicircus* included slides of journal drawings by Thoreau and performances of various works by Cage composed from the 1930s through 1987. Cage also read *Empty Words IV* (in Cage 1979a, 66–76), and M. C. Richards read her poetry. The entire performance lasted three hours (Cage 1987f). M. C. Richards recalls that she read one of her poems during the very first minutes, and then spent the remaining time observing the other performances. She also notes that her experience of the 1987 *Musicircus* was very similar to that of the 1952 untitled event at Black Mountain College (Richards 1989).

The last major musicircus to be made by Cage was at Stanford University on January 29, 1992. It was attended by one- to two-thousand people (Dworkin 1992). Performers included a Javanese gamelang ensemble, a Sufi drum group, a Gregorian chant group, an African rhythm group, a kid's Rap group from East Palo Alto, Balkan bagpipers (Kosman 1992), as well as "an employee of the San Francisco Exploratorium wearing a suit that responds with sounds to different wavelengths of light, a Cantor from a Bay Area synagogue, . . . and Martin Yan of the TV show 'Yan Can Cook' " who chopped and cooked vegetables in a wok with contact microphones (Fine 1992). Cage performed a live and taped reading of *Muoyce* (Kosman 1992). The performance lasted three hours, and as typical, the musicians were assigned chance-determined time brackets and positions (Junkerman 1993, 155). Charles Junkerman, who contacted Cage to do this musicircus, writes:

> All things considered, the Musicircus seemed to musicians and spectators like a fairly convincing mode of an anarchic community. Given the democratic distribution of space and time [through chance procedures], the refusal of money [for admission or professional salaries], and the liberated sounds, many participants thought it got close to Cage's ideal of "an art you can live in." There was no center of gravity, or at least there would have been none if John Cage himself had stayed in New York. But he was there: the guru/patriarch/elder statesman of the avant-garde, and his presence seemed . . . to orient the randomly dispersed social energy, to center this designedly uncentered event. (Junkerman 1993, 161)

The musicircus, as a genre of Cage's theatre works, has been a practical demonstration of anarchic disassociation and interplay, of the environmental use of sound and visuals in a large-scale format, and of the relative importance (or unimportance) in having a score from which to make a performance. *Song Books* (1970) and *Europeras 1-5* (1987–91) are notated examples of the musicircus idea from Cage's last period of composition, and follow in the next two chapters.

7

SONG BOOKS: GENERAL PERFORMANCES AND SPECIFIC SOLOS

Song Books (1970) is an anthology of various notations and composition methods previously employed by Cage for theatre, vocal, and instrumental performance. To compose the *Song Books*, Cage asked the *I Ching* how many solos to write. To his astonishment, the number obtained was 90 (Brooks 1982, 87). Although the *I Ching* oracle only consists of 64 numbered hexagrams, the chance-found hexagram may have changing lines, producing another. No doubt Cage found a hexagram that changed, the total of the two when added together thus equalled 90. The 19 pairs of possibilities would have been 64 + 26 through 46 + 44 (or visa versa).

The 90 solos are numbered 3 through 92. Within this body of material one could also include two earlier works, *Solo For Voice 1* (1958) and *Solo For Voice 2* (1960). *Solo For Voice 1* may be performed a cappella or with any parts from *Concert for Piano and Orchestra* (1957–58). *Solo For Voice 2* may be performed a cappella or with *Concert for Piano and Orchestra, Fontana Mix,* and *Cartridge Music*. The solos from *Song Books*, titled "Solo For Voice 3" through "Solo for Voice 92" (whether the voice is used or not), may be performed a cappella, in combination with other *Song Books* solos, or with *Concert for Piano and Orchestra* and *Rozart Mix*. The solos may be used by one or more performers, presented in any order and in any superimposition so desired. The duration of a selection of solos may fit any programmed time-length. Not all the solos need be performed, and any solo may be repeated. Other than these suggestions, Cage does not provide any method of organization other than letting the performer/s make their own choice/s (Cage 1970a, 1).

William Brooks writes that Cage decided how to compose the various solos by making. . .

> . . .a list of the ways of writing songs that he knew: composition by taste (as in The Wonderful Widow of Eighteen Springs), by means of transparencies (as in Aria, made by using the score of Fontana Mix), by use of star charts and the I Ching (as in Solo For Voice 1), and by other means. . . With these lists of known procedures at hand, Cage would be able to respond, when required to introduce a compositional technique into the Song Books, either by using one of these familiar procedures or by inventing something new. (Brooks 1982, 87–88)

Each solo belongs to one of four categories, which Cage specifies as: 1. song, 2. song with electronics, 3. theatre, and 4. theatre with electronics. In turn, each solo in any of these four categories is specified as being relevant or irrelevant to Erik Satie or Henry David Thoreau.

Considering the *Song Books* in relation to his other compositions, Cage stated in late 1970:

> *I find that the sound, the sonorous level, is much more interesting in the* Song Books. *These are works that interest me in any case. . . But at the present time to consider the* Song Books *as a work of art is nearly impossible. Who would dare? It resembles a brothel, doesn't it? (Laughter.) And even the subject seems absent: you can't find either Satie or Thoreau in it! Not even both of them! (Cage and Charles 1981, 59)*

This rather humorous self-evaluation may be largely discounted, for Satie and Thoreau *are* found throughout the score, although this may not seem to be apparent or obvious within a specific performance. And, while Cage denies that it is a work of art, *Song Books* is the most studied of Cage's theatre compositions to date, with detailed essays by William Brooks (1982, 82–100) and Janetta Petkus (1986, 153–247). Brooks encapsulates the basic conception and compositional techniques employed; Petkus further elaborates by discussing each of the 90 solos in terms of notation and aesthetics. Neither discuss actual performance practice, but are valuable studies within a musicological context.

The anarchistic quality of *Song Books* (what Cage terms "a brothel") is encapsulated in Solo 35, which is a vocal setting of Thoreau's celebrated dictum paraphrased from the opening paragraph in *Civil Disobedience*: "The best form of government is no government at all. And that will be the kind of government we'll have when we are ready for it" (Cage 1970a, 113–125; see Thoreau 1968, 343). This solo is explicitly intended by Cage to be used during all *Song Books* performances, and as such it is the central theme, the "meaning" of the entire work. Cage comments on Solo 35:

> *Hearing it, it's practically a popular tune, as popular as a slogan or a flag. But it can enter into this enlarged situation, without determining the nature of the situation. (Cage and Charles 1981, 146–147)*

The result is that in *Song Books* there is a mixture of intention and nonintention, of social statement and aesthetic process.

From the 90 solos, 48 are vocal solos, best served within a musicological context (see Petkus 1986, 153–247). Of the 42 theatre solos in *Song Books*, several have already been discussed in previous chapters as variations of *4'33"* and *Theatre Piece*. The remaining theatre solos, and representative *Song Books* performances in general, remain to be discussed.

  Song Books was first performed on October 26, 1970, at the Theatre de la Ville in Paris, by Cathy Berberian, Simone Rist, and John Cage, who performed selected solos simultaneously with *Concert for Piano and Orchestra* and *Rozart Mix*. Reviews are extremely lacking in details. Martine Cadieu mentions Simone Rist performing gymnastics, Cathy Berberian changing costume every few minutes and cooking spaghetti using contact microphones, and John Cage playing a tape machine with a recorded excerpt from Satie's *Parade* (Cadieu 1970). Antoine Golea mentions Simone Rist on a trapeze, Cathy Berberian preparing a salad, and John Cage manipulating objects while seated at a table (Golea 1970). Marcel Schneider characterized the entire performance as being in the manner of a Mack Sennett slapstick comedy with a Dada ambience (M. Schneider 1970).

  The most complete documentation of the first performance of *Song Books* is in a 1979 paper by Eleanor Hakim, unpublished and housed in the John Cage Archive at Northwestern University. Hakim writes that the auditorium was shaped. . .

> . . .*like half of a broad ampitheatre cut into three vertical sections by aisles, and sloping upwards from the stage on a steep incline. Cubicle–like balconies ranged along both sidewalls provided for the placement of additional tape recorders and instrumentalists. Other musicaians were spotted throughout the audience, sitting on the steps of the sloping aisles. The broad, deep stage was well-cluttered with a variety of sound-generating devices.* (Hakim 1979, 5-6)

A basic floorplan of the stage, based on her written description, appears in Fig. 35.

  According to Hakim, Cage spent much of his time sitting at his table. . .

> . . .*dressed in proper dark suit, copying something out of a book while smoking with an elegant black cigarette holder. Every once in a while, he would look up and smile benevolently upon the scene, or give counsel when Berberian approached him like a little girl whispering to Daddy, but without embarrassment and in full view of the audience, and clearly as an informal part of the formal action. Or, he would get up with great solicitude — as when he picked up a red balloon that had slipped from the hand of Rist, who, dressed as a nun, was about to hammer a nail through it.* (Hakim 1979, 8)

Apparently Cage concentrated more on the theatre solos, but which specific examples were performed is no longer ascertainable.

  The two main performers were Cathy Berberian and Simone Rist. Hakim notes that Rist was "puckish, child-like, and as whimsical as a clown or variety hall entertainer — French vaudeville style." Her costumes included that of a traditional French workman's outfit, an anti-riot force policeman, a nun, a Renaissance troubadour, and an acrobat in black leotard. When dressed as the troubadour, she went into the audience and gave a spectator an

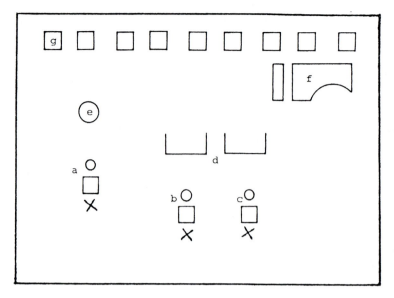

Fig. 35.   Floorplan of the first performance of *Song Books* at the Theatre de la Ville, Paris, on October 26, 1970, according to Eleanor Hakim's written description (1979). The symbols refer to: a is John Cage; b is Simone Rist; c is Cathy Berberian (the circle, square, and large X show their chair, table, and microphone); d shows the two cabanas behind Rist and Berberian, which each used for making costume changes; e is the conductor of *Concert for Piano and Orchestra*; f is the piano (on a platform) for *Concert for Piano and Orchestra*; and g shows the tape machines and microphone stands for *Rozart Mix* (the number is not actual, for Hakim does not mention how many tape machines were positioned at the back of the stage).

apple, who took a bite and then passed it on. Rist then fired a toy pistol, "shooting off" the various animal masks that were hung on the outside of her wardrobe cabana on the stage. When dressed as an acrobat, Rist at one point climbed a rope to the trapeze, and while swinging, sang "parodies of classical phrases and scales" (Hakim 1979, 9–10).

    Hakim writes that Cathy Berberian was heavily made up, wearing a bleached wig, lavender shoes, a black sleeveless pants-suit, a ruffled lavender blouse, and a great deal of costume jewelry. At other times she wore a "black tasseled dress reminiscent of a madame in a refined bawdy house," and "a 'sensible' Pucci multi-colored long jersey dress — which nevertheless conveyed the image of a slightly kooky bird of paradise." Hakim also mentions Berberian cooking spaghetti, which was served to Cage, various instrumentalists, and the audience (Hakim 1979, 10–12).

    Both Rist and Berberian performed independently. Hakim notes:

> Usually, Rist and Berberian were playing their bits at the same time, each in
> her own persona-created world, neither vying with the other nor acting in unison. At

intervals, the action was spot-lighted upon one or the other — usually while the other
was doing a costume change, of which Rist had the greater number and variety.

  However, at one point in the evening, they did come together in a "duet." Rist
— with mimed gestures that were shy, boy-childish and gallant — invited Berberian to
leave her kitchen-gadget-filled table and come over to join her in a game of chess [Solo
23]. Berberian did, like a harried, reluctantly indulgent mother. The chess board was
set so the black pieces faced Rist and the tan ones faced Berberian. There followed an
Alphonse-Gaston dumb-show routine: Rist offering Berberian the color choice of
pieces; Berberian shrugging off the choice as if it didn't matter. Then, in rapid motions,
Rist, with a black and tan piece in each fist, put her arms behind her back, motioning
for Berberian to choose. Berberian chose — the piece just happening to be the tan one,
corresponding to the way the board had been arranged in the first place. There ensued,
initiated by Berberian, a "blitz" game: pieces moved wildly, rapidly devolving into a
total disaccordance with the rules. Finally, Berberian, extending her resistance against
conforming to the courtesies and conventions of the game, capped it all off by grabbing
Rist's Queen and playing with it. The game ended in a triumphant stalemate of
anarchic chaos. Berberian then marched back to her side, while Rist pouted like a
disappointed child. So ended the "duet." (Hakim 1979, 12-13)

There is nothing else to document the first performance of *Song Books* in further detail at present.

  A phonograph recording of selected solos from *Song Books* was issued in 1976, performed by the Schola Cantorum under the direction of Clytus Gottwald, with Cage simultaneously reading from *Empty Words III* (Cage 1976e). The sound in this recording is often dense and multi-layered, as one would expect from the precedent of other musicircus recordings such as *Variations IV* and *HPSCHD*, but it is questionable to make a phonograph recording of a performance that is fundamentally not only auditory but also visual in content. For instance, one hears the sounds of typing and walking. One can easily imagine the visual counterparts to these identifiable sounds, but a more accurate mechanical recording of *Song Books* (or *any* of Cage's theatre pieces) would be better served through video tape. Because of the often dense sound it is difficult to determine which of the vocal solos are being performed. One exception is Solo 64, where a performer is instructed to shout "Nichi nichi, kore ko niche" (Every day is a beautiful day) 127 times. In this recording, it is not shouted, but whispered into a microphone at high volume, and only a few repetitions are performed.

  The only complete performance of the 90 *Song Books* solos to date was by the S.E.M. Ensemble under the direction of Petr Kotik in the spring of 1982. This was first done at the Whitney Museum in New York on March 31, 1982, and lasted over three hours. Gregory Sandow would write of this performance:

  Among other things, the performers sang a version of the Queen of Night's
second aria from The Magic Flute, *recognizable even though all the notes were*

changed [this is Solo 47]. . . Not all the performers were singers, of course. Sometimes
they chanted, or played reverberant dominoes on a table amplified with a contact mike,
or ironed a large pile of uncomplaining handkerchiefs, or walked by in animal masks,
or rasped little Bronx cheeps (not a misprint), or practiced scales on the cello. At one
point black flags of anarchy appeared, a tribute to Thoreau's Civil Disobedience, *on*
which parts of the piece were based. (Sandow 1982)

The S.E.M. Ensemble also performed the complete *Song Books* at Bonn, Germany, on April 27, 1982. A review of this performance does not add any significant details (Schüren 1982).

When Petr Kotik was recently asked about how the various solos were performed, he replied that the details of who did what are not important, and that the scores contain all the important information. When asked how various people would interpret the indeterminate notations, he replied that one doesn't need interpretation — "maybe the audience needs to make interpretations, but the performer doesn't. The score alone is important" (Kotik 1990). Kotik's lack of communication was not so much antagonistic as reflecting the ingrained, conventional view in music that the notation, rather than the performance (the interpretation of the notation), is of sole importance. (In the case of Petr Kotik, this view is also very curious, for he is himself a very sophisticated composer in using indeterminate notation.)

The other most important performance of *Song Books* made in Europe during Cage's lifetime was a staged version at the Royal Conservatory at The Hague on November 24, 1988. This was the culmination of a vocal and theatre workshop taught by the American soprano Joan La Barbara (the current specialist with Cage's songs). The 90 minute performance of 63 selected solos was performed by La Barbara with twelve students. La Barbara recalls that the idea of silences in either specific solos or in between solos was especially difficult for many of the other participants, and so she suggested some very practical ways to deal with such situations, such as looking at one's stop-watch or thinking of the next thing one was to do (La Barbara 1993).

This particular performance was supervised by Cage, with the help of La Barbara, Ivo van Emmerik, and Ron Ford. Using chance operations, Cage determined a time plan for each of the performer's solos, as well as physical entrances, exits, and stage positions. The stage floor was cross-ruled into a numbered grid of 36 stations measuring 2 by 3 meters. 81 stage lights were focused upon the 36 stations, with chance determinations for fade-in, sustain, fade-out, and intensity, "producing a change of light configurations in which the fade-ins and fade-outs were overlapped" (van Emmerik and Ford 1989, 17).

In addition, various theatrical details were determined until the last moment,
activities originating spontaneously [i.e. from the rehearsal process] and often by
chance. For instance, a chess clock that was mistakenly amplified during a rehearsal

became on Cage's request a constant background noise to the performance, as did two portable radios that softly played two different radio stations during the entire piece. Throughout the preparations Cage dispensed with all forms of decor, leaving all activity, theatrical as well as technical, visible in the hall. Thus a highly visible trap-door in the rear of the stage was further accentuated by placing an extra spotlight behind it, adding a permanent beam of light to the staging.

Cage encouraged the vocalists to think of theatrical activities for performance during the sometimes long pauses between the solos: dancing, whistling, sitting in a rocking chair, reading the newspaer, brushing teeth, climbing a ladder, etc. The singers could also choose their own costumes from the supply available at the conservatory. When it became clear that exclusively romantic evening dresses were chosen, Cage brought again this element into balance by asking some of the vocalists to wear their own clothing or to make a different choice. (van Emmerik and Ford 1989, 17)

Most of the theatre solos were performed by the students, and as is typical with so many performances of Cage's indeterminately notated compositions, specific details are lacking.

There are two groups in the U.S. that currently specialize in performances of the *Song Books* — The American Music/Theatre Group under the direction of Neely Bruce, and The Alliance for American Song under the direction of Peter Perrin.

Perrin's group recently performed 23 solos from *Song Books* in a retrospective concert of Cage's songs from 1938 through 1985 at Renee Weiler Concert Hall in New York on March 9, 1989. The *Song Books* performance took approximately twenty minutes. The stage space was rather small, and did not easily admit movement. A floorplan of this performance appears in Fig. 36. Three vocalists, with two assistants, were centered around a central (unused) piano. A second piano, at the back left side of the stage, was used as a surface for the theatre solos. The majority of the theatre solos were performed by Jonathan Bricklin at this area. Additional theatre solos were performed by Peter Perrin at front-center stage or at a chair placed in the back right corner. There were some technical mishaps, such as a slide projector that would not work when the audience lights were turned off. Perrin admits that the electronics and technology available were "very Mickey Mouse" (i.e. very simple, and crude) (Perrin 1989). The performance was nonetheless very worthwhile, and Cage himself was sitting in the audience looking very pleased with the results.

The American Music/Theatre Group, under the direction of Neely Bruce, is the specialist in *Song Books* performances. They first performed it at Crowell Concert Hall at Wesleyan University on November 6, 1979, and have retained it in their repertoire since. This version is performed by four vocalists, who do a total of 78 solos. David Barron recalls that Neely Bruce let each performer choose his or her own material, and that he would then make

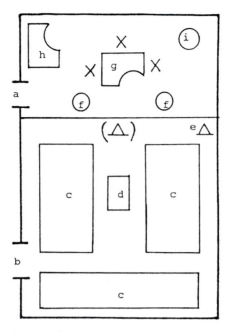

Fig. 36.   Floorplan for *Song Books*, performed by The Alliance for American Song at Renee Weiler Concert Hall, New York, on March 9, 1989. The symbols refer to: a is the stage door; b is the entrance for the audience; c is the audience; d is a piano bench with a slide projector; e is the projection screen; f shows the positions of the two assistants making electronic adjustments of the voices of the three vocalists (indicated with large Xs); g is an unused piano; h is another piano, around which Jonathan Bricklin performed most of his theatre solos; and i is a chair, used by Peter Perrin for additional theatre solos.

further suggestions to include other solos in order to make a more balanced selection (Barron 1990).

Most AMTG performances of *Song Books* have been done with prosce-nium staging. David Barron recalls that the most intersting performance, in terms of spatial arrangement, was at an art museum in Baltimore in early May, 1989, where each of the four performers were in separate rooms and the audience was free to move about the building (Barron 1990). They also performed *Song Books* at Lincoln Center on August 22, 1988, with the four individuals at different corners of the reflecting pool, however Barron feels that it is more effective when done in a frontal presentation. The most notable performance of *Song Books* by the AMTG was done simultaneously with *Rozart Mix* at the Pierre Hotel in New York on May 25, 1989, for a banquet and benefit for the Cunningham Dance Foundation, in honor of Cage's continuing commitment to the dance company and as a formal recognition of his retirement from musical performing and touring. The AMTG performers were stationed in the four corners of the ballroom, as shown in Fig. 31 in Chapter 6.

The scores and performances by Perrin's and Bruce's groups of the remaining theatre solos follows.

Solo 15 is a linguistic notation to type a sentence by Satie 38 times on a typewriter with contact microphones. This is performed by Neely Bruce in the AMTG. Bruce recalls that this solo takes about fifteen minutes to perform completely (N. Bruce 1989).

Solos 22 and 79 are variations on notated breathing, amplified with a microphone. Cage terms both solos as relevant to the subject of Satie-Thoreau, although the reference is obscure. Petkus suggests that Cage termed it relevant to the subject of Satie-Thoreau because Thoreau studied yoga and breathing exercises, and Satie wrote of his daily routine that "I breathe carefully (a little at a time)" (Petkus 1986, 187–188). Both solos are notated in spatial, visual music notation. Time is established horizontally, the duration according to the performer's discretion. The vertical space is to be interpreted as pitch (i.e. speed of inhaling or exhaling). Solo 22 notates regular and irregular breathing through the nose and mouth; Solo 79 does not explicitly notate use of the nose or mouth, but instructs to "breathe as though you had lost your voice (approach pitch — vertical space on the system — but do not arrive at it)" (Cage 1970a, 85 and 274). Above the notated breaths are two numbers, one large and one small. The large numbers (1–64) are to be related to the available number of electronic dials, using the number conversion tables in the *Song Books Instructions* supplement to relate 1 through 63 to 64. The small numbers (1–12) indicate the dial positions, including "off." Neely Bruce performs Solo 22, and Toby Twining performs Solo 79 during AMTG presentations, but neither has commented on performing their respective solos.

Solos 36, 38, and 46 involve food and are termed by Cage to be irrelevant to the subject of Satie-Thoreau. The directive for Solos 36 and 38 is that "the number given is the number of things eaten or drunk." For both solos the number below the directive is 3. Solo 36 also has the nonsense quotation: "I can drink without eating, but I certainly can't eat without drinking," which Cage explains as a quote from Peggy Guggenheim (Cage 1982b). Neely Bruce performs Solo 36 by eating an apple, drinking a glass of water, and drinking a glass of brandy (N. Bruce 1989). David Barron also performs Solo 36, by eating an apple, drinking a glass of water, and eating a hoe cake (Barron 1990).

Solo 46 is a variation on Solos 36 and 38, the directive being to "prepare something to eat." Neely Bruce performs this solo by preparing hoe cakes, or corn-meal pancakes, by bringing water to a boil on a hot-place on a small table, then measuring some corn meal and salt into a bowl. Boiling water is then poured over this to moisten. The remaining water is poured into a cup with the astrological sign of Aquarius (Satie's birth-sign) to make Cranberry Cove tea (a brand of herbal tea by Celestial Seasonings, the symbolism of cranberries being a reference to a native American plant, hence to Thoreau). Bruce then performs other vocal and theatre solos for about one hour and fifteen minutes. Towards the conclusion of the group's ninety-minute performance, he then concludes Solo 46 by frying some hoe cakes in a cast-iron skillet on the hot-plate and gives one to David Barron to eat. Neely Bruce then eats a hoe cake and drinks the Cranberry Cove tea (N. Bruce 1989).

Solos 41 and 42 are termed theatre with electronics and irrelevant to Satie-Thoreau. In Solo 41, feedback is to be produced three times; in Solo 42 feedback is produced two times. Both solos were performed by Peter Perrin's group in a very inventive way. Perrin did not have access to electronic equipment that would produce feedback, so he made a tape of an American oratorio, *Daniel*, by George Frederick Bristow, composed in 1866. The tape had loud choral passages, which caused a system overload when played at high volume on a cheap "ghetto-blaster." During the *Song Books* performance, Perrin played the tape offstage quietly, and when the chorus sang a word very loudly, he turned up the volume and opened the stage entrance door. Perrin says that he wanted to keep the performance simple, and that he used the ghetto-blaster because it is increasingly difficult to produce feedback with contemporary electronic equipment (Perrin 1989). Ironically, the most technologically sophisticated version of the *Song Books* to date is by Neely Bruce's group, but they perform neither of these two solos.

Solo 43 is theatre with electronics and *i*s termed relevant to Satie. A short sentence by Satie is notated in four different typographies. The performer is instructed to improvise a melody for each of the four versions, recording each improvisation. The first time it is sung 17 seconds; the second time 49 seconds; the third time 52 seconds; the fourth time 53 seconds. This recording, with a total duration of approximately 2'51", is then played. The performer then repeats this procedure on a different recording machine. When the second recording is finished, both recordings are played simultaneously, resulting in a unique type of unintended counterpoint. Phyllis Bruce performs Solo 43 very scrupulously following the score. She states:

> It is different every time. Since I'm a classical singer, this lets me do my thing, using high notes, different rhythms, and different keys. So it is fun to do! The total duration lasts about nine minutes. (P. Bruce 1989).

(The nine minutes that Phyllis Bruce mentions includes all the stages of the score — singing, rewinding the machine, playing the tape, rewinding, again singing, rewinding, and playing the first and second recordings together.)

Solo 51 is termed theatre with electronics and is relevant to Thoreau. The directive is to "play a recording of a forest fire." The relevance to Thoreau is explained in Cage's 1974 essay "The Future of Music," which concludes by relating the story of when Thoreau accidently set fire to the woods and the resultant discoveries made concerning music, sound, and nature. After the fire, . . .

> *Thoreau met a fellow who was poor, miserable, often drunk, worthless (a burden to society). However, more than any other, this fellow was skillful in the burning of brush. Observing his methods and adding his own insights, Thoreau set down a procedure for successfully fighting fires. He also listened to the music a fire makes, roaring and crackling: "You sometimes hear it on a small scale in the log on the hearth."*
>
> *Having heard the music fire makes and having discussed his fire-fighting method to one of his friends, Thoreau went further: suggesting that along with the firemen there be a band of musicians playing instruments to revive the energies of weary firemen and to cheer up those who were not yet exhausted.*
>
> *Finally he said that fire is not only disadvantage. "It is without doubt an advantage on the whole. It sweeps and ventilates the forest floor, and makes it clear and clean. It is nature's broom. . . Thus huckleberry fields are created for birds and for men." (Cage 1979a, 187)*

Solo 51 is performed by both Perrin's and Bruce's group. Concerning this solo, Peter Perrin states:

> *I failed. We played the sound of an erupting volcano! I went through the sound-effects bin at Tower Records, and couldn't find a forest-fire recording. (Perrin 1989)*

When further asked if he tried the 1930s radio sound-effect of crinkling cellophane close to the microphone, Perrin said that he tried it but that it did not sound good on tape. Solo 51 is performed in Neely Bruce's group by Toby Twining. Twining states that Neely Bruce had found a thirty-second recording of Christmas trees burning. Twining re-recorded this onto tape for a duration of approximately 5'30". The thirty-second fire recording was re-taped several times, with thirty-second "pauses" (silences) interspersed (thus, if one began with the recording, there would be six repetitions, with five in-between silences) (Twining 1990).

Solo 57 is theatre without electronics and is termed relevant to Satie. The basic directive is: "Immobility (interior, exterior)," which is a quotation from Satie's *Vexations* (Cage 1982b). *Vexations* received its first complete performance at the Pocket Theatre in New York from 6:00 p.m. September 9 to 11:00 a.m. September 10, 1963 ("Music: A Long, Long, Long Night [and Day] at the Piano" 1963). Twelve pianists, including Viola Farber, John Cale, David Tudor, Christian Wolff, Philip Corner, and John Cage, played the entire score in continuous twenty-minute relays. As one pianist would finish, he/she would slide over for the next one to continue. *Vexations* consists of a 180-note passage that is to be repeated 840 times.

Cage's experience in organizing and helping to perform in *Vexations* is noted in Solo 57 when he amends the above, basic direction with this humorous aside:

> *If one does not have this, try obtaining it by vocalise and use of friends names and famous names as words for any commonly known tunes such as "Merrily We Roll Along," "America the Beautiful," etc., the tunes repeated many times, varying the words and sometimes inventing cadences. If that doesn't work, take a nap on or off stage.*

This alternate solution, in singing banal tunes, is reminiscent of Charles Ives's musical sense of humor. Taking a nap is an autobiographical reference to Cage's own earlier experience while performing Satie's *Vexations* in 1963. The *New York Times* review noted that Cage. . .

> *. . .played* Vexations *75 times himself, then retired to sleep soundly on a foam-rubber pad down in the basement. ("Music: A Long, Long, Long Night [and Day] at the Piano" 1963)*

Cage would comment on this performance:

> *The effect of this going on and on was quite extraordinary. Ordinarily, one would assume there was no need to have such an experience, since if you hear something said ten times, why should you hear it any more? But the funny thing was that it was never the same twice. The musicians were always slightly different in their versions — their strengths fluctuated. I was surprised that something was put into motion that changed me. I wasn't the same after that performance as I was before. The world seemed to have changed. I don't know quite how to say it. A moment of enlightment came for each one of us, and at different times. (Stein and Plimpton 1982, 235)*

Solo 57 is performed three times during the American Music/Theatre Group's version of *Song Books*. Phyllis Bruce comments on her interpretation:

> *I take the easy way out. I get in a fetal position and don't move. I don't really sleep but do deep relaxation for about ten to fifteen minutes. (P. Bruce 1989)*

Neely Bruce performs Solo 57 by first singing "Merrily We Roll Along" beginning with the names of their three children — Richard, Lucille, Maryweather — then continuing with names such as Hector Berlioz, John Singer Sargent, and Ollie North. He then lies down to take a short, pretend nap (N. Bruce 1989). Toby Twining also performs Solo 57, either by singing the names of friends to the tune of "America the Beautiful," or by sitting down on the floor with crossed legs, and remaining quiet in that posture until the entire performance concludes (Twining 1990).

Solo 71 is theatre without electronics and is termed relevant, as it refers to the cards and notes of Satie (Cage 1982b). The direction is to "write a card or note with sketch in ink." Phyllis Bruce performs this solo by. . .

> *. . .writing to whoever I want to. I use note paper which I then stick in an envelope and seal. It takes however long it takes to write a card, usually three to five minutes. (P. Bruce 1989)*

Thus, the relatively indeterminate content suggested in the score is determined by the performer's own life.

Solos 69 and 80 are paired pieces. The score of Solo 69 consists of 53 rectangles with punctuation marks in between. Each rectangle is divided into three horizontal lines, representing the three lower rows of keys on a typewriter. An "o" represents the relative position of a key to be depressed. An excerpt from Solo 69 appears in Fig. 37.

Solo 69 is theatre with electronics and is termed irrelevant to the subject of Satie-Thoreau. The sound of the typewriter is to be amplified with contact microphones. The text produced by the performer then provides the vocal text for Solo 80. The text produced in performing Solo 69 consists of isolated alphabet letters without reference to grammatical or syntactical

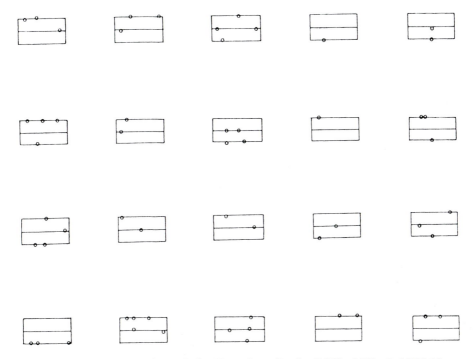

Fig. 37. A score excerpt from Solo 69 in *Song Books* (1970, 249); © 1970 Henmar Press Inc.

meaning. Concerning this situation, Cage has stated:

> *I hope to let words exist, as I have tried to let sounds exist.... That's why I insist on the*
> *necessity of not letting ourselves be dragged along by language. Words impose feelings*
> *on us if we consider them as objects, that is, if we don't let them, too, be what they are:*
> *processes. (Cage and Charles 1981, 151)*

Solo 80 is theatre with electronics and is termed relevant to Satie. In the *Song Books Instructions* supplement is a page containing 55 notes written in the treble clef. Cage states that the notes come from Satie (Cage 1982b). The performer cuts up the different notes (33 quarter notes, 13 dotted half notes, 9 half notes) using a contact microphone for amplification. Each cut-up note is placed into separate containers, appropriate to the duration. Following the time values below the empty staff lines provided into Solo 80, one draws out a corresponding note from the appropriate container, writing the found note within the empty staff. This produces a melodic line, which one uses as a vocalise with the text produced from Solo 69. (This method is remisniscent of Duchamp's *Musical Erratum* [1913] or Tristan Tzara's instructions for how to write a Dada poem, but the simplicity of this chance composition method is not typical of Cage's other works.)

When the melody and vocal text are transcribed, the instruction is that "the song is then ready to be practiced and/or sung. If there is any applause, repeat the song: if not, not." Solo 80 is in the key of C major, 3/4 time, and is 33 measures long.

Solos 69 and 80 are performed by David Barron in the American Music/Theatre Group. He performs Solo 69 using a manual typewriter with a contact microphone on the carrier. It takes him about three minutes to type the entire text. He then performs nine other solos before doing Solo 80. It takes him about 1'30" to cut up the notes, which are contact-miked on the scissor. It then takes about 2'30" to transcribe the notes onto the empty staff, and another 1'30" to transcribe the text. This is done with a contact microphone on a pencil. Barron then rehearses the piece for another two minutes using a pitch pipe (Barron 1990). Although he has performed Solos 69 and 80 for over ten years, Barron says that when it comes to actually singing the song, it really is rehearsed during public performances, for the chance procedures always result in a new work to be learned. With the performance of these two solos, the spectator also is able to witness an elementary example of the process of chance composition in a public format.

Solo 78 is theatre without electronics and is irrelevant to Satie-Thoreau. The complete score reads:

> *What can you do?*
> *"I can take off my shoes and put them on."*

This may appear to be reminiscent of the comic routines of Stan Laurel and Oliver Hardy in their 1930s films, or of the dialogue between Didi and Gogo in Samuel Beckett's play *Waiting for Godot*, however Cage states that this is a quotation from Gertrude Stein (Cage 1982b). The source has not been identified. Solo 78 is performed by both the Alliance for American Song and the American Music/Theatre Group. Peter Perrin performed this with the AFAS. He comments:

> *The principle was to keep it simple. At the back of the stage, the performer's left, I had a pair of moccasins placed underneath a chair. I went to the chair and took off the boots I was wearing and put on the moccasins. (Perrin 1989)*

Perrin used the moccasins as his own reference to Thoreau, which, while not literally following Cage's score for this solo, is still in the spirit of the *Song Books* in general. David Barron performs Solo 78 in the AMTG for about forty-five seconds by sitting down in a chair and taking off and putting on again the same pair of shoes. The shoes are walking shoes with laces. Barron says, "I do it very slowly and deliberately. I do a 'sitting dance'" (Barron 1990).

Solos 81 and 86 are both theatre with electronics and are relevant to Thoreau. The direction for Solo 81 is to "project four slides relevant to Thoreau." The direction for Solo 86 is to "project twenty-two slides relevant to Thoreau." Both solos were programmed for performance by Peter Perrin. He had a slide projector in the middle aisle of Weiler Concert Hall, the machine placed on a piano bench. For Solo 81 he projected four slides of the Whole Earth Flag floating in water. Solo 86 was planned for performance, but the technical problems with the electric wiring (turning off the house lights also turned off the socket for the slide projector) caused it to be cancelled. These slides were taken by Perrin of rural landscapes in New England. Both the Whole Earth Flag and New England scenes were chosen for their relevance to Thoreau (Perrin 1989).

Solos 81 and 86 are also performed by Phyllis Bruce. She explains that each slide is shown for approximately five seconds, thus Solo 81 takes about twenty seconds and Solo 86 takes about two minutes (P. Bruce 1989). Neely Bruce further comments that their slides are a photographic essay of late-twentieth century Concord, Massachusetts, rather than a sentimentalized version of Concord that Thoreau might recognize today. Thus, there are slides of the Concord High School football team practicing, the street signs showing the intersection of Thoreau and Emerson Streets, a Gulf Station, Henry Thoreau Elementary School, and the city dump near Walden Pond (N. Bruce 1989).

Solo 82 is theatre with electronics and is relevant to Satie. The direction is:

Using a Paris cafe cognac glass, serve yourself the amount above the line. Drink, using throat microphone to make swallowing very audible.

This solo is not performed in either Perrin's or Bruce's group. Very likely it was performed by Cage himself during the first performance in Paris in 1970 since it is so similar to his performances of *0'00"* in the mid-1960s. The relevancy to Satie is a reference to his cognac trick in Paris cafes:

> It was the custom at that time [ca. 1900] to serve cognac in small graduated carafons of a conical shape and divided into three sections, each containing what was supposed to be a normal dose. But Satie observed that the bottom section contained a slightly larger dose than the other two. He would therefore ask for an extra glass to be brought, explaining to the mystified waiter that as he only wanted to consume the bottom portion of the carafe he would pour the remainer away. When told he ought to "take it as it comes," and that if he wanted the bottom portion he had only to drink the others first — "Not at all," he would gravely reply; "I prefer the underneath portion because it hasn't been exposed to the air; and, what's more, I am legally entitled to drink only the middle portion if I choose; and if I don't it's solely so as not to cause you any inconvenience." Whereupon he would pour away the two top portions and empty the remainder into his coffee. (Myers 1968, 125)

Solos 32, 37, 44, 54, 55, and 88 are all linguistic movement notations for various exists and entrances. All these movement solos are termed theatre without electronics and irrelevant to Satie-Thoreau. Several of these solos were performed by Jonathan Bricklin in the Alliance for American Song group and by all four members of the American Music/Theatre Group.

The complete directive for Solo 32 is: "Go off-stage at a normal speed, hurrying back somewhat later." This was performed by Jonathan Bricklin in an inconspicuous manner, his stage absence being less than five minutes. Toby Twining also performs Solo 32, his stage absence being about two or three minutes. David Barron also performs this solo. He comments:

> I just walk off like I'm going for a drink of water. For returning I put something in my head like "I should have been back two minutes ago" for motivation, which is totally unnecessary, but it helps me focus. It's about fifteen seconds to go off, five seconds to re-enter, and four to five minutes total. (Barron 1990)

Solo 37 reads: "Leave the stage at a normal speed by going up (flying) or by going down through a trap door. Return in the opposite direction very quickly." This solo is currently unperformed. The use of flies and traps is reminiscent of the Venice *Music Walk* performance in 1960, and Cage probably wrote Solo 37 to make use of the actual theatre in Paris for the first scheduled *Song Books* performance in 1970. (He was a very practical composer, but few theatres are normally equipped with floor traps.)

Solo 44 reads: "Go off-stage at a normal speed, returning somewhat later also at a normal speed." This was performed by Jonathan Bricklin, at the very beginning of the Alliance for American Song version. Bricklin was off-stage for a few minutes. No one in the American Music/Theatre Group performs this solo.

Solo 44 is perhaps the least difficult of all Cage's theatre pieces to perform. The notation itself is deceptively easy in being relatively determinate, explicit in content. It is indeterminate, however, in several respects: to "go" in this context usually means to walk, although there are many possible ways to "go off-stage;" a "normal speed" could mean one's everyday pace, although pace (or tempo) changes with environment, time of day, and age and health; and "somewhat later" is somewhere in between soon and after a while. There is virtue in using such obvious indeterminancy through linguistic movement notation, for the performer is to make an everyday action in an everyday manner. A walk is not simple, but Cage does not over-complicate the process through obscure movement notations (such as notating a walk in Beauchamp-Feuillet, Zorn, Stepanov, Laban, or Benesh). In the notation of Solo 44, Cage uses language both concretely and evocatively, determinately and indeterminately, to notate a disciplined action in the least symbolic way as practically possible.

Solo 54 reads: "Leave the stage by going up (flying) or going down through a trap door. Return the same way wearing an animal's head." This is one of the signal solos in *Song Books* performances. Eleanor Hakim mentions that both Simone Rist and Cathy Berberian used various animal masks in the first performance in 1970, but does not provide further specifics. Jonathan, Bricklin used a lion's head in the version by the Alliance for American Song. It was impossible to use flies or traps, so he went behind a curtain at the back of the small stage and re-entered wearing the animal head. Bricklin then wandered around the stage for about five minutes. Peter Perrin states that a mask relevant to North American wildlife was originally intended, however no such mask was available (Perrin 1989). All four performers in the American Music/Theatre Group do this solo, with changes from one performance to the next — Neely Bruce with a giraffe's head, Phyllis Bruce with a wolf's head, Toby Twining with an elephant's head, and David Barron with a Zebra's head. Traps and flies have not been used by any of these performers. When asked if Solo 54 was a reference to shamanism, Cage replied that that was not at all what he had in mind, but that one could interpret it that way if one chose to do so (Cage 1982b).

The directive for Solo 55 is: "Leave the stage and return by means of wheels (e.g. skates, small auto). Let speed of exit and entrance be 'normal'." Jonathan Bricklin performed this with a skateboard, going up and down the left-side audience aisle for about two minutes. Toby Twining also uses a skateboard among the audience, again for about two minutes (Twining 1989).

David Barron performs this with a red children's wagon, one knee inside, for three to four minutes (Barron 1990).

The directive for Solo 88 reads: "Leave the stage through the audience returning to the stage without leaving the theatre. Do this very slowly." This is performed by Phyllis Bruce, who comments:

> I just leave. If I can, I go outside and come back through a different entrance if possible. It takes about five minutes. I'm outside most of the time. (P. Bruce 1989)

Solo 89 is the last theatre solo in the *Song Books*. It is termed theatre without electronics and relevant to Thoreau. The directive is to take from the *Song Books Instructions* supplement the transparency with two straight lines intersecting in the center at right-angles and to place this anywhere over the seating plan of the theatre. One is then to make a gift "of an apple or some cranberries to this member of the audience. If no one is seated there, simply place gift on empty seat."

This solo may be used as a possible ending for the *Song Books* in performance. It was used at the conclusion (simultaneously with vocal solos) in the Alliance for American Song version. Jonathan Bricklin wore a box on his head, with a portrait of Thoreau on all four sides. A seating plan of the audience was blown-up to poster-size. Peter Perrin then spun Bricklin around a few times, and Bricklin put his finger on the poster, indicating a seat in the audience, much like in the party game "Pin the Tail on the Donkey." Perrin then took the box off, and Bricklin went to the appropriate seat and gave that person an apple. Perrin states that it was done this way because otherwise the score would not be seen by the audience, and this way they could see what was happening (Perrin 1989).

Solo 89 is also performed by Phyllis Bruce and David Barron in the American Music/Theatre Group. Both usually use an apple, because of the rather limited cranberry season. Both use the transparency on a piece of paper rather than on a poster. Phyllis Bruce comments that by doing the solo this way, the audience does not know what is being done, that "the action doesn't telegraph what you are doing," and this in turn "destroys the barriers between daily life and public performance" (P. Bruce 1989).

Song Books marks a culmination of the musicircus idea from the 1960s. William Brooks, in his seminal study of this work, also feels that it is a concrete definition (albeit, now early) of Cage's current composition in general, through the "use of pre-existing material, collage, and traditional notation" (Brooks 1982, 86–87). The idea of the musicircus, and the return to determinate notation, as exemplified in the *Song Books*, finds its most unified expression in *Europeras 1 & 2* (1987), discussed in the next chapter.

8

EUROPERAS 1–5: THE FINAL THEATRE PIECES

Europeras 1 & 2

Europeras 1 & 2 was commissioned by Heinz-Klaus Metzger and Rainer Riehn for the Frankfurt Opera at Frankfurt am Main in Germany. It would take Cage, with the assistance of Andrew Culver and Laura Kuhn, over two years (from 1985 through 1987) to compose the entire work. Instrumental music, lighting, decor, costumes, stage action, and arias were selected and composed according to chance procedures using an *I Ching* computer program designed by Andrew Culver. There is no complete "master score," only individual parts, a practice Cage had employed since the 1950s as in *Concert for Piano and Orchestra* (1957–58), *Theatre Piece* (1960), or *Song Books* (1970). Much of *Europeras 1 & 2* is in determinate notation, and is Cage's most determinately notated theatre piece since *Water Walk* and *Sounds of Venice* in 1959. It is, with the exception of musicircuses, the longest and most complicated of all his theatre pieces. It is also the most reviewed theatre piece of Cage's career; and with Laura Kuhn's 1992 Ph.D. dissertation (at 720 pages), is the most minutely documented and intellectually interpreted example (as yet) of any of Cage's theatre pieces. My independent study will only provide a brief summary.

The production of *Europeras 1 & 2* is a somewhat curious story. The premiere was scheduled for November 15, 1987, but on November 12 there was a fire which completely gutted the Frankfurt Opera House. The fire was supposedly started by an unemployed East German emigre with a history of arsonist activities, who had apparently broken into the Opera House looking for food. The man later turned himself in to the police, and there was speculation that he was working for a radical political group, although nothing was proved. Cage took his setback in his usual optimistic stride:

> *I think it shows very clearly that this society is in transition, we hope, to another society in which there won't be that great separation between those who have what they need and those who don't. I haven't seen the man or talked with him, but it seems he must not only have been hungry but somewhat out of his mind. It's not his fault, but the fault of the whole society. The opera in society is an ornament of the lives of the people who have. I don't feel that so much with my work, but with more conventional operas, it's clearly an ornament that has no necessary relation to the 20th century. (Durner 1988, 13)*

The production was quickly reassembled, and first performed on December 12, 1987.

Europeras 1 & 2 was widely reviewed in the German press, as it had become not only an aesthetic but a social event as well. Reviews were in general kind but also a bit nonplussed. The arias sung by the various singers were chosen from the standard European opera repertory, which prompted two reviewers to liken Cage's work to a musical puzzle or identification quiz (Koch 1987; and Herbort 1987). Gerhard Koch interpreted the collage of traditional arias as a musical correlation to Marcel Duchamp's found-objects and readymades (Koch 1987). Lotte Thaler would note that "Europeras" is a pun on "Europe" plus "Operas" which is, in standard American English, pronounced as "Your-Operas" (Thaler 1987). (In America we pronounce "Europe" similar to "You're Up," with the emphasis on the first syllable.) Hans-Klaus Jungheinrich interpreted the work as a parody of traditional opera, which neatly summarizes the general critical mood of the European critics (Jungheinrich 1987).

The audience reaction is not documented in the European reviews, but is included in a news story on European Journal, shown on American Public Television in February, 1988. The general critical agreement among professional journalists was apparently not shared by the average person in attendance:

> *While the opera's playing to packed houses, audience reactions have been decidedly mixed.*
>
> Man: *My first impression is that I was confused!*
> Girl: *It's as weird as it should be!*
> Woman: *It's like a big Fairy tale with lots of fantasy.*
> Woman: *The MUSIC I don't like — At all!*
> (C. Harris 1988, 3)

Europeras 1 & 2 was first performed in the United States at Purchase, New York, by the Frankfurt Opera on July 14, 16, and 17, 1988. This was also widely reviewed by the American press and was again generally interpreted to be a parody of traditional opera. One reviewer characterized the piece as "a very funny, though repetitive and overlong, takeoff on opera" that "resembles not so much an 18th-century nut house. . . as a space backstage where singers are rehearsing various operas, dancers are warming up and stagehands are trying to get props in place" (Gouvels 1988). Two reviewers would compare it to the Marx Brothers's 1935 film *A Night at the Opera*, wherein Groucho, Chico, and Harpo riotously lambaste and circumvent the conventions of opera staging and its commonly perceived pomposity ("Cage-y: opera guyed" 1988; and Sweeney 1988). One reviewer would write that "Act 1 wears out its welcome. Act 2 is 45 minutes of the same. . ." (Taylor 1988), while another would write "I found the first half cute but hadn't yet overcome my lingering resistance to Mr. Cage's old tricks. But in the second half, I became mildly diverted" (Rockwell 1988).

The interpretation of *Europeras 1 & 2* as being a parody of conventional opera, however, is not an aspect of Cage's own intentions or aesthetics. Cage would state in 1965:

> *Our situation as artists is that we have all this work that was done before we came along. We have the opportunity to work now. I would not present things from the past, but I would approach them as materials available to something else which we were going to do now. They could enter, in terms of collage, into any play. . .*
>
> *Let me explain to you why I think of past literature as material rather than as art. There are oodles of people who are going to think of the past as a museum and be faithful to it, but that's not my attitude. Now as material it can be put together with other things. (Kirby and Schechner 1965, 53)*

Cage had used pre-existing material in works such as *HPSCHD* (1969) and the *Song Books* (1970). It would be more accurate, according to Cage's aesthetics and previous theatre pieces, to interpret *Europeras 1 & 2* as a use of historical tradition as a fluid potential for creativity rather than a fixed or unalterable object of dumb reverence.

Andrew Porter would provide the most complaining review, criticizing that the arias "are sung at any old pitch, and not necessarily in tempo" and that the chamber orchestra added "a dreary, unrelated sound. . . Spotting the tunes through the irrelevant noises provided mild diversion for a while" (Porter 1988). The most negative review was by Peter Goodman, who wrote: "The work is open to anything. That is because it is nothing. I didn't pay for my tickets. You shouldn't either" (Goodman 1988).

The production would also engender unequivocal praise. Mark Swed would comment that the "openness, this demystifying of opera" begins "to explain the strong emotions that *Europeras 1 & 2* can generate. . . a celebration of the human spirit and of the environment" (Swed 1988b). Richard Kostelanetz considered it to be one of Cage's five greatest works (with *Sonatas and Interludes* [1946–48], *Williams Mix* [1952], *HPSCHD* [1967–69], and *Roaratorio* [1979]), adding that Don Gillespie (Cage's music editor at C. F. Peters) considers it to be the "quintessential Cagean piece." Kostelanetz summarizes by noting:

> *What is remarkable is that Mr. Cage, after 50 years of ignoring opera, in an age when "everything has been done" produced an opera that is truly avant-garde. It is also true that by achieving such originality in his 70s Mr. Cage reaffirms that he will be an innovative presence for the rest of his life. (Kostelanetz 1988b)*

Most reviewers and audience members found it amusing, which is exactly what Cage intended the opera to be. He writes in the American program notes:

> *Europeras 1 & 2 would not have been composed had not Heinz-Klaus Metzger and Rainer Riehn asked me to do so. The fact that the work is comic followed Gary Bertini's suggestion that it be in the spirit of* Hellzapoppin'. *(Cage 1988a, 49)*

Hellzapoppin' was the most commercially successful Broadway show of the 1930s, playing 1,404 performances from 1938 through 1941. It starred the Vaudeville and film comedy team John "Ole" Olsen and Harold "Chick" Johnson who, with an eclectic supporting cast, presented a plotless succession of verbal and visual gags.

The production began with a filmed introduction "in the form of a newsreel, in which a Yiddish-accented Hitler, a Harlem-drawling Mussolini, and a gibberish-speaking FDR [President Franklin Delano Roosevelt] were all exhorting crowds in praise of *Hellzapoppin'*" (Green 1971, 164). The live action included such elements as:

> ...pistol shots... an amply proportioned deadpan lady fiddler... a magician whose tricks didn't work... a ticket seller hawking good seats to I Married an Angel... pistol shots... a man riding an eight–foot unicycle... a lady looking for Oscar (eventually Johnson invited her up on the stage. After he shuffled her off into the stage wings a shot was heard and Johnson reemerged wiping blood from a sword)... eggs and bananas tossed into the audience... a trio of movie–star impersonators... a gorilla dragging a girl out of a theatre box... a man rolling around on stage all evening trying to get out of a straightjacket... pistol shots... (Green 1971, 164)

The influence of *Hellzapoppin'* on Cage's *Europeras 1 & 2*, however, is questionable. Andrew Culver does not recall it being used as a conceptual basis during the composition process (Culver 1988). Instead, Cage decided "to make a collage in the way I have worked for many years with Merce Cunningham," by extending the independence of music and dance to the independence of all other theatrical elements (Cage 1988a, 49).

The instrumental parts are for a chamber orchestra of strings, wood-winds, brass, and percussion. Each part is independent and was composed by chance procedures by determining excerpted measures (1 to 16) from opera scores by Gluck through Puccini (Durner 1988, 10). Above each musical fragment in the individual parts are two sets of numbers denoting clock times for beginning and ending. *Europera 1* has a total duration of one hour, twenty-nine minutes and thirteen seconds; *Europera 2* has a total duration of forty-four minutes and fifty-seven seconds (Cage 1987d). There is no conductor. All the performers, whether instrumentalists, singers, assistants — as well as stagehands manipulating flats or changing the lights, follow a videotaped digital time-display on television sets placed in the orchestra pit, and at the back and side-wings of the stage. A tape-collage of 101 superimposed opera recordings entitled *Truckera* supplements the live percussion. *Truckera* is played from time to time (at about fifteen-minute intervals), fading in through the right and fading out through the left side speakers in the auditorium, like a truck passing by (Cage 1987c; and Cage 1988a, 49).

At the Purchase performances, the majority of the orchestra was in the pit. Two brass players also were at the very back of the stage. The pit was on a platform which at various times moved the orchestra up or down. At times the heads of the musicians were below stage level, at other times the neck or torso was at stage floor level. The sound had a very light texture and had a somewhat pointillistic quality reminiscent of Anton Webern. During one performance, a brass player inserted an "instrumental laugh" (descending "wah-wah-wahs"), which does not appear in the score. Apparently the musician was reprimanded for taking such personal liberties, for this did not appear in subsequent performances.

The instrumental parts and *Truckera* tape are available on rental for performance from C. F. Peters. Most of the other notated parts are published for sale, which includes an introduction written by Cage previous to the premiere performance, the list of the original singers scheduled, the floorplan of the (now destroyed) Frankfurt Opera Stage, a list of flat cues, the actions of the singers and assistants, a props list with description of the prop and its use, and twelve sets of alternative "synopses" for the two acts (Cage 1987d).

The floorplan from the score appears in Fig. 38. It is marked out like a chessboard, with numbers from 1–64 in reference to the *I Ching*. At Purchase the stage floor was painted with white lines and numbers exactly like the notated floorplan. The movements of the singers and assistants, and the positions of flats, were all choreographed according to this spatial plan. Much of the computer work done by Andrew Culver was in predicting and then avoiding any physical collisions on stage which occurred from using chance procedures (Cage 1988a, 49).

The actual composition process began by first determining the occurrence and duration of each action for a singer or an assistant. Cage, assisted by Andrew Culver and Laura Kuhn, looked up nouns and verbs from the second edition of *Webster's Unabridged Dictionary* to determine what an action might be (as in doing *Theatre Piece*). Andrew Culver comments on how this was accomplished:

> You just enter the total number of dictionary pages into the computer, and ask it for how many choices [by using the I Ching]. I think there were about 200 or so, so you would ask for 200 numbers between 1 and the total number of pages, and out would come 200 numbers.
>
> Then, one by one, you would open to that page and then read the definitions until an action occurred to you. So there was a choice, although you can imagine if you do this over and over and over, it's not so much a matter of seeing all the possible

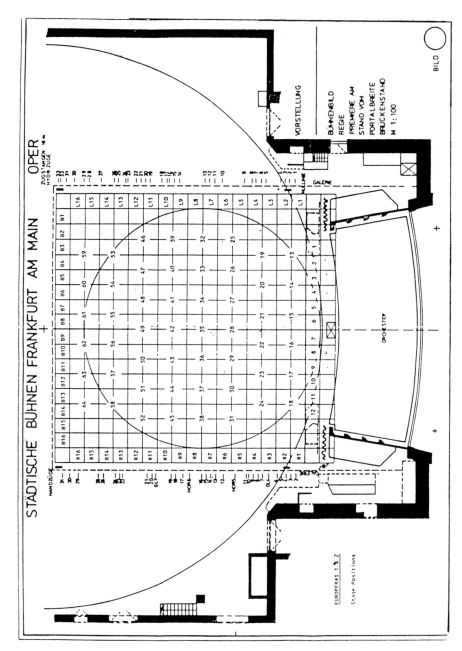

Fig. 38. The floorplan for *Europeras 1 & 2*, © 1987 Henmar Press Inc.

actions on a page and then choosing the one you like the most, it's more likely that you would just read until something occurred to you and say "Oh! That's good!," write that down, and go on to the next thing. And if you got to the end and nothing had occurred to you, you'd go back, but you wouldn't sort of scan the page and be so judgmental — there was no need to be that way. We'd just read along.

Say you landed on the page that started "Ka" at the top — this happened. You'd read along and you'd see there would be "kayak" — "Oh, Kayak!, that's very nice," write that down, and then go on to the next thing (laughs).

Then we got a list of possible activities. This is an interesting indication of how John works. He didn't find out how many activities he needed and then look up in the dictionary exactly the number of activities. He looked up and came up with many more activities than were necessary. Then, when he needed one, he chose one by chance. John often works that way with chance — he'll make a chance determination, and then he'll make a chance determination on that chance determination, and so forth. (Culver 1988)

Having determined a list of possible actions, chance procedures were then applied to the durations of the singers and assistants, and their movements on the stage floorplan. Culver states that the computer was particularly useful for first chance-determining spatial movement, and then for avoiding collisions. There are six female and four male singers in *Europera 1* and three female and six male singers in *Europera 2*. There are twelve assistants, both male and female, who perform in both *1 & 2*. The first page of the action score appears in Fig. 39.

To make the action plan more intelligible, one must refer to the stage floorplan. A few comments on the abbreviated format are also in order. At the top left hand corner is *"Aria"* and below it is "Num" (number) which gives the number of the singer. The first singer in *Europera 1* is "106.1" which is read as follows: the first "1" means that this is *Europera 1*, the "0" means a female, the "6" means the sixth female singer, and the "1" after the dot means the first aria for that singer. The next singer notated is "151.1" which means a male singer, the first male singer, singing his first aria in *Europera 1*.

"Ptime" means Performance time. In this column the first number refers to the hour, the next set to minutes, and the third set to seconds. Both *Europeras* begin at a 0'00" clock time. The next column "Dur." means the duration of time from initial occurrence. "Who" means either a singer ("S") or an assistant ("A") or two assistants ("AA"). The next two columns — "From" and "To" — give the entrance points and stage floor positions for the respective performer, according to performance time and duration. When a performer is stationary, as is 106.1 at 0:00:00, the numbers for "From" and "To" are the same.

The two columns "A1:A2" give the number of which of the twelve assistants is being notated with an action. The next two columns — "Pos/1:2" — indicate the respective positions of the two assistants relative to the singer,

```
                                      ACTION
Europera 1                                                    Page   1

ARIA
Num   Ptime    Dur.  Who  From  To  A1!A2  Pos  Sings?   Description
                                        1!2
```

```
106.1
  1  0:00:00  3:36  S     13   13   -    - - -   no       S on chair1 and mynah bird in
                                                          igloo
```

```
151.1
  2  0:01:57  0:10  SAA   R5   38   1    2 R L   no       S held up by AA
  3  0:02:07  0:20  SAA   38   29   1    2 R L   Seraglio S held up by AA; face turns
                                                          violet
```

```
106.1
  4  0:02:10  0:02  A     L2   64   -    4 - -   NA       en route
  5  0:02:12  0:23  A     64    7   -    4 - -   NA       en route
```

```
151.1
  6  0:02:27  0:20  SAA   29   27   1    2 R L   Seraglio S held up by AA; profile
                                                          violet
```

```
106.1
  7  0:02:35  0:43  A      7   60   -    4 - -   NA       en route
```

```
151.1
  8  0:02:47  0:40  SAA   27   39   1    2 R L   Seraglio S held up by AA; violet fades
                                                          out
```

```
106.1
  9  0:03:18  0:08  A     B5   13   3    - R -   NA
 10  0:03:18  0:08  A     60   13   -    4 - L   NA       en route
 11  0:03:26  0:05  AA    13   13   3    4 R L   NA       unzip igloo sides
```

```
151.1
 12  0:03:27  0:55  SAA   39   B5   1    2 R L   Seraglio S held up by AA
```

```
106.1
 13  0:03:31  0:05  AA    13   13   3    4 B F   NA       unzip igloo front and back
 14  0:03:36  0:24  A     13    5   3    - - -   NA       dance                          dance!
 15  0:03:36  0:32  A     13   59   -    4 - -   NA       dance                          dance!
 16  0:03:36  4:00  S     13   13   -    - - -   Ballo    S sitting; bird flies          fly!
 17  0:04:00  0:47  A      5   21   3    - - -   NA       dance                          dance!
```

```
104.1
 18  0:04:02  1:54  SA    R5   31   5    - L -   Carmen   A carries on screen upstage
                                                          of S
```

```
106.1
 19  0:04:08  2:09  A     59   12   -    4 - -   NA       dance                          dance!
 20  0:04:47  0:33  A     21    6   3    - - -   NA       dance                          dance!
 21  0:05:20  1:21  A      6   57   3    - - -   NA       dance                          dance!
```

```
104.1
 22  0:05:56  0:19  SA    31   28   5    - L -   Carmen   A carries screen upstage of S
```

Fig. 39.   The first page of actions for *Europera 1;* © 1987 Henmar Press Inc.

whether to the singer's right ("R"), left ("L"), back ("B"), or front ("F"). The next column "Sings" refers only to the singer. If a horizontal line (such as at 0:04:08) has "NA" this means that it is not applicable; if it has a "no" this means that a singer does not sing for the notated duration; if a singer sings, the abbreviated title of the opera from which the aria was chosen appears.

Cage sent all the prospective singers a list of durations for singing their respective arias, and each singer used these durations to decide (by personal choice) which arias they would sing from their repertory which could fit the required time limits (Cage 1987b). An example of the arias chosen by a singer according to the given durations appears as follows from an unpublished worksheet during the composition process:

105.1	*Dido and Aeneas*	*When I am laid*	*7:30*
[105.2	*information missing]*		
105.3	*Migon*	*Connais–tu le pays*	*4:30*
105.4	*Babiere*	*Una voce poco fa*	*6:00*
105.5	*Fledermaus*	*Ich lade gein mis*	*6:00*
105.6	*Cenerentola*	*Nacqui allaffano*	*7:00*

(Cage 1987b)

Although Cage does not mention it in his introduction to the published score, it would probably be just as accurate to perform *Europeras 1 & 2* by having singers choose arias other than those suggested in the published score. This is rather indeterminate, for in the final score version only the title of the opera appears, and the actual aria selected is not indicated.

Andrew Culver states that not all the original singers initially scheduled to perform actually appeared in the German premiere, nor did all of those singers perform in the United States. In the process, other arias were chosen by the replacement singers, and the published information on operas from which to choose arias is only an indication of the general type of material to be used (Culver 1988). (For instance, I only know one opera well — Henry Purcell's *Dido and Aeneas* — yet although this is mentioned in the published score, I did not recognize it during any of the three American performances. Either it was not sung but was replaced with an aria from a different opera, or with the great overlapping of various arias and instrumental parts it became lost in the sound mix.)

The final column in the action part is "Description" which is an abbreviated description of the action for the singers and assistants. In comparison with *Theatre Piece*, these are very determinate actions, although examples such as "en route" (at 0:02:35) or "dance" (at 0:04:47) must still be finally determined through actual performance.

In the very right column are uncategorized notations such as "dance!"

or "fly" (beginning at 0:03:36). Andrew Culver explains that these were originally personal remarks made during the composition process and should be edited out from the final score (Culver 1988).

A more completely determinate action description is in the published score of the props. Each singer, identified by the numerical code of opera (1 or 2), female or male (0 or 5), number of singer, and number of aria, is provided with a prop description and action column. (A third column, with the number of a figure or illustration, is in the score; however the figure to be referred to is not included in the published version.) For the beginning of *Europera 1*, the first two singers have the following notations from the props score part:

Description	Action	Fig
106.1		
zippered igloo, chair 1 and mynah bird	*igloo onstage from 0:00 with mynah bird and S sitting in chair 1 inside. . .AA unzipper bag, S sings, bird flies, AA dance. . .AA rezipper bag, igloo pulled off by stage-hands with S inside, AA dance and exit*	*1*
151.1		
light: follow spot	*arms held aloft by AA, moves as in old age; face turns violet*	

(Cage 1987d)

Other examples of props include a bathtub, a coffin, a door, a swing, potted plants, a large tricycle, a rug pulled with ropes, a jeep, and four posters with the letters "M," "A," "N," and "E" held by assistants 9–12 spelling the various combinations "MANE," "EMAN," "ENAM," "NEMA," "NAEM," and "NAME" (in *Europera 1* from 1:00:33 through 1:03:28).

The published score also has a list of cues for the movement of flats. What is notated is the duration of a flat coming in or going out; the position on stage (indicated by the pipes on the stage floorplan); the number of the flat, the image, and a blank remarks column (used during composition but not needed in published form). There are thirty-six flats used in each *Europera*. The images for each flat were in black-and-white, chosen by Ursala Markow from late-eighteenth through early-twentieth century images researched from the Stadt- und Universitats-bibliothek in Frankfurt. The images were then sent to New York, and Cage made croppings by chance procedures. Images included birds, serpents, composers (Mozart), and famous historical opera singers (Caruso).

What is significant in Cage's composition of the flats is not only that the plastic imagery is an independent element, but that the imagery extends chance procedures to bring purely visual art-works into the realm of performance. Cage's own purely visual works, such as the *HV* series (1983), reveal much of the same rationale employed in composing the flats for *Europeras 1 & 2*. The *HV* series consists of thirty-six monoprints made by chance determinations of the choice of printing material (velvet, cloth, carpet), the color to be used, and the horizontal and vertical dimensions on the sheet of paper. For Cage, part of the rationale behind the stage flats was to apply Duchamp's statement pointing to "the impossibility of transferring from one like image to another the memory imprint" (Durner 1988, 13), resulting in a visual music in chance counterpoint to all the other elements.

The lighting plan is available on rental from C. F. Peters. Cage writes that there are 3,726 light cues, "each having from one to fifty events" (Cage 1987b). Andrew Culver further comments:

> The lighting is what John considers to have been the most significant contribution that this opera made to theatre, because lighting is the most antiquated thinking of all in theatre. He said, 'We'll take all this information and compose it, we'll use chance, and we'll make it independent of the action so it will be an element all to itself." (Culver 1988)

In all, Culver recalls that 181 lamps were used, independently, with 30 or 40 different gells of different whites. The choice of variant white lights was a conceptual decision from Cage's personal taste, for the stage floor was grey, the props were various greys, and the flats were black-and-white. There are only two examples of colored lighting. The first has been previously noted with the reproduced action page in Fig. 39, where singer 151.1 turns violet for thirty seconds beginning at 0:02:27. The second instance is when singer 154.2 turns greenish-yellow at 0:27:53 for one minute and fifty-five seconds. In both cases, the colored lighting effect was included as an action, rather than as part of the lighting plan. The general effect of the various white lights was of different changes of illumination over the entire stage. There were often unlit areas during a particular moment, however since there were so many lamps being used, there was always a general overall subdued illumination.

The costume plan is also not included in the published score. Costumes were originally found through chance determinations from a fourteen-volume nineteenth century encyclopedia of world fashions. Slides were made and sent to Germany. Another version of the costumes, among Cage's unpublished papers, lists each singer and each aria with a traditional national costume. An example from this unpublished score part is reproduced below, showing the national costumes to be worn for each of the seven arias by the sixth female singer in *Europera 1*:

106.1 *Poland*
106.2 *Norway*
106.3 *Morocco*
106.4 *South*
106.5 *Spain*
106.6 *Sweden*
106.7 *China*

(*Cage 1986a*)

The costumes, of course, had no relation to the aria being sung. All of the costumes were very ornate and colorful, and made the singers more noticeable and isolated figures within the overall scheme of greys and whites. The assistants wore various shades of grey — some dressed in dancer's tights, others in loose-fitting exercise-type clothing, which made them appear as a transitional element between the decor and the singers.

The final part of the published score consists of twelve pairs of opera synopses. These were composed by chance from historical opera synopses. In Frankfurt there were twelve different programs — an audience member did not have access to the other eleven. When performed in the United States, all twelve synopses were published in the program, with the individual given the choice of which to choose from. One example of a synopsis for *Europera 1* is the following:

> *She gains admittance to the palace. He accepts a commission to outwit the two lovers. However, she kills him at her feet and assists the lawyer who cannot resist her invitation to the palace. He tries prayers. He displays a white dove and wins the hand of the princess. (Cage 1987d)*

None of the synopses have any connection to the stage action in Cage's *Europeras 1 & 2*, indeed there is no plot or narrative progression in Cage's work. However, if one is hard-pressed to agree with the general interpretation of the European and American critics that *Europeras 1 & 2* is a parody of conventional opera, this may be an accurate view of the synopses, for Cage plays with the rather tawdry and melodramatic situations, and exposes them as being just that. It might also be interpreted that in making the synopses, Cage is also playing with the tradition of opera performance in America, for a typical program contains a brief written story outline for the average theatre-goer to follow the plot of a work sung in a foreign language. Here, Cage is perhaps making a wry commentary on the general incomprehensibility and boredom that many Americans feel towards traditional, European opera.

The production at Purchase was more complete than the hastily remounted original production in Germany (Rockwell 1988). Upon entering the auditorium, one saw a silent color film by Frank Scheffer entitled *Wagner's*

Ring, a three minute and forty-second stop-action abridgement of *Europera 2*. This was also shown as a film loop during the intermission.

Visually, *Europeras 1 & 2* was very entertaining. The singers wore colorful costumes, which made them stand out against the grey stage, grey properties, grey-clad assistants, and black-and-white flats. Some of the assistants were ballet-trained, others were not, and this difference in movement style created an intriguing yet inconsistent tension in the production. Again, some of the singers were decidedly "hammy," while others sang their arias and performed their unrelated actions without any overlaying of dramatic pretention or pomposity.

The most noticeable, and intentional, bit of added business was done at the first Purchase performance by Heinz Hagenau before his second aria beginning at 0:27:43 in *Europera 1*. Hagenau was dressed in a medieval knight's costume, wearing his everyday eye glasses. He leaned on his sword, then took off his glasses in a rather obvious and forcedly flippant manner, and did a short, silent prepartory gesture as if to say "Now, I'm going to give you all the low-down." He then began to sing his aria, from *Fidelio*. This personally inserted "schtick" was not included in the two subsequent performances, in part because it did not engender the expected audience reaction (people did not laugh), and because it was a "cute" and personal expression which was totally incongruous with Cage's score. Mark Swed, writing about performances of *Europeras 1 & 2* in the winter of 1988, would note that after Cage left Europe and was not attending the performances, that some of the performers were beginning to take unintended liberties with the score and "playing to the audience" (Swed 1988a). Andrew Culver recalls that such instances of incongruously added elements worked better with German audiences, and that Cage later lectured the performers not to do this, but to simply and accurately do the events as notated (Culver 1988).

The most enjoyable aspect of the performance was in the precision and accuracy with which the majority of performers attempted to realize Cage's complex score parts. In the three Purchase performances, there were no major differences other than the minor variations that naturally occur in live performance. Perhaps the most spectacular event in the entire production was a radio-controlled miniature zeppelin. This was brought on stage by Assistants 9 and 10 in *Europera 2* at 0:37:06. The zeppelin was then allowed to float out into the auditorium for the concluding minutes of the second act. On each side was a banner, which read 'europera 3'' and "europera 4." This was greeted with spontaneous applause each evening.

Europeras 1 &2 is one of Cage's greatest achievements in theatre composition. It is his most important theatre piece since *Song Books*. It is his most detailed and determinately notated theatre piece, and may be considered to be a summation of his ideas in theatre since the early 1950s. It is didactic in being an example of style and content for further realizations of the indeterminate notation in *Theatre Piece*, but it is also a work of great charm and aesthetic integrity in itself.

Europeras 3 & 4

The promise of *Europeras 3 & 4*, originally advertised on the dirigible in *Europera 2*, was fulfilled with a commission from the pianist Yvar Mikhashoff who, as artistic director of the Almeida Festival in London, England, wanted Cage to make a new piece. Andrew Culver, Cage's assistant, recalls:

> *I have a very, very fond relationship with* Europeras 3 & 4, *and I think that John did too. For one thing, they didn't have any of the anxieties that 1 & 2 had in their creation or their production. He knew it wouldn't be a big problem that way; and he'd always thought, even while we were composing 1 & 2, he'd wanted to have a concert version as a relief to the stresses of dealing with an opera company. (Culver 1992)*

Yvar Mikhashoff recalls that Cage's initial idea was to write a piece for brass, percussion, and singers, but by late 1989 decided to make it a minimalist theatre piece for singers, phonographs, and pianos (Mikhashoff 1993). The two paired operas were composed in late 1989 and completed in early 1990 (Culver 1992).

Europera 3, at 70 minutes, is for six operatic voices, two pianos, six players each using two electric 78 r.p.m. phonographs, lighting, and the *Truckera* collage tape. *Europera 4*, at 30 minutes, is for two operatic voices, lighting, *Truckera* tape, solo piano, and solo Victrola. Each of the performers's parts were generated by chance procedures using Culver's *I Ching* computer program. The director's part, which serves as both a practical introduction to the other parts as well as being an instruction for the general production, is similar to the director's part in *Europera 5*. In *Europeras 3 & 4* the director is to mark the stage into a numbered grid of 64 squares, which is then used for the stage positions of the various singers's arias, as well as for determining the positions of the instruments and stage properties (primarily chairs, tables, and lamps). A video clock serves as conductor.

In *Europera 3*, the six singers are provided with the beginning times and stage positions for nine different possible performances, in order to sing six arias chosen from their repertoire. The arias are to be in the public domain, and between arias they may sit in the provided chairs. The six record-player performers play from 300 two-sided 78 r.p.m. recordings of opera arias on electronic phonographs, each performer working two machines. Their parts list the record, the side, the dynamic, and beginning and ending time in seconds for each minute. The lighting plan is on a specially designed computer software program, adaptable to each individual performance space and available resources. The *Truckera* tape is played eight times in 20″ parts, fading in to a very loud volume and then fading out again from side to side, like a truck passing by. The two pianists are each provided with seventy chance-determined excerpts from Franz Liszt's *Opern-Phantasien*, with excerpts from one to sixteen measures. Preceding each excerpt is a time in seconds, referring to the silence within a specific minute before one begins to play. The pianists are also provided with nine different lists of random-ordered numbers from 1 through 70 to determine the actual order of the piano transcription excerpts. Andrew Culver, in his performance notes, writes: "It is not required that all 70 excerpts be completed in the opera's hour and ten minutes: play until time is up." As with all the other performers's parts, one "may wear whatever you wish" (Cage/Culver 1990). While it is not obvious when reading the score parts, *Europera 3* is a very dense-sounding piece in performance.

Europera 4, by purposeful contrast, is a much more sparse work. The two singers again have times to initiate their performance of public domain arias, but within a more minimalist context. The lighting is no longer focused on the stage grid, but on the walls and ceiling, creating a soft, ambient effect. The *Truckera* tape is only played three times, in 52″ parts with a "peak volume of bare audibility." The solo pianist plays three opera transcriptions beginning at 1′30″, 9′15″, and 19′41″. Culver's performance note is:

> Create or play 3 piano arrangements of operatic material, making sure that their durations do not run into the performance times of the next. The third must end before 30:00. (Cage/Culver 1990)

The first two transcriptions are performed by "shadow playing," where one is only to graze the keys, unintentionally producing tones. The last is to be played normally. Yvar Mikhashoff recalls that the original idea of "shadow playing" was to perform with gloves or mittens: "I didn't like that idea, because it would be difficult to control and very dissonant." His solution was:

> Well, there is a way you can play backstage that you can play when you don't want to disturb other people, so you just skim over notes. In Europera 4 I look as if playing really actively, and with all the same gestures, but occasionally a note comes out. The third excerpt was to be played out [with normal dynamics], but it was to be played very quiet. What I chose was "Oh, Star of Eve" from Tannhäuser — of all opera excerpts it is a very gooey and hackneyed piece — it is often recorded. It is a symbol of opera of the past. It is overly sentimental, but exactly what you need to communicate the mood of nostalgia. I played it extremely slowly. Normally it would take about seven minutes, but I performed it to be eleven minutes. (Mikhashoff 1993)

Europeras 3 & 4 was first performed at the Almeida Theatre, London, on June 17, 19, and 20, 1990, and subsequently toured to Berlin, Strasbourg, and Paris. It was performed without a curtain on a bare stage, and directed by Andrew Culver, who recalls:

> I had to deal with the stage locations, and the lights through chance operations — the choice of lamps, the focus, gels, the cues — and then I took on the more conventional role of director, which was talking to the cast and running the rehearsals. I did some acoustic balancing on the relative strengths of the pianos and the phonographs. The singers have their own strength, and actually it's amazing, but voices are not difficult to balance. It really doesn't matter whether a voice is very loud or quite soft, it still can be heard. (Culver 1992)

Culver also recalls that the general dynamics range in *Europera 3* was from mf to f, and p to mp in *Europera 4*; and that the clothing of the performers "looked a bit like a scene from a late-1950s or early-1960s Hollywood 'in-crowd party,' in other words, they looked like opera singers, they were perfect!" (Culver 1992).

Journalists wrote generally mixed reviews. Meirion Bowen provided the most negative criticism: "Occasionally an uninterrupted bit of Verdi or Wagner surfaced and the few silences were golden: otherwise, it was inexpressibly tedious. . .Avoid" (Bowen 1990). Paul Driver, typical of most reviewers, found *Europera 3* "onerous and footling," but *Europera 4* "affecting through and through, . . . a serene epilogue to 19th century opera" (Driver 1990). The most positive review was provided by Nicholas Kenyon, who characterized the works as. . .

> . . .a random tapestry of operas past, lovingly woven and dauntingly extended in order to remind ourselves how completely batty is our approach to the great art-work, the grand statement. . .
> . . .it served to show that Cage, so often accused of being anti-musical, could never be said to hate music. . . I've spent far worse evenings with opera. (Kenyon 1990)

Europeras 3 & 4 was later staged by the Long Beach Opera, with direction by Andrew Culver, at Long Beach, California, in November, 1993. An audio recording was issued in 1995. Listening to this production is rather surprising in comparison with the critical reviews. I do not find *Europera 3* to be overwhelming, nor *Europera 4* to be as sparse as suggested by reviewers. Missing, of course, is the visual aspect of performance, although the accompanying booklet to the two-CD set includes several photographs. The *Europera 3 & 4* CDs nonetheless document a careful, accurate production of a work which is unlikely to find a place within the repertoire of opera companies, given the paucity of new music performance in general, and the difficulty of finding the 78 r.p.m. records and phonographs (Cage 1995).

Perhaps most intriguing content of reviews is the general critical opinion that Cage's dense sonic collage in *Europera 3* was a tedius, uninteresting repetition of his earlier ideas; and that contemporary music has since moved on to other concerns. Of course, one could say the same thing about contemporary productions of any antique opera by Verdi or Wagner. The great difference is that nineteenth century composers have become culturally enshrined, while Cage is as yet considered to be of only marginal, novelty value. Andrew Culver, in this context, provides the most cogent insight:

> *Opera is one of those things — it's like improvisation — that is impossible to do, and therefore* intriguing *to attempt. That's why it won't go away. And it's also the perfect post-modern medium. It's perfect! It is post-modern, by definition, because it has to do with incongruous elements that can never be brought together, that can only be juxtaposed. You have to stick, you know, A against B, and then a little something else tacked on top; and you can make a statement in post-modernism, but you can't unify all the elements behind your statement. It's like those sculptures by John Chamberlain that are made up of old car-parts (laughs). That's sort of what it's like, it's like an old junk-yard (laughs). (Culver 1992)*

I agree with Culver's assessment, and add that the supposed unification of elements in conventional opera really only seems to be so because of the linear narrative structure. By shearing away the narrative structure of opera, Cage's isolation of elements provides a reflexive de-synthesis which exposes and informs the integrity of individual components and performers. Cage was respectful but not protective of tradition, using the past as a fluid source of pre-existent material for critical (and emotional) insights into our present situation.

The emotional, "elegiac" sparsity of *Europera 4* would find its final, complete expression in *Europera 5*.

Europera 5

Europera 5 (1991) is Cage's last theatre piece composition. Several performance organizations were interested in doing *Europera 4* as a single piece, but Cage refused, stating that *Europeras 3 & 4* could only be performed together as a set. Finally around Christmastime of 1990, Cage told Yvar Mikhashoff "I have a solution for you wanting to do *Europera 4* — I'm going to write *Europera 5* so you can travel around, have a completely portable piece that you can take on the road" (Mikhashoff 1993).

Europera 5 was commissioned by the North American New Music Festival and De Ijsbreker (Holland), and was first performed at the SUNY-Buffalo Department of Music on April 18, 1991 (Behrens and Young 1992). The score is for a pianist, two singers, a Victrola, electronic sound including radio and television, lighting, and a director. The list of properties include a grand piano, several old lamps, five old chairs, and the tape and 64 stick-on numbers to mark a symmetrical or asymmetrical grid on stage. As typical with

Cage's mature compositions, each performer has a separate part and there is no "master score." The piece is sixty minutes.

The two singers each sing five arias chosen from their repertoire of classical opera. Nine different performance versions are provided in the score, with time of occurrence and position on the grid or offstage. Culver, in his performance notes, writes that each singer "may wear whatever you wish." Also noted is the stage position and duration for wearing a "head and shoulders animal mask." Yvar Mikhashoff recalls that the typical masks employed in various performances have been a bear and a wolf (Mikhashoff 1993).

The piano part lists six time occurrences to begin playing piano arrangements of operatic material. The first, third, and sixth pieces are played with normal dynamics; the second, fourth, and fifth are in the "shadow playing" style of *Europera 4*.

The Victrola part is to play six early 78 r.p.m. operatic arias on a wind-up horn phonograph. The score notes that if "the sixth ends before 60:00, play it again, stopping at 60:00. Perform with great care" (Cage/ Culver 1991). Although not explicitly noted, "early recordings" would mean records made before the use of the electronic microphone in the 1920s.

The sound part plays the *Truckera* tape as well as a radio and mute television. The *Truckera* tape is played in six 30" installments fading in and out from either left to right or right to left. The radio is turned on and off four times from 00:30 through 48:30. The television is played twice, from 41:30 through 50:00, and 58:00 through 60:00.

The lighting performer's part is on IBM floppy disk, which gives detailed instructions for using the floor grid and available lights and gells, in chance operations. This performer also controls a VCR which has a video-tape clock that shows the minutes and seconds of the hour-long work on television screens placed for reference by the other performers. At the conclusion, the "light performer blacks the lights and video, and anyone still making sounds stops" (Cage/Culver 1991).

A 15'01" excerpt of *Europera 5* was recorded and released by the journal *Musicworks* in the CD accompanying their Cage issue from 1992, with Jan Leibel (soprano), Darryl Edwards (tenor), Jack Behrens (piano), and Noel Martin (Victrola). This studio recording, based upon the premiere performance, has a delicate, "spacey" quality that is eerily ghostlike yet tender and almost comforting (Cage 1992b).

A complete recording of *Europera 5*, made during the dress rehearsal at the State University of New York at Buffalo on April 12, 1991, was released on CD in 1994. Although it is not the first public performance, this rehearsal was the first time the work was enacted in its entirety, and in that sense is the actual "premiere." The delicacy of the composition and the care with which it is done, make this one of the finest audio recordings of any Cage composition to date. While it would more accurately have been documented on video tape (to include the visual components of performance as well), what remains is extraordinary nonetheless. Because it is so soft, one must listen to the recording at almost full volume on one's home equipment. If one judges an opera as being "great" by tears from reception (as from Purcell's *Dido and Aeneas* or Puccini's *Madama Butterfly*), Cage's *Europera 5* is a truly classic opera that is affecting without seeming affected (Cage 1994b).

Europera 5 received its first New York City performances on July 31, and August 1, 14, 15, 21, and 22, 1992, in the Sculpture Garden at the Museum of Modern Art with the singers Cheryl Marshall and Lisa Wilson, pianist Yvar Mikhashoff, and Andrew Culver as the director (Program 1992a). I attended the performances on August 14 and 22, and Cage's recent death from a stroke on August 12 made the already whistful theatre piece seem all the more poignant.

The stage grid was basically asymmetrical because of the sculptures and reflecting pool in the museum's Sculpture Garden. The audience sat in the round, with the performers in the center. There was a general ambient low-lighting in the performance area, and at various times there were more intensely illuminated lights focused upon the trees. The sound level was generally very low. I could barely hear the radio, but at times it sounded like static, at other times a jazz station. The video clocks for the performers were also visible to most of the audience. On August 14 the television programs shown were the situation comedies "Step by Step" and "Dinosaurs;" on the 22nd an underwater documentary was being broadcast. The singers wore fashionable evening dresses; Mikhashoff, a button-down shirt and tie; the other performers in casual attire. As there was only one television for ambient program broadcasts, I sat in the area where it would be visible. The *Truckera* tape was the loudest sonic element. The Victrola and piano were slightly amplified because of the outside space and lack of concert hall acoustics.

The singers's arias, without accompaniment or electronic amplification, made an eerie contrast to the wind-up phonograph, like unintended echoes between the living and the dead. The unhurried, serene, and elegiac mood was also a delight because of the actual setting. I would look up and see a jet plane pass over-head, or listen to the interpenetration of the city traffic sounds just beyond the museum wall. As it was in August, the sunset was around 8:00 p.m. (the beginning of the performance). The dusk light slowly faded to night, and the electric lighting on the trees became more noticeable through the hour. Several audience members walked about the garden, perhaps from boredom or disappointment, but for me this only increased my attention to the intended (composed) and unintended (ambient) events that occurred.

Reviews of the *Europera 5* New York performances were kind but not especially enthusiatic. Adam Horvath wrote that it was "yet another John Cage puzzle," and wondered "is the pastiche of European operatic tradition satiric, or sentimental?" (Horvath 1992). James Oestreich wrote that it "lacked the visceral impact and sustained intensity of the equally inscrutable 'Europeras 1 and 2';" and that "Only the rolling juggernaut of the 'truckera,' overwhelming even the street noises beyond the wall, periodically swept the listener into the melee" (Oestreich 1992). Mark Swed would write the most positive review, noting that it was "brilliantly directed by Andrew Culver," and that. . .

> . . .the work is most affecting in the way it magnifies the performers. Hearing arias sung without accompaniment and often with unrelated musics happening simultaneously exposes the singer's art and puts a listener in much closer contact with the performer. It also forces the singers to focus to an unprecedented degree, since they are not only unaccompanied but in competition with everything around them. (Swed 1992)

Perhaps the most accurate critical assessment of *Europera 5* is from Paul Zukofsky's general statement on Cage's last compositions:

> In these works. . . Cage's philosophical and structural sensibility remains much the same, but the surface changes dramatically. There is less activity; the average duration of single notes [or an event] is much longer; the music is more elegiac, calm; and there is an extreme simplicity of musical means. All these together allow a perceiver to reconsider how Cage relates to aspects of classical music, especially, aspects that Cage's earlier music eschewed. In addition, I do not find hyperbole in my personal feeling that many of Cage's recent [i.e. final] works are similar in concentration and beauty to Monet's Waterlilies. (Program 1992)

The nostalgic, sentimental, elegiac quality of *Europera 5* is something which may perplex critics of Cage's work, particularly because of his aesthetic of avoiding personal taste, likes and dislikes. In practice, Cage was never able to completely free himself from personal expression. Yvar Mikhashoff agrees that both *Europera 4* and *Europera 5* are bittersweet and sentimental works, but notes that the sentimental reception is from the fact that Cage wanted familiar, middle-class operatic references; and that his taste only came in with using the familiar, and with it, the attendant personal emotional responses that may ensue (Mikhashoff 1993).

I find *Europera 5* to be particularly sentimental not from the use of antique opera but in the use of technology, which at hindsight perhaps is a semi-autobiographic record of the social changes that occurred during Cage's lifetime. The Victrola dates from Cage's childhood. I remember once arriving at his loft in the late 1980s for an interview. Before we could sit down and talk, he had to walk a few blocks to a Veterinarian to pick up his cat. Would I mind coming along? No, of course not. As we walked, I asked him if his parents had a Victrola at home when he was a little boy. Yes they did, he replied. Well, what kind of records did your family have? John replied that his mother was the one most interested in records, and that mostly she listened to the popular music of the period. He then remembered that her particularly favorite record was "Dardenella," but I wouldn't know that song, would I? Yes!, I did, my maternal grandmother also liked that song; and I also grew up listening to a 78 r.p.m. recording of that once-popular tune.

The nostalgic reference of changing technology, as embodied in the Victrola, also extends to the radio (an invention that became widespread commercially during the 1920s), the television (which became widespread commercially in the US only after 1948), and the computer (emblematic of Cage's involvement with new technology throughout his career, but particularly with the computer, of his final years as a composer.)

With *Europera 5* Cage came full circle, and was able to make a chance-determined collage of conventional art through a selective microcosm of audio and visual technology from throughout his lifetime. With his unexpected death just a few weeks before his 80th birthday, his presence at the final Summergarden performances was missed. For many years, at both performances of Cage's work in concert or with the Cunningham Dance Company, he was often in the audience, and it was not uncommon to overhear people whisper "Look, that's John Cage!;" and because many knew that he was in attendance, the applause afterwards was perhaps more for him personally rather than for the performers or the actual composition. Knowing that he was also in the audience became in itself a part of the total performance experience. The following, and concluding chapter, will thus survey a variety of different genres in which Cage himself was integral as a performer of his own compositions.

9

JOHN CAGE AS A PERFORMER

Many of the previously discussed theatre pieces were either first or subsequently performed by the composer as a solo (e.g. *Water Walk* and *Sounds of Venice*) or as a simultaneous solo in duet with David Tudor (e.g. *Music Walk* and *Cartridge Music*). On the most trivial level, much of the popular success of the various musicircuses has been because Cage was either a simultaneous performer or known to be in attendance. Historically, with the exception of *Dialogue* with Merce Cunningham, none of the previously discussed theatre pieces have depended upon his presence as a performer but as a composer. Aside from the interest by some intellectuals, Cage's entire body of work has been, and continues to be, performed by an eclectic variety of people on both the professional and amateur level. Much of his adult career had been in composing works that were practical, feasible to perform. (As noted in Chapter 1, Cage learned the practicality of performance with composition in the 1942 radio play *The City Wears a Slouch Hat* with Kenneth Patchen.)

This chapter will begin to address the previous imbalance of viewing Cage primarily as a composer, by looking at his career as a performer. John Cage began performing previous to composing, as a child during piano recitals. As an adult he began giving lectures in the early 1930s, conducted his percussion ensemble during the latter 1930s and early 1940s, accompanied Merce Cunningham as a pianist in their early joint recitals in the mid-1940s; and made physical-action performances from the 1950s through the latter 1980s. Cage retired as a musical and physical performer in 1989, but continued to give lectures and poetry readings. In addition, he continued a very demanding music, verbal, and visual composition schedule until his death.

John Cage first began to study the piano with Fannie Charles Dillon in Santa Monica, California, around 1922 (when he was ten years old). The Cage family moved to Glendale around 1923. He later commented on these earliest experiences:

I asked my parents to get a piano for me, which they did when they moved from Santa Monica to a home near Glendale. I studied no longer with her [Dillon], but with my Aunt Phoebe [Phoebe James, on my mother's side], and she taught me to sight read. She wasn't so interested in the scales as the other one, and the Los Angeles Public Library had a very fine music section so that you could borrow sheet music, and I became familiar with a great deal of music in that way. My Aunt Phoebe told me not to pay attention to Bach or Beethoven, "That, I wouldn't like!," but anything else would be perfectly alright (laughs). I was in the fifth–sixth–seventh grade, that sort of thing.

Aunt Phoebe gave piano recitals with most of her students. Most of her students performed "Pianologues" — do you know what they are? You play the piano and you speak at the same time, and we also performed in costume, appropriate to whatever we were talking about. If the Pianologue was Spanish, for instance, you'd come in a Spanish costume; or if it was Wild-Western, you know, you'd come as a cowboy.

These were very popular. That was in the 'twenties. I just remember that at children's recitals [not as part of Sunday School or Public School recitals.]

[Question: Was there any movement with the Pianologues, other than walking to the piano, sitting down, playing and speaking, then getting up and walking off?]

No, because you're sitting at the piano, playing, and you're in costume, and you're talking. That's enough! (laughs). It was more like a travelogue at the piano, that sort of thing, or a very short story, you might say. (Cage 1987e)

Ironically, perhaps, Cage as an adult was a very nondemonstrative and untheatrical pianist. Cage has been disparaging of his pianistic abilities, saying that he never liked to practice (Cage 1987e). David Tudor states that Cage was never a virtuoso pianist, but that Cage never had any desire to become one, and that he could not play technical, intricate passages well but that he knew what he could perform effectively (Tudor 1989c). The virtuoso pianist Grete Sultan, who has known Cage since the early 1940s, recalls hearing him perform Erik Satie's *Nocturnes* and his own *Sonatas and Interludes* sometime in the early 1950s and that "he played very beautifully," although again mentioning that he did not like to practice (Sultan 1989).

Cage's pianism with his earlier compositions is documented in the live recording at Town Hall in 1958 as the accompanist for Arline Carmen (contralto) in performances of *The Wonderful Widow of Eighteen Springs* (1942) and *She Is Asleep* (1943). *The Wonderful Widow* is an abridgement from page 556 in *Finnegans Wake* (1939) by James Joyce. The vocal setting is in the style of a simple, evocative chant. The piano is played using the body of the instrument — underpart of the body, front of the keyboard lid, back or higher part of the keyboard lid, and closed top of the piano. His performance on the piano-body is very emotionally expressive, using a wide range of dynamics with rubato (slightly speeding up or slowing down the tempo) (Cage 1958d). On the phonograph recording, some of the piano-body events sound quite loud, but Cage has explained that the actual performance was quite soft, and that the loudness is a distortion from recording (Cage 1987e).

She Is Asleep documents Cage's playing the prepared piano. The sung text is a vocalise with ascending and descending sliding tones. There is again a very limited range for the pianist. *She Is Asleep* uses only the keyboard, playing only prepared tones, and does not have the gestural quality inherent in *The Wonderful Widow*. Cage's pianism in *She Is Asleep* again is very emotionally expressive through a wide range of dynamics and rubato (Cage 1958d). In listening to both of these works, Cage reveals a very subtly expressive, intently focused, yet somewhat mysterious persona.

Other than his own occasional performances of *Sonatas and Interludes* in the 1950s and early 1960s, the most extended piano work that Cage performed in public was *Cheap Imitation* (1969). *Cheap Imitation* is a 30-minute work based on Erik Satie's *Socrate* (1918), using Satie's original rhythmic structure and substituting notes by chance procedures. It would be his final work for public performance as a pianist. Cage would later recall that because the arthritis in his hands had become so painful, he knew that he had to retire as a pianist (Cage 1987e). Philip Corner recalls attending a live performance of Cage playing *Cheap Imitation* in the early 1970s, and remarks that Cage's hands were very badly swollen, but that he played "excellently" (Corner 1989).

A phonograph recording of Cage playing *Cheap Imitation* was released by Cramps, in Italy, performed in early March, 1976, and listening to this performance documents why Grete Sultan said that Cage played Satie's *Norturnes* so beautifully in the 1950s. In playing *Cheap Imitation*, Cage did not use any intentional contrast in dynamics or use rubato. It is soft throughout, and has an unhurried, fastidiously unchanging tempo (Cage 1976c). One feels that the pianist is not being at all expressive, but is simply a blank conduit for sound — austere, focused, disciplined, yet mysteriously evocative and hypnotic in effect. While Cage did not perform as a pianist after the mid-1970s, he continued on occasion to "try out" various compositions privately on the keyboard, such as *ASLSP* (1985) (Cage 1987e).

The last period of Cage's musical performances is with his compositions *Child of Tree* (1975), *Branches* (1976), and *Inlets* (1977). All of these are in linguistic notation, and are indeterminate in character. *Child of Tree* is an eight-minute percussion solo, using two to ten plants as instruments. Two of the instruments are specified in the score — one is a pod rattle from the Pornciana tree (found near Cuernavaca, Mexico); the other is a cactus "or part of one (live or dry) of a genus having a solid body and spines which are relatively free of other spines" with contact microphones for amplification (Cage 1975). The other eight instruments may consist of other pod rattles and/or cacti, or other plants not requiring amplification, such as claves, tepanaxtli, or sticks broken or slapped against one another. The majority of the score is a detailed notation for the performer to use the *I Ching* coin oracle method to obtain chance determinations for the number of parts within eight minutes, which instruments are to be used and how many in each part, and the timings of the parts. This information is then to be written down and used as the score for actual performance. Cage's directions conclude by stating:

> *Using a stop-watch, the soloist improvises, clarifying the time structure by means of the instruments.*
> *This improvisation is the performance. The rest of the work is done ahead of time. The performer shall take as much care as possible during a performance not to make any other sounds than those he makes with his instruments. (Cage 1975)*

In *Child of Tree* the title is, in part, a generic classification of the performer's use of instruments, as well as a poetic reference to James Joyce's *Finnegans Wake* used in Cage's *Wonderful Widow of Eighteen Springs*, where "infantina Isobel" is celebrated as "neath of the whitethorn, child of tree, like some losthappy leaf, like blowing flower stilled" (Joyce 1939, 556). The improvisation that Cage notes in the score is not purely spontaneous, but requires the use of specific chance procedures according to specific use. Improvisation is, rather, the actual rhythmic or arhythmic performance of the various plants according to the resultant time plan.

Branches (1976) is a brief handwritten indeterminate score and is a variation of *Child of Tree*. One is to refer to the instructions for *Child of Tree* to produce a percussion solo, duet, trio, or "orchestra (of any number of players)" (Cage 1976b). *Branches* may be performed for longer than eight minutes, with periods of one to eight minutes of silence in between parts. Tom Johnson would write of Cage's performance of *Branches* at The Kitchen in New York in December, 1977:

> *A large pine cone, a small cactus, and materials less easy to identify were mounted on a small table, and Cage performed alone... All the plants were amplified, via a unique sound system designed by John Fulleman, so we heard the plants through a dense layer of technology. Furthermore, Cage performed the piece, which lasted about 23 minutes, with intent concentration. He followed a stop watch, watched his score, and produced each sound with great care.*
> *The sounds of the plant materials in* Branches *were extremely delicate, with ample silence between them. The technology could be heard so much as the plants, and many of the sounds benefited from echo or reverb effects. (Johnson 1978)*

The score of *Branches* may also be used as accompaniment. The music then "stops when what it accompanies stops" (Cage 1976b). *Branches* was performed by John Cage, David Tudor, and Takehisa Kosugi as the music for one of the Six Events by the Merce Cunningham Dance Company at the 69th Street Armory in New York in June, 1983. I recall that the performance lasted approximately ninety minutes, and that the music was very sparse, quiet, with several sections of slow ostinati (repeated rhythmic patterns). Cage was visible behind the electronic equipment at the back of the dance area, and he seemed totally focused upon his activities. His playing the amplified spines of various cacti was particularly reminiscent of a slowed-down passage from his prepared piano works of the 1940s, and hence had a "pianistic" quality.

Inlets (1977) is a linguistic notation for three percussionists who play conch shells filled with water. A tape recording of fire sounds is also played. The score very briefly instructs that there are twelve water-filled conch shells — three very large, three medium-large, three medium, three small sized — and that each performer uses four different shells. Sound is produced by slowly tipping the shell. These sounds are amplified by microphones. The total duration may be "Any amount of time," but halfway through the performance the sound of burning pine cones — "(If possible this should be live.)" — is to be heard. The score concludes:

> *Then at any point post-central in the total time, the conch used as trumpet is to be played for as long as the player can hold a single tone. . . it is best to have a hall with a very high ceiling and good acoustics. (Cage 1977)*

Tom Johnson describes a performance at The Kitchen in New York in December, 1977:

> Inlets *offered the most unusual sounds. I became quite caught up in the little gurgles, glugs, and swishes that resulted as Cage, David Tudor, and Takehisa Kosugi manipulated their water-filled conches. . . Garrett List blew on a conch, making a shocking loud entrance, continuing without interruption for several minutes, and sounding quite grand. John Fulleman's crackling fire tape played a less important role, but combined nicely with the other sounds. (Johnson 1978)*

The score of *Inlets* was also performed as the accompaniment for Merce Cunningham's same-named choreographic work of 1977. When performed in New York at the City Center Theatre for Cunningham's performances during the early 1980s, Cage, Tudor, and Kosugi were in the orchestra pit and not visible to the audience. The sounds were very soft and pleasant, like listening to a backed-up sink.

Cage, with the assistance of two Irish folk musicians, performed *Inlets* as a concert work previous to a performance of the Cage/Cunningham version of *Roaratorio* at The Brooklyn Academy of Music in October, 1986. Cage sat in a spot-lit auditorium box on the left, with various conch shells ready on the floor. His gestures were very slight, his facial expression blank in concentration. The indeterminacy of actual events was of interest, because he might tip a shell in some direction for ¼ or ½ an inch, or for a few inches, and there would not necessarily be any resultant sound. Or, he would tip a shell, and a sound would appear a few seconds after the action. At other times, the slightest tipping of a shell would produce a quick succession of various water sounds within the shell chamber. The sounds that Cage produced were thus beyond his immediate control, yet throughout this was the quiet constancy of his disciplined, inwardly focused attention and the integrity of his personal presence.

Philip Corner characterizes Cage's musical performance persona by stating:

> *There's a certain kind of human presence, charisma, and an inner sense of*
> *pleasure and satisfaction. With Cage there is an earnestness and intensity, almost like*
> *study, working hard at doing it. (Corner 1989)*

As a musician, there was also a great clarity and precision in Cage's performances. There was no element of "playing to the audience" or making large, obvious, "theatrical" gestures. Like David Tudor, John Cage's gestures in performing music were not to call attention to himself, but merely necessary actions to be made in order to produce sound. When asked if he ever experienced "stage fright" before a musical performance, Cage replied "Of course!" When asked how he dealt with this anxiety, if he used any relaxation or meditation techniques, he said "No," and then after a pause replied, "Well, you just have to do what you have to do. That's all" (Cage 1987e).

With the exception of the percussion ensemble during the late 1930s and early 1940s, Cage was rarely a conductor of his instrumental compositions. A photograph published in the *Life* magazine issue of March 15, 1943, shows Cage conducting his now famous percussion concert at the Museum of Modern Art in New York ("Percussion Concert" 1943, 42). In the photograph, he wears the formal tails of a classical orchestra conductor. He holds a baton, and his eyes are looking down at the score. His face is seemingly expressionless, in deep concentration. A review of Cage conducting the premiere performance of *Imaginary Landscape No. 4* at Columbia University in 1951 also mentions the qualities of concentration and earnestness in his conducting style (Berger 1951).

A rare instance of Cage conducting in recent years was the performance of *Score (40 drawings by Thoreau) and 23 Parts and/or Voices; Twelve Haiku followed by a Recording of the Dawn at Stony Point, New York, Aug. 6, 1974* (1974) by students at Bucknell University on March 10, 1977. The score of *Score. . .* is made in the same manner as *Renga* (1976), previously mentioned in Chapter 6, with drawings from Thoreau's *Journals* superimposed on a time plot. The first line from the conductor's score and the first line in parts I and II appear in Fig. 40.

The conductor's score is the only part to include the complete drawing. All of the 23 individual parts consist of fragments, or black spaces, from a complete drawing. In the written instructions Cage notes that the horizontal space equals the conducted time, and that the vertical space equals the relative pitch of the voice or instrument. None of the parts have any indication for instrument or voice. Cage would later elaborate:

approximately fifty-five minutes. Cage's conducting resulted in a rather soft, unhurried, pointillistic interpretation by the students. This is not necessarily the only way that this notation could be performed, because of the very indeterminate nature of the score. However, Cage was at ease during the entire performance and did not appear to be at all dissatisfied at the conclusion.

A more recent instance of Cage conducting one of his compositions is the complete performance of *Atlas Eclipticalis* (1961–62) in simultaneous performance with *Winter Music* (1957), recorded live at the Cornish Institute, Seattle, in December, 1983, and released as a three-record set by Mode in 1985. This recording, almost three hours long, is the definitive documentation of simultaneous performance of both works; however, Cage adds in the linear notes:

> *I am glad that this record exists, though, as I have frequently stated, I, myself, do not use records. I just listen to the sounds around wherever I happen to be.* (Cage 1985a)

The recording is a soft, pointillistic music with several extended silences. It sounds very much like the Bucknell University performance of *Score. . .*, and gives further credence to Cage's undemonstrative, yet disciplined presence.

The influence of Cage's personal presence as a conductor, and the resultant interpretation by the various musicians under his direction, may be concretely seen by comparing his own conducting of *Atlas Eclipticalis* and *Winter Music* with another recording by a different conductor. *Atlas Eclipticalis* with *Winter Music* and *Cartridge Music* were performed simultaneously under the direction of Rainer Riehn, and released by Deutsche Grammophon around 1971. When conducted by Riehn, the music is a dense, continuous, rather loud and abrasive wall-of-sound, with a duration of approximately thirty minutes (Cage ca. 1971). True, the very nature of indeterminate notation will result in far different interpretations by different performers, however the orchestra under Riehn's direction is a completely opposite result from Cage's realization. Much of the negative criticism or misinterpretation by critics of Cage's work has been because reviewers rely on their experience of a specific performance, rather than first studying the score and then comparing the two. With Cage, unlike Beethoven, there can be far different results for a particular score in different performances. The comparatively insensitive realization under Riehn's direction is a prime example of a performance which might lead some reviewers (and even some academics) to state that in Cage's work, "anything goes" or that it is an exercise in "anti-music." That is not the case in either Cage's scores, nor is this the case in performances under his own direction.

Conducting is Cage's most conventional example of movement or physical-action performance. Physical-action compositions in a more experimental context would include previously mentioned works such as *Music Walk, Water Walk, Sounds of Venice, Theatre Piece, 0'00"*, selected solos from *Song Books*, and *Dialogue*. Three miscellaneous works in this genre may be used to further trace Cage's work in physical performance from the early 1960s.

Variations III (1963) was done by Cage in simultaneous performance with David Tudor (playing *Variations II*) at the Avant-Garde Festival at Judson Hall in New York in August, 1963. Ironically, the reviewer for *Newsweek* magazine would reverse the usual critical response to the previous Cage/Tudor duets by writing that Cage had "the virtuoso role" ("Is It Music?" 1963). The most complete synopsis of his performance appeared in the *New York Times* review:

> It started mildly enough as his actions in untangling cords of an electronic circuit caused a number of cracklings and explosions to come from the loudspeaker. But then he wired himself for sound, and one heard the sounds he made putting on spectacles, smoking a cigarette, flicking ash into an ashtray and writing a letter. . .
>
> The biggest sensation, the sound of Mr. Cage drinking a glass of water, enormously amplified by a loudspeaker at the back of the hall, made a definite climax. An informant left behind reported that the sound was rendered unbearable in its intensity because Mr. Cage did his drinking while a cord containing a microphone was wrapped around his throat.
>
> Many left the hall because the extent of the amplification hurt the eardrums. But those who remained for the last mammoth gurgle, it is said, gave Mr. Cage and his partner, David Tudor, a standing ovation. . .
>
> He [Cage] did all these things in a dead–pan manner. . . (Parmenter 1963)

It will be noticed that Cage's performance of *Variations III* is similar to *0'00"*.

The score of *Variations III* is similar to *Theatre Piece* and *0'00"* in that all three pieces require the performer to make a disciplined action or actions. *Variations III* consists of two transparent sheets, each measuring 8½ by 11 inches. One sheet is blank. The other has 42 circles, each with the circumference of a United States 25¢ piece. One is to use the transparencies according to the short written instruction. In brief, the instruction tells the performer to cut up the transparency with circles into 42 squares, then to drop each circle onto a piece of typing-sized paper, removing all circles that do not overlap with at least one other circle. Over this is placed the blank transparency, for the very practical reason of keeping the cut-outs in place. This is then to be read in the following manner:

> Starting with any circle, observe the number of circles which overlap it. Make an action or actions having the corresponding number of interpenetrating variables (1 + n). This done, move on to any one of the overlapping circles, again observing the number of interpenetrations, performing a suitable action or actions, and so on.

Some or all of one's obligation may be performed through ambient circum-
stances (environmental changes) by simply noticing or responding to them. (Cage
1963a)

An example of one possible result in dropping circles onto a sheet of
paper appears in Fig. 42. There is no information to suggest that this overlay
appears like the one that Cage used. It does, however, follow the score
instructions. For illustrative purposes, Fig. 42 includes all 42 circles, that is, if
a circle fell off the paper, it was redropped until it hit. There is no mention in
the score to do this. Five of the circles, indicated with an X, would be removed
from the paper as they do not overlap with any other circle, and hence would
not be operable for making a performance. The number of actions indicated
by overlapping circles have been included in this overlay example. This
brings up the question of how to use numbers with actions. For instance, is

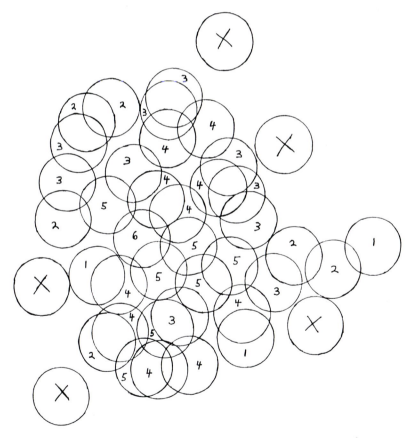

Fig. 42.   An example of *Variations III*, showing a superimposition of score materials
with added number of actions; © 1963 Henmar Press Inc.

putting on and taking off a pair of contact-miked spectacles one action or two actions (putting on and taking off), or three actions (putting on, using for sight, then taking off), or four actions (reaching for, picking up, putting on, taking off), and so on. It is this very perplexing question of how to number and hence to analyze an action or actions, that later led Cage to be dissatisfied with *Variations III* for the very reason that it forced counting (Kirby and Schechner 1965, 65).

Cage's three unpublished notes for *Variations III* provide a glimpse into both his own variety of actions, as well as his personal thinking behind the score and performance. The first piece is a typed, conventional free-verse poem about two influential teachers during the 1930s — Galka Scheyer, for exposure to the paintings of Klee, Kandinsky, Jawlensky, and Feininger; and Mark Tobey, for learning "to see the world around me." The poem concludes:

> There are — let us say — two ways of hearing. One has to do
> with hearing sounds with a work of art.
> The other has to do with keeping ones ears
> open during ones daily experiences.
> This second way is in my opinion the more
> useful. Certainly one can do it more often.
> > (Cage 1963b)

This poem, apparently, was one of the possible choices for an action in performance.

The second piece is the list titled "THINGS I CAN DO," which consists of 28 actions, including:

> Answer questions
> Smoke
> Write
> Walk back and forth
> Think
> Put on or take off my glasses
> Drink water
> Listen (to David [Tudor])
> > (to ambient sounds)
> Do a timed action (stop–watch)
> Do a spaced action (choreography)
> Speak after putting something in code
> Ask questions
> Talk (see other sheet)
> > (Cage 1963b)

The "other sheet" that Cage refers to is unclear, but may mean the free-verse poem, or the third piece of paper discussed below.

The third piece is a collection of various philosophical reflections written in pencil, and scattered about the page in a non-linear arrangement.

An abridged reading of these statements could appear as:

> *the mind not as "me" but as an instrument*
>
> *Our insts. [instruments] are becoming like tools*
> > *a knife is a tool*
> > *a the [i.e. a noun or object] is an inst. [instrument]*
> > *electronics?*
>
> *imitation of nature*
> > *= art follows science in a kind of "folk" way*
>
> *composition? Interpenetration [in] any direction*
>
> *time[:] the function of × quantities in chance*
> > *operation + indeterminacy*
>
> *all is vibratory, i.e. musical — mikes to hear*
> > *what is small → inaudible*
>
> *think of electronics in terms of what we know,*
> > *we use it for reproduction instead of revelation*
>
> *mystery of "outer world," e.g. tech. sc. [technological sciences]*
>
> *as knowledge increases, possibilities diminish*
>
> *[mystery] of "inner world" feelings, drama*
>
> *as mystery increases[,] so does fluency*
>
> *sober + quiet the mind thus:*
> > *conversation with others*
> > > *"   " ourselves*
>
> *cues + timelessness + theatre*
>
> *my notion of "cue" = the actions of others give me*
> > *less obligation to act myself*
>
> *no parameters*
>
> *out of chaos or the most necessary in any direction*

(Cage 1963b)

What is perhaps most extraordinary with Cage's performance notes to *Variations III* is the combination of philosophical content with mundane physical actions. The list of physical actions are practical, almost autobiographical events which Cage could enact with relative ease. What is especially telling is the sheet of random reflections, where Cage refers to himself/the performer as a tool or instrument in objective, egoless terms; and then gives credence to the "inner world" of subjective emotions — an "interpenetration" of art and life to make a seamless process involving "no parameters." Cage's greatest concern with this piece is the unforeseen "mystery" integral with indeterminacy — the indeterminacy that exists in both the score as well as in everyday life. The complexity of the score, and the analysis then required to make simple everyday actions, however, still results in a work of art. Although the ideal was "no parameters," the discipline involved in realizing the score ultimately becomes a hinderance to unbounded activity.

The freedom from constraints, which Cage only partly fulfilled in *Variations III*, would be further addressed in *Variations VIII* (1967). Cage recalls:

> *You perform without having anything to do, with no proper equipment. The first time was at Skowheggan, in Maine, when Merce and I thought we should go up there for a vacation when we didn't have to perform. And so we rented a car and drove up, and the closer we got, the more advertisements there were of a performance that we were going to give. We had nothing with us to do, and so that was the birth of* Variations VIII *— with what you do when you don't have any material to do anything. It was very difficult. This was in May, 1967. (Cage 1990a)*

The score for *Variations VIII* was written and published in 1978, dedicated to Heinz-Klaus Metzger and Rainer Riehn, who wanted to perform a new Cage score in Germany. Cage recalls that notating the previously unwritten score was "like killing two birds with one stone — it was practical" (Cage 1990a). The score includes the history of the piece as "accept invitation to a distant place" with "no music/no recordings." The central box of text on the single page reads: "What am I to do? Nothing. No concert? No lecture? Nothing." The original performance is noted as being prepared by exploring "the building for machines, movable or not: *plug them in (and turn them off)* whether they work or not." The lower right-hand corner of the page concludes with Cage's self-documentation of his performance:

> *I'd brought no music, no recordings. Spent sleepless night. In the morning found sounds with the microphones of the recorders by moving them in the air in relation to the loudspeakers (that also came in with them). (Feedback.) Moving across the air, the floor, the wall. Scanning (silent performance). Keith McGary arrived unexpectedly and offered to perform with me. Sound board of piano was effective. That evening we performed for one hour and a half without stopping. (Cage 1978)*

Cage would later perform *Variations VIII* in simultaneous performance with *String Piece* by Alison Knowles at The Museum of Contemporary Art in Chicago on October 23, 1967. Knowles recalls:

> *Hundreds of people came, first to a bar adjacent to the Museum, and then they went to the opening. And people had a great deal to drink, but we did the performance anyway. We did some nice work this night, in spite of it all.*
> *John sat on the stage tracing and cutting out mushroom silhouettes, and then pinned them against the back wall. While John was doing that, I was doing* String Piece *within the audience, which was to tie a single figure on the stage — John was over to the side doing the tracing — and one of the people who had driven the* Big Book *[a 1964 work by Knowles exhibited at the opening] from Canada was placed in the center of the stage, and I tied him in with the environment for, I'd say, about half an hour. (Knowles 1989)*

Knowles no longer recalls whether the scissors that Cage used had contact microphones attached or not, nor does Cage recall that performance, but given the precedence of similar works such as *0'00"* and *Variations III*, it is quite possible.

One final stray work of action/music performance is *Sound Anonymously Received* (1969). There is no score. Cage would recall:

> *That was done at the University of California at Davis. I had a box for my mail at the University, and once there was a whistle in it, so I call that* Sound Anonymously Received *because I didn't know who sent it or what it was for. I had been asked to make a piece of music, and I decided to blow the whistle once as long as I could, for the situation where they wanted some music. (Cage 1990a)*

Whether or not Cage had the intention of making *Sound Anonymously Received* an example of Zen, his performance is similar to the story of Kakua. Kakua went from Japan to China to study Zen (Ch'an) Buddhism. On his return, the emperor wanted him to preach Zen for his enlightenment:

> *Kakua stood before the emperor in silence. He then produced a flute from the folds of his robe, and blew one short note. Bowing politely, he disappeared. (Reps n.d., 60–61)*

John Cage is most known, however, as a vocal performer, primarily as a lecturer and poetry reader. Several of these performances have been documented with audio recordings. In one very rare instance, he has also been an actor.

Cage's verbal performances began during childhood. The Pianologues, previously mentioned, included talking in addition to playing the piano. However, while Cage and other children performed in costume, they were not necessarily being "actors" in the sense of being a character in a play. Children of his generation also had to regularly memorize and recite poetry or famous works (such as poems by Longfellow or Lincoln's Gettysburg Address) in school (Faxon 1913). Cage has not commented on reciting poetry in school but dates his earliest work in verbal performance with the Boy Scouts's radio show he produced when he was about fifteen years old. He recalled:

> *I did have a radio program — have you read that story? [spoken in the recording* Indeterminacy *(1959a) and published in* A Year from Monday *(1967, 132)] — and I did a good deal of piano playing on that. I got any scout who played anything. I was constantly trying to find people who could play, something to fill the hour.*
>
> *This was an hour show, every week, while I was in High School. It was on KNX, and it was four to five o'clock on Fridays in Los Angeles, and the year was about 1926–27. It began with a ten-minute talk by an older person. I thought I was going to be a minister, and on the radio program I always had some minister or rabbi or someone from some religious organization, who would give a ten-minute talk at the beginning of the hour, a kind of inspirational character.*

Then it involved correspondence from listeners — not telephone calls the way they do now, but the exchange of letters — and miscellaneous filler-material, like jokes or stories, games, someone describing some kind of game that one might play. And then in between that verbal material would be musical interludes. The performances of it might be a trombonist or a clarinetist, or a violinist and a pianist. I was mostly the pianist, or sometimes I played the accompaniments for the other musicians. We did have rehearsal for this [the musical portions]. I found the other boys on the telephone. And, I was the announcer.

This was on about two years. Only the radio sponsored it, because the Boy Scouts refused to, and they refused to cooperate as an organization. I went to the Boy Scouts's office and said that KNX was willing to have a Boy Scout program, and would they cooperate with it? They said no, but that it was alright to do it. Then when it became popular they took it over, and then it stopped after two weeks, because they used it to advertise themselves.

The radio was fairly fascinating to us at the time. It was in its infancy. And my father wasn't given credit for it, but he invented the first radio to be plugged into the electric light system. Listening to the radio programming at that time must have interested me, otherwise I wouldn't have thought of having a radio program.

I think as a child one thinks of all sorts of things to do — at least I did — such as publishing a newspaper for children. I remember having some kind of children's newspaper that I could count the characters, you know, type it all up — but the idea of having a radio program was more interesting, I think, to more people. (Cage 1987e)

During High School Cage was also involved in the Oratory Club, winning the Southern California Oratorical Contest at the Hollywood Bowl in 1927. His winning speech, "Other People Think," is the earliest of his juvenile writings to be published (in Kostelanetz 1970, 45–49). "Other People Think" is concerned with relations between the United States and Latin American countries, in which he makes the still relevant comment that "Latin American is a Land of the future."

Cage, who graduated valedictorian, was the class commencement speaker for the class of 1928 from Los Angeles High School. A contemporary would later recall:

John was being graduated from Los Angeles High School; I had been graduated six months previously. He was to be a graduation speaker. In a class of more than five hundred, he was notably among the brilliant and promising. He was practicing his talk; I was his audience.

His subject was something like "Eating Flowers." Neither of us knew anything about mushrooms in those days, but we liked to think we were exotic, or maybe the word for what we hoped we were was avant-garde. But I had doubts about flower eating as a commencement topic.

"Everybody will think I mean more than I do," John countered, laughing. At least that's what I remember. I think I felt it amused him to imagine people would take seriously what he didn't intend to take seriously. . . I think now his object was indeed serious, that he wanted people to listen to something. To listen really. (Hendrick 1972)

Cage entered Pomona College in the fall of 1928 with the objective of studying for the ministry. While at Pomona he became influenced by Gertrude Stein's writings and decided he was to be a writer. He left college after his second year and traveled in Europe studying piano and architecture, writing poetry and painting. In 1931 he returned to California and took a job as a gardener in a Santa Monica auto court. To supplement his income Cage enlisted a group of women from the Santa Monica area together for a subscription series of lectures on modern art (Tomkins 1968, 78–81). While none of these early lectures survive, it is significant that Cage, as a young adult, first turned to lectures rather than music in order to make a living.

Cage's first adult lecture — "The Future of Music: Credo" (in Cage 1961, 3–6) — was originally written and delivered in 1937 because he had been asked to explain then-contemporary trends in music theory, composition, and new instruments and technology (Cage 1987e). The vast majority of his literary writings since the late 1940s are performance pieces, including lectures, diaries, and poetry. This study can not be comprehensive with this large amount of material, however a few selected examples will serve as representative from this genre.

Very little study has been done of Cage's literary output as yet. Marjorie Perloff notes how Cage's first mature lectures (from 1949) and stories (from the 1950s) are striking in "their literal empiricism, their stubborn and insistent literalness," an "oddly unemotional" situation poised "between sense and non-sense" (Perloff 1981, 311–316). In later essays, she provides some narrative and philosophical exegesis of later works such as "Where Are We Eating? and What Are We Eating?" (Cage 1979a, 79–97) and the radio piece *Roaratorio* (Cage 1985b), attempting to include performance concepts into a primarily literary methodology (Perloff 1982, 4–16; and 1989, 193–228). Arthur Sabatini has written of Cage's literary writings as being a "silent performance," in that "Cage creates conditions which undermine, or challenge the reader" through spatial arrangement on the page and the use of various typographies. In the process, this supplements "the inherent significations of postmodern writing . . . through the introduction of Duchampian aesthetics" by using texts as found-objects through chance procedures (Sabatini 1989, 74–96).

Both Perloff and Sabatini make for engaging reading, however neither seem to directly discuss the performance aspect of Cage's literature. Perloff, for instance, does not write much about actual performance, but is more concerned with general aesthetics in contemporary art. Similarly, Sabatini becomes involved in literary theory, and while it is a charming term to call much of Cage's literature a "silent performance," this is not unique to Cage. All reading, when not spoken aloud, is a silent performance (an active *doing*, including eye movements and neurological activity in the brain).

The first of John Cage's lectures that could be said to be a "performance piece" (apart from the traditional aspects of conventional vocal delivery) is the 1954 lecture "45' For A Speaker" (in Cage 1961, 146–192). It may be read aloud simultaneously with *34'46.776" for a Pianist* or *31'57.9864" for a Pianist* (both 1954), as well as with *26'1.1499" for a String Player* (1955) and/or *27'10.554" for a Percussionist* (1956). An example from "45' For A Speaker" appears in Fig. 43.

Each line takes two seconds to speak. Each page equals one minute. Each minute, each page, also includes unspoken time references for performance (at the left margin), and various auxiliary vocal sounds and physical gestures (at the right margin). Cage would perform this lecture on occasion through the mid-1960s. A review of Cage's solo performance, at Louisiana State University in January, 1964, would note: "It was one of the most unique and perplexing compositions for the whole human body that will probably ever be seen or heard on this campus" ("Cage Speech Is Termed 'Astounding' " 1964).

"45' For A Speaker" has a generic title, for it is literally forty-five minutes for a speaker. In this lecture, Cage tells about his composition methods, and Zen-influenced philosophy and aesthetics. The use of auxiliary vocal sounds and physical gestures may reflect the influence of Artaud in being responsive to a body-based, "total theatre" style of presentation. The structure of having each line take a maximum of two seconds may be an application of Charles Olson's "projective verse," where one writes poetry according to the use of the breath in order to determine line lengths (Olson 1966, 15). Cage knew Olson from Black Mountain College, but when asked if he was using Olson's idea, he replied that he did not really understand what Olson meant at the time, but that he liked the idea now (Cage 1988b). Rather, Cage's lectures from the late 1940s and early 1950s were made analogously to his music compositions. He would later explain:

> When M. C. Richards asked me why I didn't one day give a conventional informative lecture, adding that that would be the most shocking thing I could do, I said "I don't give these lectures to surprise people, but out of a need for poetry."
>
> As I see it, poetry is not prose simply because poetry is in one way or another formalized. It is not poetry by reason of its content or ambiguity but by reason of its allowing musical elements (time, sound) to be introduced into the world of words. Thus, traditionally, information no matter how stuffy (e.g. the sutras and shastras of India) was transmitted in poetry. It was easier to grasp that way. (Cage 1961, x)

These early lectures, written as music, describe methods of chance composition techniques, his basic aesthetics, and concepts from Zen. They are informational, but in an unconventional way. Thoughts are not developed and expounded upon, as in a linear progression of ideas, but are presented in

12'00" It is the continuity of a
piece of music.
Continuity *today*
when it is necessary.

A fugue is a more complicated game; but
10" it can be broken up by a single sound,
say, from a fire engine.

(Cough)

20"

Now

(Laugh)

30"   getting sleepy & so on.
Very frequently no one knows that
contemporary music is or could be
art.
He simply thinks it was irritating.   (Clap)
Irritating one way or another
40" that is to say
keeping us from ossifying.
It may be objected that from this point
of view anything goes. Actually
anything *does* go,——but only when
nothing is taken as the basis. In an utter emptiness
50" anything can take place.

The feeling we are

getting nowhere

Fig. 43. A page from "45' For A Speaker" (1954), as published in *Silence* (Cage 1961, 160). Reproduced courtesy of the University Press of New England.

fragments. Thus, Cage will begin to describe chance procedures employed for a specific work, then go into Zen, talk of theatre, and go on to another related or unrelated topic. As "45' For A Speaker" goes on, various topics reappear without any logical preparation. The result is that while the style of writing and presentation is not logically sequential as cause and effect, the ideas mentioned throughout gain an evocatively resonant and immediate quality. Silences allow for the listener to make unexpected self-reflections on the spoken material, as well as providing opportunities to listen to the ambient sounds of the surrounding environment. We are invited to share, however vicariously, in the composer's experience of the world, and rather than simply "soaking in information" as with a conventional lecture, we are also allowed to passively and silently participate through our own personal thoughts as they may occur. The urgent, persuasive quality of such lectures is in part from Cage's "insistent literalness," but also from the liminal, inbetwixt and inbetween occasions that provide the listener (or reader) to make his/her own personal discoveries and reflections.

Cage's vocal style of the 1950s is documented in the 1959 Folkways four-sided recording *Indeterminacy*. This was first given in 1958 at the Brussels World's Fair and consisted of thirty stories without accompaniment, each lasting one minute. In the spring of 1959 Cage was asked to lecture at Columbia University and wrote another sixty stories. Simultaneous accompaniment was performed by David Tudor playing the solo piano part from the *Concert for Piano and Orchestra* with radios as auxiliary noises (Cage 1961, 260). The ninety-minute version is the one recorded, with the inclusion of *Fontana Mix* tapes (Cage 1959a).

The recording exists as a separate version from the printed stories. Fifty-six stories are published as "Indeterminacy" in *Silence* (Cage 1961, 261–273); an additional thirty-nine stories are published interspersed among other writings in *A Year from Monday* (Cage 1967, 20; 25; 34–35; 49; 69; 72; 84; 88; 111; 132; and 162). Thirty of the *Indeterminacy* stories are also included in "How To Pass, Kick, Fall, And Run," which consists of thirty-six one-minute stories read as the accompaniment for Merce Cunningham's same-named choreographic work in 1965 (Cage 1967, 133–140). David Vaughan recalls that Cage performed "How to Pass . . ." sitting at a table on stage left, speaking into a microphone, and occasionally taking sips of champagne (Vaughan 1989). Not all of the stories on the phonograph record are published, and several of the published stories are not on the phonograph record. Thus, while there are several versions of "Indeterminacy," this work does not exist as a fixed or final object.

The stories in the *Indeterminacy* recording consist of autobiographical anecdotes about his childhood, family, friends, studying music and philosophy, composition, and retellings from reading. Three of the published stories, as found on the recording, give an example of the overall unconnected narrative sequence:

> *I was surprised when I came into Mother's room in the nursing home to see that the TV set was on. The program was teenagers dancing to rock–and–roll. I asked Mother how she liked the new music. She said, "Oh, I'm not fussy about music." Then, brightening up, she went on, "You're not fussy about music either." (Cage 1967, 111)*
>
> *One day down at Black Mountain College, David Tudor was eating his lunch. A student came over to his table and began asking him questions. David Tudor kept on eating his lunch. The student kept on asking questions. Finally David Tudor looked at him and said, "If you don't know, why do you ask?" (Cage 1961, 266)*
>
> *There was an international conference of philosophers in Hawaii on the subject of reality. For three days Daisetz Suzuki said nothing. Finally the chairman turned to him and asked, "Dr. Suzuki, would you say this table around which we are sitting is real?" Suzuki raised his head and said Yes. The chairman asked in what sense Suzuki thought the table was real. Suzuki said, "In every sense." (Cage 1967, 35)*

These are examples of shorter stories. In order for a shorter story to last one minute, Cage made improvised (non-predetermined) silences in between words or phrases. Other stories are rather long, and are spoken very fast. Whether speaking a few words and having silence, or then speaking very fast, Cage's performance makes for unexpected breaks in the text, or runs together otherwise separate sentences into a rush of information.

In *Indeterminacy*, as with all his lectures and poetry readings, Cage is not being an "actor," but is, rather, a "nonmatrixed performer" who, unlike an actor, is not in a matrix of "pretended or represented character, situation, place, and time" (Kirby 1987, 4). He speaks as himself rather than as someone else. There is only one story during the entire recording where Cage does an impersonation, speaking in a comic Japanese old-man accent. In this story Cage gives the "history" of haiku by reciting three poems of a sad bird on a willow tree. The first is "vely krassicar" (very classical), the second "nineteenth centuly" (century), and the third is "vely contempolaly" (contemporary). The humor in this story, however, is not so much in Cage's impersonation as in the fact that all three "different" examples of haiku are, with the minor variation of an excluded or added word, essentially the same work.

Cage's voice on the *Indeterminacy* album seems very reminiscent of the vocal quality of the actor Vincent Price. Both Cage and Price have a somewhat nasal tone, are soft-spoken, and have a gentleness tempered with a fulsome sense of humor. Both also are able to give very subtle inflections to words that result in the listener interpreting the material in several ways. Mr. Price is most popularly known for his B-movie horror roles. The comparison of the two is concretely shown in Cage's most uncharacteristic vocal performance, as an actor in Igor Stravinsky's *L'Histore du soldat* ("The Soldier's Tale").

L'Histore du soldat (1918) was performed under the direction of Lucas Foss at Philharmonic Hall in New York on July 15, 1966. For the three vocalists, three American composers were chosen — Aaron Copland was the narrator, Elliott Carter was the soldier, and John Cage was the devil. The *New York Post* review would note that they wore "white jackets, black bow ties and pants" (Harrison 1966). The *New York Times* provides the most complete description of the event:

> It could not have been merely random chance to have chosen Mr. Cage to portray the devil in this little morality play. Much can be read into the casting, for Mr. Cage's name is anathema in academic circles. One does not wish to read more meaning into the circumstances, but it must be noted that Mr. Cage stole the show.
> He devoured his part, breathing fire and smoke and coloring his lines as the old man and then as the old woman with great intensity. It was Bela Lugosi cum Boris Karloff, and the audience loved it.
> Mr. Carter, soft-spoken, gentle and shy, was the perfect soldier. Duped at every turn, taken in completely by Mr. Cage, he was innocently pathetic.
> Mr. Copland's dry, rasping nasality as the sly narrator made the trio complete. The three composers traded lines with rhythmic precision such as they might have demanded of a percussion section. In all, it was a lesson in dramatic recitation, and a delight to hear. (Klein 1966)

(It is interesting to speculate what would have happened if Cage, like Oscar Levant, had pursued a career as a character actor in addition to his musical activities. Cage almost did become a film actor when he was in Italy in 1959. Federico Fellini, who saw Cage on the television quiz program *Lascia o Raddoppia*, offered him a part in the film *La Dolce Vita*, but Cage turned down the offer [Tomkins 1968, 133].)

The more recent style of Cage's vocal performance during the last twenty years was based upon song rather than speech. He recalls his first experiences as a singer:

> When I was in the sixth grade, I wanted to join the Glee Club in grammar school, and they said I couldn't join until they had tested my voice; and when they tested it, they said "You don't have a voice." And so I actually believed that until I was thirty-five years old, that it was improper for me to sing. Then for one of Merce's dances [Experiences (1945)] I made a song which I could sing, I thought, and I sang it so that the audience couldn't see who was singing it. And afterward, Alan Hovaness, the composer, came back stage and asked who had sung this song. And I said why do you want to know? And he said "I want that voice in my next opera." So then I told him! (Cage 1987e)

Cage's singing in recent years has been documented with a recording from *Empty Words*. *Empty Words*, written in 1974–75, is in four parts, each made by *I Ching* chance determinations to find words, phrases, syllables, and letters from Henry David Thoreau's *Journals*. Cage read *Empty Words Part III* several times during the latter 1970s. A *New York Times* review of a performance at the Gotham Bookmart characterizes him performing this piece "in a manner almost to the point of inaudibility . . . it was received enthusiastically by the audience" ("'Little' Magazine Gets a Big Boost at Gotham Mart" 1976). Of a later New York performance, with Grete Sultan playing *Etudes Australes* (1974–75) for piano, at Town Hall, the reviewer would note:

> *Mr. Cage and Miss Sultan are formidable stage personalities. However one construed their particular activities, Saturday's experience of watching and listening was unified by the gentle composure of their presence, and the static, spacious sense of being it seemed to embody. (Horowitz 1977)*

The Town Hall concert was similar to the one I attended at Bucknell University in March, 1977. Sultan began the concert with the first eight *Etudes Australes.* Cage then read from *Empty Words Part III,* and Sultan concluded the evening with the next five pieces in the *Etudes Australes* series. (Sultan's performance of the complete piano work, recorded in 1978 and 1982, was issued as a four-record set by Wergo in 1987.) At Bucknell, Cage sat at a small table at the front of the stage at the right-side of the audience. The stage was darkened to allow the projection of slides made from drawings in Thoreau's *Journals.* He had a small desk lamp and used a microphone close to his mouth. He spoke very, very softly, chanting a very slight melodic line, with several extended silences. His performance lasted approximately fifty minutes, and about half the audience walked out during much of the reading. During the entire time, he did not give any perceptible notice of the negative audience reaction, but concentrated on reading/singing the text.

Cage's performance of an excerpt from *Empty Words Part III* was again done recently in New York, in a concert of spoken music organized by the S.E.M. Ensemble at the Paula Cooper Gallery on February 6, 1990. On this occasion Cage used a section from the text and sang an improvised chant which was very reminiscent of the melodic line in his earlier song *She Is Asleep* (1943). This performance was approximately twenty-two minutes. It was done, as is usual, sitting at a table with a small desk lamp and a microphone. No slides were shown on this particular occasion. The respect shown by the audience for Cage was striking. There were many extended silences throughout the performance, during which the audience sat very quietly, not trying to add any of their own sounds to the environment. The conclusion consisted of several minutes of silence. Cage sat very quietly looking at the paper and referring to the watch in front of him on the table. The end of his performance was signaled by gathering up the pages and looking up at the assembly.

Empty Words Part IV was first performed at the Naropa Institute in Boulder, Colorado on August 8, 1974. The performance is described as follows:

> Slide projections of drawings appeared and disappeared as John Cage, sitting at a table, [his] back to the audience, his text lit by a small lamp, performed the sounds of vowels, consonants and silences of his piece. Some of the audience filled in the silences with sounds ranging from guitar playing and bird whistles, to catcalls and screams. Through it all Cage managed a fierce concentration on his piece. (Waldman and Webb 1978, 217)

The extremely volatile and hostile audience reaction on this occasion may have been prompted by the unconventional text, but may also have been a misreading of Cage's sitting with his back to the audience as indicative of an antagonistic disregard. (This was not in character.) There followed a question and answer period, with Cage defending himself by saying "This isn't the first time people have tried to make me appear as a fool" (Waldman and Webb 1978, 217).

One questioner asked about a particularly relevant and often misunderstood aspect in Cage's aesthetics:

> Q: Haven't you said that you want to incorporate outside noises into your work?
>
> J.C.: I haven't said that, I've said that contemporary music should be open to the sounds outside it. I just said that the sounds of the traffic entered very beautifully, but the self-expressive sounds of people making foolishness and stupidity and catcalls are not beautiful and they aren't beautiful in other circumstances either. (Waldman and Webb 1987, 220)

Aside from the lack of etiquette, this specific audience seemed to make the mistake that because Cage uses chance and silence, that "anything goes." Chance, however, is Cage's method to avoid self-expression, and silence is a way of allowing unintentionality to enter into the work. Paradoxically, while Cage tried to avoid personal taste, likes and dislikes, he still had very definite ideas of what he wanted to achieve. And, while chance procedures are a model of anarchy, Cage had very high ideals that society and the individual be involved not in foolish or destructive activities, but in responsive, disciplined actions with the world we live in.

A recording of a complete performance of *Empty Words Part IV* was made at Cologne, Germany, on September 4, 1984, and released as a two-record set by Michael F. Bauer in 1987. The entire performance is two-and-a-half hours. Cage's rendition is again an improvised chant, reminiscent of *She Is Asleep* (Cage 1987a).

The published text of *Empty Words* (in Cage 1979a, 11–77) is, according to the composer, a "transition from language to music" (Cage 1979a, 65).

Language is not used for referential, intellectual meaning, but purely as sound. The pages include selected drawings from Thoreau's *Journals*, which have no contentual reference to the chance-determined text. The typography of words, phrases, syllables, and letters is spatially arranged on the page, again according to chance procedures. The first page from *Empty Words Part IV* appears in Fig. 44. The published version of *Empty Words*, however, is a primarily literary work that *may* by performed, rather than a specifically designated performance score. There are no explicit time indications for silences or durations of sounds other than what the individual reader might infer from space equal to time.

An example of notation used by Cage for actual performance appears in Fig. 45. This is a typed version of a manuscript page that appears as an illustration in the 1987 *Empty Words Part IV* recording. The original is on blue-lined yellow paper in blue ink. The horizontal lines of the original manuscript paper are retained in the typed version, for this shows the time — the top half of a space equals one second, the bottom half shows the next second, etc. Not shown in either the published or unpublished version are any notations of tonality or dynamics. Cage almost always performed this very softly, in a chanting style. Also not notated are the actual sounds of the vowels or consonants. For example, when listening to the recording, "A" is pronounced "ah," and a "T" is sung as "Tah" for a duration of one to almost three seconds (Cage 1987a).

Cage's voice changed in his elder years. Comparing his vocal quality in *Indeterminacy* from 1959 with *Empty Words* some thirty years later, he became softer, more mellow. He no longer had the nasal quality of thirty years before. The voice acquired a somewhat frail quality, with a less variable range of dynamics but with a greater tonal range. Giving up cigarette smoking in the early 1970s probably helped Cage to use his voice in a more subtle and seemingly effortlessly expressive and evocative manner. It was not uncommon for him to read for ninety or more minutes without once having to clear his throat or take a sip of water. When speaking, either in a public reading or in private conversation, he did not use any mimicry in voice or gesture. There was a great sense of concentration and purpose in his delivery.

Cage was always disparaging about his vocal capabilities when I talked with him, but some of his later vocal expertise (and endurance) can be attributed to his informal voice lessons with the virtuoso singer Joan La Barbara. La Barbara also disparages the effect/influence of these lessons during the mid- to late-1970s/early 1980s, but comments:

> *I showed him the warm-ups I do before I sing, which consists of neck relaxation; the shoulders; the back; and then the tongue. If you do these exercises you*

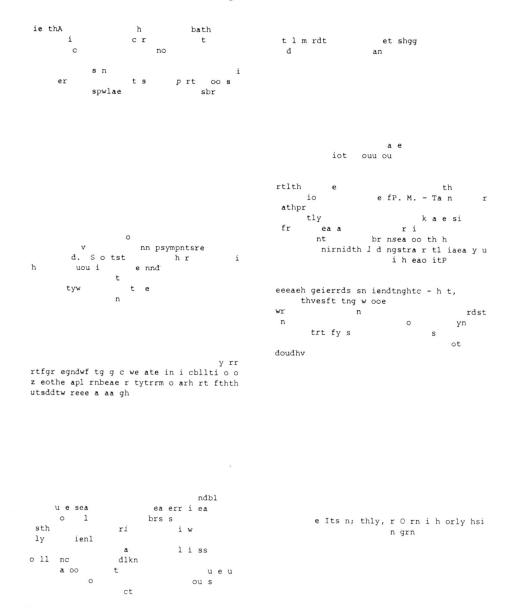

Fig. 44.   The first page from the published version of *Empty Words, Part IV* (in Cage 1979a, 66). Reproduced courtesy of the University Press of New England.

literally bring blood up to the vocal chords. The breathing exercises increase capacity.
The back exercises are to strengthen the lower back, and then to actually match inhale to exhale, portion the amount of air depending on the amount of air required for the phrases you have to carry. The warm-ups I do are silent, but they prepare the whole body to do what you have to do. (La Barbara 1993)

0'00"		41" i		
	52"	43"		
	55" o	46" l		
	57"	r		
		50"		
13" i	1'03" n	53" t		
1	o	s		
th	07"	57"		
A		2'00" b		
21"		rt		
24"		04"		
26"		07" oo		
29" b		s	3'00"	
a		11"		
th		14" sp		
35"		wl		
38" i		a		
40"		l		4'00"
43" c	31" s	22"		
r	n			
47"	35"			
50" t		28" sbr		
		30"		

Fig. 45. John Cage's performance version of the beginning of *Empty Words, Part IV*, typed from a photographed manuscript page (in Cage 1987a).

The change in vocal delivery, and its influence on his literary writing, was to become central to the composition and performance of works such as *Empty Words*, and much of his literary writing until his death. The increasing disinterest in language in writing, with reference to vocal lessons to maximize the breath, was made explicit by Cage in a 1992 interview:

To me it seemed to be that as I got closer to music, the breath became more important. When I was with language, what was important was not so much my breath as it was a phrase, or getting from a beginning to an ending. For instance, a stanza was important. When the breath begins to take over — when it begins to be more music than literature — such things as paragraphs, sentences, and what–not are not as important as breathing, it seemed to me. (Smith 1992, 51)

Apart from *Empty Words*, Cage's most distinctive verbal works in his later years were readings of mesostic poetry. The writing of mesostic verse is influenced by the work of the poet Jackson Mac Low (Cage 1973, ii). An example of one of Mac Low's works is *Stanzas for Iris Lezak*, written in 1960, which is a series of chance poems based on an acrostic structure of single words or word-strings made from various source texts (Mac Low 1972). Cage's mesostics are similar, but are spelled down the middle rather than at the beginning of a line. Three examples — *Roaratorio* (1979), *An Alphabet* (1982), and *I–VI* (1988–89) — exemplify Cage's final major vocal/literary compositional out-put.

Roaratorio, An Irish Circus on Finnegans Wake is Cage's example of a musicircus made for his own performance. Made as a Hörspiel ("Ear-play") for WDR in Cologne, Germany, it was first broadcast on October 22, 1979 (Cage 1985b, 71). It is his major work for radio since *The City Wears a Slouch Hat* in 1942, and reveals Cage's mature ideas for the radio medium in a theatre context.

The basis of *Roaratorio* is the 1979 composition ⎯⎯⎯⎯⎯⎯⎯⎯⎯ (title of composi-tion)' (article) (adjective) *CIRCUS ON* ⎯⎯⎯⎯⎯⎯⎯ (title of book)', which consists of a series of detailed instructions to make a book into a performance piece. In brief, the instructions state that one first chooses a book, and then using the name of the author and/or title of the book, writes a series of mesostics made from each page of the source text. Reading through the text, one finds "the first word in the book that contains the first letter of the row [mesostic line] that is not followed in the same word by the second letter of the row" (Cage 1979b). Having gone through the entire book according to the instructions, one then makes a vocal recording of this text "using speech, song, chant, or sprechstimme, or a mixture or combination of these." This then becomes a visual text (on paper) and temporal document (on tape) to determine the other parameters of performance.

After having made the text, one then makes a list of places and sounds mentioned in the source book, and collects as many recordings as possible. These recordings are then superimposed to "make a chance determined total program for each having at least twice as much silence as music," which are then reduced to one tape, with the result that "the material is then in a plurality of forms" (Cage 1979b).

To make the spoken text, Cage chose to use the name James Joyce throughout. A list of 1083 places mentioned in *Finnegans Wake* were recorded from between 30 seconds to five minutes; a list of 1210 sounds mentioned in Joyce's text (such as thunderclaps, earthquake sounds, laughing and crying, farts, musical instruments, bells, guns, animals, birds, and water) were also included (Cage 1985b, 147). In addition, Irish musicians were employed to make vocal and instrumental performances of traditional Irish folk music during the hour-long radio musicircus.

Roaratorio, like the typical live-performance musicircus, is a varient mix of many different musics, however the visual element is absent. The central focus is in listening to Cage's speaking/singing his mesostic text, and in that sense it is a personal work as well as being a composition that incorporates internationally inclusive pluralities. Cage used his voice in all the possibilities suggested in his basic score instructions, and while his voice is often obscured by the simultaneous place, nature sounds, and Irish folk music, what finally emerges is a personal performance that, paradoxically, was made by impersonal, rule-bound procedures. *Roaratorio* won the Karl-Sczucka Prize in 1979, being cited as an example "in which the listener is able at will to experience and at the same time is exposed to sounds, which the radio, normally restricted to the mediation of one-dimensional information, cannot normally offer" (Cage 1985b, 153).

Norman O. Brown has criticised Cage's mesostic versification of *Finnegans Wake* as "getting rid of the syntax/getting rid of the cadence/getting rid of the puns" (Brown 1989, 110), and faults Cage on the basis of Nietzsche's Dionysian/Apollonian duality, in that . . .

Chance operations are an Apollonian procedure
a perfectly sober procedure
the Apollonian "I" remains in control
          (Brown 1989, 109)

and that

Chance operations avoid real uncertainty
the negative capability of being in uncertainties,
    mysteries[,] doubts, and
darkness   (Brown 1989, 111)

One should, however, not be led to be overly protective either of Joyce's text, nor of Nietzche's often-used standards of art criticism.

Marjorie Perloff notes that Cage's *Roaratorio* mesostics are not entirely arbitrary, but a combination of both his pre-determined rules as well as personal taste (Perloff 1991, 149–161). As an example of how one might use Joyce's text according to the score instructions, the following lines appear as excerpted from Cage's last-used page in *Finnegans Wake*:

> *Diveltaking on me tail. Just a whisk brisk sly spry spink spank sprint of a thing theresomere, saultering. Saltarella come to her own. I pity your oldself I was used to. Now a younger's there. Try not to part! Be happy, dear ones! May I be wrong! For she'll be sweet for you as I was sweet when I came down out of me mother. My great blue bedroom, the air so quiet, scarce a cloud. In peace and silence. I could have stayed up there for always only. (Joyce 1939, 627)*

At the most minimal, one could make the following mesostic based on James, as:

> Just
> A
> theresoMere
> saultEring
> Saltarella

or one could make a mesostic on Joyce, as:

> Just
> Of
> pitY
> Came
> mE

The first example on James is rather nonsensical and very unpoetic. The second example on Joyce is not in the best school-book grammar, but makes some intellectual and emotional sense. However, the way that Cage used Joyce's text to make the concluding mesostic in *Roaratorio* is:

> Just a whisk
> Of
> pitY
> a Cloud
> in pEace and silence
> (Cage 1985b, 68)

Cage's example is poetic, and creates its own syntactical meaning in the most conventionally understood and assumed standards of literature. It seems almost autobiographical, and certainly reveals the sometimes whistful and sentimental undercurrent of his later work. "Just a whisk" may be taken to be a self-description of his approach to writing through Joyce's text; the "pity" might refer to the gentleness in Cage's personality and public persona (although he was not, nor wished to be "pitiful figure"); and the "cloud/in peace and silence" is certainly relevant to Cage's compositions and aesthetics from and after 1952.

Cage stated that his intention with *Roaratorio* was to:

> *. . . introduce people to the pleasures of* Finnegans Wake *when it is still on the side of poetry and chaos rather than something analyzed and known to be safe and law-abiding. (Cage 1985b, 163)*

The alternative context that Cage thus created through his rule-bound yet personal mesostics is a combination of respect to Joyce's text without being literal, as well as being a playful, nonacademic approach to the source material that is just irreverant enough to be, by turns, surprising and comforting. The Apollonian aspect of Cage's work is in the thoroughness and care with which the text and music were made; the Dionysian element still exists (although far different from Joyce) in listening to the actual performance, for in the true spirit of celebration and drunken abandon, it is easy for the listener to become disoriented (whether one is aware or not aware of Joyce's novel).

James Joyce, Marcel Duchamp, Erik Satie: An Alphabet (in Cage 1983b, 53–101) is Cage's work that is the closest to what might be considered to be "a play." The subject is a fantasy on the ghosts of Joyce, Duchamp, and Satie meeting and interacting with each other, with occasional appearances by other ghosts — such as Brigham Young, Henry David Thoreau, Henrik Ibsen — and then-living persons such as Robert Rauschenberg, Teeny Duchamp, and the late Morton Feldman. The narrator who comments upon the actions and sounds, in addition to making personal asides, is not identified but may be interpreted as being John Cage.

The text is written entirely in English, and uses the names of Joyce, Duchamp, and Satie as the structure for the mesostic verses. There are also several paragraphs with excerpted material from the writings of all three "ghosts" (the works by Duchamp and Satie being translated from French). The first two stanzas appear as follows:

> *what Joy*
> *to hAve*
> *theM*
> *on thE*
> *Same stage same time*
>
> *even though the subJect*
> *Of*
> *the plaY*
> *is the Curtain*
> *that sEparates them! (Cage 1983b, 55)*

This example shows all the basic features of Cage's mesostic versification. All letters are in lower-case except for the middle row (in this case, the three names) from which the text is structured. Also, it will be noticed that the letter following a middle-row name is always different from the next middle-row letter (that is, in the case of "JAMES," the "J" is not followed by an "a;" the

"A" is not followed by an "m;" the "M" is not followed by an "e," etc.). As is typical with all of Cage's mesostic compositions, it has a rather deft, light touch. *An Alphabet* is not typical of other mesostic works (such as *Roaratorio* or *I–VI*) in that it is not composed from source texts but from personal, intuitive exposition.

The original, published version of *An Alphabet* was performed by Cage at the Mudd Club in New York in the summer of 1982. He read for an hour, sitting on a stool, speaking at a microphone in a soft, conversational tone of voice. Before the reading, he explained to the audience that it was a radio play. Cage read it in the manner that it is published, that is, as a monologue. There is no separation in the text of different voices, sounds, or described visual elements. All of these components, which would be separated in a conventional playscript, are treated as equal events. Aside from the interest in hearing Cage reading his own work, this performance of *An Alphabet* had a very austere, rather untheatrical quality.

The radio play version was broadcast on July 6, 1983, by Westdeutscher Rundfunk in Cologne, Germany (Henck 1985, 330). Except for the three excerpts from James Joyce's *Finnegans Wake*, Cage's text was translated into German (by Klaus Reichert) and arranged (by Klaus Schöning) for fourteen voices. The cast included Klaus Reichert as the narrator, John Cage as James Joyce, Daniel Charles as Erik Satie, George Brecht as Marcel Duchamp, Christian Wolff as Henry David Thoreau, and Teeny Duchamp as herself. Other than reading their parts, there was no dramatization with added sound effects or music.

An Alphabet was later performed in New York City as the finale of the 2nd Acustica International Sound Festival, on April 29, 1990. The entire work was revised by Schöning for sixteen voices and retained Cage's original English-language text. This was directed by Cage and Schöning, and was recorded in live-performance for later radio broadcast in Germany. This second New York performance, and the first New York performance of the radio-play version, is arguably the most all-star cast realization of a Cage theatre piece since *Theatre Piece* in 1960 or 1965. The cast for this *Alphabet*, which reads almost like a "Who's Who" in the New York avant-garde, was:

Narrator	*Klaus Reichert [1]*
James Joyce	*John Cage [2]*
Erik Satie	*Alvin Curran [3]*
Marcel Duchamp	*Charles Dodge [4]*
Rrose Selavy	*Mimi Johnson [5]*
Teeny Duchamp	*Melissa Curran [6]*
Buckminster Fuller	*Dick Higgins [7]*
Henry David Thoreau	*Christian Wolff [8]*

Robert Rauschenberg	*Jerome Rothenberg [9]*
Mao (as a child)	*Park Tao Fay [10]*
Brigham Young	*Jackson Mac Low [11]*
Jonathan Albert	*David Vaughan [12]*
Veblen	*Malcolm Goldstein [13]*
Oppian	*Philip Corner [14]*
Ibsen	*Charlie Morrow [15]*
Isou	*Richard Kostelanetz [16]*

The cast was seated on stage as in the floorplan of Fig. 46. Each person on the floorplan is identified with the bracketed number in the above cast listing.

The performance began with the opening of the curtain. Each person was seated at his/her own microphone, set of papers on a music stand, and small reading light. When the reading began, the stage lights were at a minimal level, and the individual reading lamps appeared like individual stars in the night sky. After ten minutes of darkness, the full stage lights gradually came on for forty minutes, and then darkened again during the remaining ten minutes. While it was probably not intended, the visual mise-en-scene was reminiscent of the cemetary scene in the third act of Thornton Wilder's *Our Town*, where various "ghosts" sit in chairs (their "graves") and talk among each other. It would be a mistake, however, to ascribe any kind of "stylized naturalism" to Cage's work, for this does not exist when reading *An Alphabet* on the page, and the formality of performance was not a replication of everyday experience. Apart from the eyes and vocal cords, the only perceptible movement of the participants was in

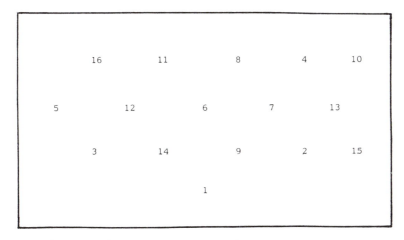

Fig. 46. The floorplan for *James Joyce, Marcel Duchamp, Erik Satie: An Alphabet,* performed at the 2nd Acustica International Sound Festival, New York, on April 29, 1990.

following the text and turning the pages. There was only a soft level of speaking thoughout, and there was no mimetic vocal delivery. Everyone spoke in their normal, conversational tone of voice.

An Alphabet is a very human, optimistic, and accessible work. It is designated by Cage as a fantasy (Cage 1983b, 55). On the page it is a fantasy of imagined voices, sounds, and visuals. When listened to, it is a fantasy of visuals and unheard musics. It does not make any attempt to explain or analyze the works or aesthetics of the three main "ghosts," but allows us to enjoy their imagined presence and to celebrate the continuing importance of their achievements in our contemporary consciousness. There is no linear narrative, it is simply a series of discontinuous events, like celestial telephone calls, that continually interrupt and interpenetrate with our mundane existence.

I-VI, a series of six lectures written mesostically from various source texts, were delivered as the six Norton lectures at Harvard University in 1988–89. The complete title for the lectures, which also gives the mesostic structure for composition, is: *MethodStructureIntentionDisciplineNotationIndeterminacy-InterpenetrationImitationDevotionCircumstancesVariableStructureNonunderstandingContingencyInconsistencyPerformance.*

This is Cage's most prestigious lecture. It is also his longest. *I-VI* is published with two accompanying cassette tapes. One is a complete recording of *IV*; the other is an edited version of various questions and answers from various sessions. The printed pages contain the mesostic verses, and at the bottom are the transcriptions of the question-and-answer sessions. The book concludes with the various source texts — including Cage's own writings, and those of other authors such as Emerson, Thoreau, Wittgenstein, and articles from the *New York Times, Wall Street Journal,* and *Christian Science Monitor* — that were used to make computerized *I Ching* word determinations (Cage 1990b).

Each of the six lectures last approximately ninety minutes. Cage also read a brief (about twelve minutes long) excerpt from *IV* at the 2nd Acustica Festival in New York on April 29, 1990. As usual, he simply sat at a table with a reading lamp and a microphone, and read in a soft voice. The posture that I have seen Mr. Cage use most frequently in various public readings during the last fifteen years appears notated as a stick-figure in profile in Fig. 47. While reading, he often had his knees bent slightly behind the front of the chair with the feet bent upwards on the ball of the foot, and at rest and in balance on the floor. He always bent the upper torso towards the table, and held the paper about one to two inches above the table top. He typically did not have his elbows on the table, but sometimes rested the middle of his forearms on the surface. He spoke very closely to the microphone, slightly hunched over at the shoulders. When speaking in public, he did not make any glancing

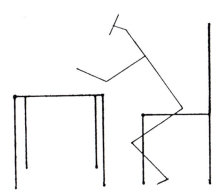

Fig. 47.   A stick-figure portrait of John Cage as he appeared, typically, during a public reading.

eye-contact with the audience but concentrated on the page he was holding. When speaking to someone apart from a formal, public performance, he always made eye-contact during conversation. Either way, there was an undeniable sincerity, an optimistic and evocative "interfacing" in his speech.

I–VI is written as a performance score. For the notation employed, Cage writes:

> *The lectures are written to be read aloud. A space followed by an apostrophe indicates a new breath. Syllables that would not normally be accented but should be are printed in bold type. (Cage 1990b, 5)*

A brief excerpt, from the beginning of *IV* reads:

> are as Much
> is **not** ' finitE
> Trouble '
> and Heavy
> **tO**
> only **neeD**
> with **the** ' caMpus
> arE
> iT
> **Has**
> exist amOng
> of hurDles **nobody**
> all huManity ' **now**
> or tastE
> To
> current **pH**ysics
> **Or** ' opposition of
> fishes **think** Does not exist '
>
> (Cage 1990b, 215)

These lectures are, in keeping with his other lectures from the past forty years, not designed to transmit information, but are written from a need to make poetry. In *I-VI*, language is used unintentionally. There is no explicit "meaning," yet when reading, or listening, one eventually begins to see and hear things that are not there. One enters into the text, makes connections between disparate words, makes one's own meanings. Language becomes transparent, seemingly empty, yet also ripe, full, intellectually and emotionally expressive. Language is not used to circumscribe or set limits, but to express the inexpressible potential of direct experience. It is a language of the unexpressible, similar to Ludwig Wittgenstein's concluding statement in his *Tractatus Logico-Philosophicus*: "Whereof one cannot speak, thereof one must be silent" (Wittgenstein 1922, 189). Depending upon one's point of view (and knowledge of Cage's work), *I-VI* is either a fatuous waste of typography on paper; or Cage's final literary masterpiece, a last summation of his application of his mature ideas and practice of linguistic composition.

John Cage's last three public performances were of vocal works. He read/sung *Empty Words IV* (split into two sections) on July 10 and 11, 1992 as part of the Cage Summergarden festival at the Museum of Modern Art in New York. Barbara Moore recalls that Cage was "as always" in his *Empty Words IV* rendition (Moore 1992). Alison Knowles, also in attendance, provides the most eloquent description:

> John sat at a table in front of an open window and read a text. He spoke the text at a normal volume. Listeners, even those who sat very near him, were barely able to understand him. Even when they listened carefully, they caught only fragments of words, for the chirping of the birds outside in the evening was deafening to the ears . . . After about twenty minutes, the birds gradually went to sleep and John's voice seemed to grow louder and louder as the singing of the birds subsided. When the last bird had turned silent, John's reading voice, although no louder than before, sounded extremely clear. (von Berswordt-Wallrabe 1992, 23)

Cage's very last performance piece is *ONE*[12] (1992). The unpublished score is subtitled "for a lecturer," and consists of one page of brief handwritten notes. Using a computerized version of the *I Ching* by Andrew Culver that generates 640 numbers between one and twelve, one is then to read the randomly generated numbers and improvise a vocal text with the following key:

> 1 = *empty word (connective pronoun, conjunction, article)*
> 2-11 = *whispered/vocalized vowels/consonants of each number*
> 12 = *full word (noun, verb, adj., adv.), in each case spoken*
>
> (Cage 1992d)

ONE[12] was first performed by the composer on June 22, 1992, at Perugini, Italy. A reviewer for the *Neue Zürcher Zeitung* would write:

> *In it he sings a diatonic scale of about one octave small tone groups, continuously different, very soft, in a meter of quarters and eighths, with rough voice and intentionally incomprehensible text articulation; the performance which radiated a quiet and beauty of its own, lasted for thirty minutes. ("About Music furthered in the Italian Tradition" 1992)*

Cage's second performance of *ONE*^{12}, and the last of his long life and career, was incorporated in a simultaneous piece titled *FOUR*^{6} (1992) with Joan La Barbara (soprano), William Winant (percussion), and Leonard Stein (piano) at Central Park, New York, on July 23, 1992. Joan La Barbara recalls that he was in good voice, and that his sung pitch choices were very harmonic with the environmental sounds and the other simultaneous performances: "I remember how in tune he was with the circumstances — they were very musical decisions" (La Barbara 1993).

This live performance was privately recorded. During the half-hour, Cage sung approximately twelve short vocal fragments ranging from approximately one-half to four seconds in duration, with several extended silences in between (Cage 1992c). His voice was very soft and, as typical, relied upon the microphone for amplification. What is so extraordinary is that, in making his scored improvisation, Cage chose pitches that were harmonically related to the other three performers — a rare example where Cage actually fulfilled his *Variations III* notes so that "the actions of others give me less obligation to act myself" (Cage 1963b). In this instance, Cage was not making a totally independent simultaneity so much as an example of conventional counterpoint. Although probably unintended, it is both ironic and bittersweet that Cage's last performance would be a concrete demonstration of using his ears in a sensitive awareness to others' actions, as well as a demonstration of his sensitivity to conventional triadic harmony.

Cage's sudden death from a stroke, on August 12, 1992, was a shock to all who knew him. As a fitting public memorial, Essential Music (John Kenney and Charles Wood) and Andrew Culver produced *Cagemusicircus* at Symphony Space, New York, on November 1, 1992. This was titled *Cagemusicircus* because it was not an actual musicircus by Cage, and unlike the typical Cage musicircus, this event was devoted exclusively to Cage's own compositions. The performance groups and individuals read like a "Who's Who" of those closely associated with Cage, including Essential Music, Continuum, The Downtown Ensemble, The New Music Consort; and Laurie Anderson, William Duckworth, Yoko Ono, Don Gillespie, Jackson Mac Low, Anne Tardos, Takehisa Kosugi, James Tenney, Jean Rigg, and Yvar Mikhashoff (Program 1992b).

Altogether almost sixty of Cage's works from throughtout his career were performed for three-and-a-half hours. Kyle Gann would write that it "was the most compelling Cage concert I'd ever heard; and if you couldn't grasp what the man was aiming at in this glorious welter of noises, gestures, and quotations, you're just not susceptible" (Gann 1992). Ellsworth Snyder recalls that usually three or four pieces were being played simultaneously, other times it was much more silent, but that something was always going on within the total space; and compared the experience to glancing through a newspaper, picking up headlines or a few words, then shifting one's attention to something else (Snyder 1993). Alex Ross, also enthusiastic, would note the appropriately sentimental conclusion:

> *Toward the end, the carnival became an elegy. Essential Music, the percussion-and-piano ensemble that organized the event, delivered an intense performance of "Credo in Us," a tightly structured work from 1942 with a searing climax. During its epilogue, the hall darkened. For a minute at the end, the [center] stage was held only by a desk, a lamp, a glass of water and a gray jacket draped over an empty chair. In the mind's eye, John Cage walked out and began to read.* (Ross 1992)

CONCLUSION

In general, there are at least eight basic concerns which one may see throughout John Cage's theatre pieces and performances from 1952 through 1992 — 1. chance, 2. an experimental use of notation (often through indeterminacy), 3. structure, 4. an alternative use of time, 5. focus upon process, 6. the non-matrixed performer, 7. an innovative use of space, and 8. the central role of each individual's perception. These categories may admittedly be condensed into fewer items, such as structure and process, but ultimately the blurring of distinctions is in keeping with Cage's aesthetics and practice.

The concept of chance has run throughout these pieces. Many of the works discussed, from *Water Music* to *ONE^{12}*, were made by use of the *I Ching*. The systematic use of chance procedures used in Cage's composition process, however, is only rarely employed by the actual performer — as in Solos 6, 10, 19, 31, 76, and 77 from the *Song Books*, or *Child of Tree* and *Branches*. Rather, Cage typically used chance in either making determinate notations (as in *Water Music, Water Walk*, and *Europeras 1 & 2*), or in making indeterminate notations (as in *Theatre Piece*). The concepts of chance and indeterminacy must not be understood as being synonymous; however, when one uses an indeterminate notation, one "takes a chance," according to popular terminology, in that one takes a gamble, a risk, with no explicitly predictable result.

The innovative use of notation may be seen in all of Cage's theatre pieces, although this may not always be obvious. *Water Music* uses conventional notation systems, but does so in an experimental manner, in part because all the conventional symbols are spatially notated in time, and because the juxtaposition of conventional notation systems requires the reader and performer to become aware of the freedoms and limitations that thus exist through notation. The latent indeterminancies that exist in conventional notation systems would be further explored by Cage, resulting in his complex indeterminately notated scores such as *Concert for Piano and Orchestra, Music Walk, Cartridge Music,* or *Variations III*. Indeterminacy is, in Cage's work, primarily a concept tied to notation. No notations are completely determinate, and what Cage did was to make this situation so much more obvious through his own experimental notation systems where the performer must make the final determinations of what is actually to be done.

Whether the score is in determinate notation made by chance procedures, or in indeterminate notation, all of Cage's theatre pieces are structural in concept. The use of structure, rather than content being predominant in the act of composition, dates to Cage's earlier work in the 1930s. In the theatre pieces it is not a structural use of information or linear progression of chronological narrative, but a use of disparate content which, in either score reading or actual performance, makes structure itself important. The use of structure, whether in a chance or indeterminate context (as in *Water Music* or *Music Walk*), is a demonstration of "nature in her operation." Cage ultimately breaks down structure until it seems to be haphazard, although it is, paradoxically, still controlled (whether this be on the level of the individual performer's enactment of the requirements of a specific score, or the perception of the audio-spectators).

The concern with structure also involves the use of time. In Cage's work, time is not used as typically a chronological, cause and effect, linear progression of past-present-future, or beginning-middle-end. Nor do any of Cage's theatre pieces exhibit a circular model of time. (The one exception in Cage's compositions that uses a circular structure is the ballet score of *The Seasons* [1947] where the beginning measures are also the concluding measures.) Jonathan Kramer characterizes Cage's use of time as "vertical" or "now time," which is represented by a vertical, rather than a horizontal, arrangement in the score (or in perceived performance) of isolated, non-progressive events; and that the "present that the work extends suggests itself as infinite. Past and future disappear as everything in the piece belongs within the horizon of now" (Kramer 1988, 384–388). In scores such as *Music Walk* or *Cartridge Music*, one does not necessarily read the score (and hence, the time, the occurrences of events) in a linear, left-to-right arrangement on the page. Rather, all events are visually displayed at once in the score, and it is the performer who, in using the notation, must finally determine the sequence of events, as given in the written instructions. The use of time as structure is seen in all of Cage's theatre pieces. Most typically, the theatre pieces are performed with reference to a stop-watch or clock. It is only in very rare works — such as *0'00"*, *Rozart Mix*, *Sound Anonymously Received*, or *ONE* [3] — where there is no prescribed duration other than an intuitively made personal choice during actual performance.

Cage's theatre pieces, in the use of chance, innovative notations, structure, and use of time, are works which focus upon process rather than object. Particularly with the indeterminately notated works, there can not be said to be any final, fixed version. Instead, a performance is based upon a notation, and it is the performance itself, rather than the score, which becomes of crucial interest. In Cage's work, the process involved in performance can only be critically viewed in terms of the relative faithfulness to or ignorance of the score. In *Theatre Piece*, for example, one might easily term David Tudor's performance to be the most exacting, and Nam June Paik's performance to be the least exacting in accordance with Cage's score. Yet, neither are finally what one could call "definitive, end-all" performances of the specific work in question; and both were, apparently, very engaging and rewarding experiences for the audiences in attendance. In my opinion the example of David Tudor's use of indeterminate scores should be the model for later performers to employ, at least in terms of making an exacting and imaginative use of the score materials and instructions, however I can not suggest that one would necessarily be doing "correct" performances of Cage's indeterminate scores by doing a "David Tudor imitation."

The performer in Cage's theatre pieces is typically non-matrixed; that is, the performer is not playing a character (or animal, vegetable, or mineral) within a narrative context. The performer is him- or herself, and is simply doing what is required for a performance of a specific work. The "Cagean performer" may only be said to be "matrixed" in that one may be using a score from which to make the performance; or if there is no score, that one is involved in a situation with other people (whether this be a solo performance and the "others" are the audience, or if one is doing a simultaneous performance with other performers).

The innovative use of space in Cage's work may be seen throughout his theatre pieces. The untitled event at Black Mountain College in 1952, the first performance of *Theatre Piece* in 1960, and various musicircuses, have all involved a "theatre-in-the-round" rather than a separation of performer from audience through a centralized or frontal focus of visual and sonic attention. Cage, however, also used traditional, proscenium staging throughout his career as well, as in *Water Music, Water Walk, Europeras 1 & 2*, and in a typical lecture or poetry reading. With perhaps the single exception of *HPSCHD*, Cage did not employ environmental staging to transform the performance space to be anything other than what it already is, whether it be a dining hall, a gallery, a theatre, a pavilion, or an out-of-doors area. Cage's use of space was, in common with the role of the performer, very literal and functional.

The involvement of audience perception is crucial in Cage's work, as he said that each person is at the center. It is with this concern that Cage's theatre pieces most cogently reflect his Zen-influenced aesthetic practice. In particular, Cage often stated that his favorite Zen writer was the nineth century Chinese sage Huang Po, who in answer to the question "What is the Buddha?," replied:

> *Your Mind is the Buddha. The Buddha is Mind. Mind and Buddha are indivisible. Therefore it is written: 'That which is Mind is the Buddha; if it is other than Mind, it is certainly other than Buddha.' (Huang Po 1958, 78)*

Through the perception of interpenetrating and nonobstructing events, one is invited to "split the stick," to pass "a camel through the eye of a needle." The term "audience" ("those who listen") is admittedly limited, for one is also a "spectator" ("one who sees") as well. With each person at the center, this includes both those who perform as well as those who witness. Thus, when an individual performs, it is not necessarily to do something that can be heard or seen by everyone else. In the situation of simultaneous rather than solo performance, each audience member notices various events differently from each other person, thereby differently structuring the experience. Cage's theatre pieces typically involved both seeing as well as hearing, and may be termed "total theatre," but his was not a Wagnerian "Gesamtkunstwerk." Where Wagner idealized a fusion of theatrical elements into a single and unified experience, Cage used theatrical events as independent elements. There is no fusion, no interconnection, no casual relationship among events except if the individual wishes to make such connections. In keeping with Cage's Zen aesthetics, it is the performer, and ultimately the individual audio-spectator, who rather than the composer, must "do it."

There have been many critical philosophical or theoretical interpretations of Cage's work. I have concentrated not upon philosophy or theory but on notation as the stimulus to begin an inquiry into interpretation. From notation, it was actual performance which thus became my focus. Indeterminate notation is only viable when it is actually used; and in its use, Cage's aesthetics then become meaningful.

Cage's theatre pieces were not "drama," a narrative conflict or crisis to require a resolution. Theatre was not a reflective emotional fiction but a demonstration of life in a non-judgemental structure/context. At his best, as in *Music Walk* or the solos in *Song Books*, Cage's theatre pieces are graceful and thought-provoking, charming but also at times irritating/disruptive of expectation. His theatre pieces were art and not actual everyday life; but Cage did not presuppose art to be more than a model. If there was a major failure by Cage to implement his aesthetics into actual performance practice, it was in the fact that he never fully gave up his own subjective taste, in either composition or performance.

It is difficult for me to provide or suggest any kind of closure to this study. There will be many more future performances and studies of Cage's work, hopefully in a variety of contexts which one can not yet imagine or foresee. I continue to enjoy Cage's work, despite its contradictions, human and humane, limited and idealistic; and can only say a yes, and then let's go on . . .

And let the music *play*.

APPENDIX 1

JOHN CAGE ON TEACHING

(The following comments are from an interview with John Cage on June 11, 1987, when he discussed the classes at the New School for Social Research (1956–60), as well as his general approach to teaching. Most of the questions are edited out from the tape transcript but occasionally appear in square brackets to clarify the progression of thought.)

[Question: What was your teaching method at the New School?]

The principle of my teaching was not to teach — not to teach a body of information, but simply to lead the students, to tell them who I was in terms of what we were studying, which was composition — then, the rest of the time would be spent with what they were doing — so there was a conversation. I told them if what they were doing was not, so to speak, experimental, that I would nudge them in that direction.

We did whatever the students had to offer — and I told them not to compose something that could not be performed in that room by those people, but to compose something that we could actually perform. The person who always had something to perform was Jackson Mac Low, and the next dependable for having something was Allan Kaprow. And between the two of them there never was anything to worry about, because there was always something to be shown, you know, something to be heard.

[Question: Was there any syllabus, any readings?]

No, no . . . If I were teaching a class now it would be different from what it was then. I was about to write the *Concert for Piano and Orchestra* [1957–58], so I already had the idea of space equal to time in terms of notation, so I explained that to them, and it made it very simple for people who weren't even musicians to write music. Some could and some couldn't, but with space equal to time it didn't make any difference.

I never performed any of my own compositions, I just talked about the ideas and the composing means. The room had a few percussion instruments in the closet that the school already had. There was a piano — a rather poor one. That's all there was. But I didn't find that to be a limitation. I insisted that they be able to perform it in the room. I wasn't transmitting information, I was trying to encourage the students to find their own way of doing things.

[Question: How did you teach earlier classes at other places — for instance, what did you do teaching WPA recreation camp counselors in California in 1939?]

My teaching was similar. It was connected with camp counselling, though, which is taking care of children in country situations where they would go for the summer, you know, for a camp. What I would do would be to take the prospective counselors on a walk through the woods, and what they were looking for were not edible plants, but sounds. I told them to look for things that would make sounds. And then when we got back they would play with those to make sounds — stones, sticks, and whatever they happened to find. It could be tearing a leaf. It was just that we were looking for instruments, really we were looking for sounds. And then when we had those sounds, then we'd come up to question composition, what to do. They were interested in camp counselling, in teaching, but they were aware of the possibility of letting children discover their own instruments.

[Question: Have you ever had any problem with discipline?]

I don't think we had the problem of discipline, because these were all serious people. I *have* had problems with children.

There was one time at the New School where I knew that the class we were having was the last one before the Christmas vacation, and so, since it was almost a two-week period, I thought it was my duty to go to tell each person what he might do during the vacation to improve his work. And I came to Toshi Ichianagi, and I told him his work was very interesting but I thought it could be a little more interesting, and so I told him the direction — I forget what it was — that I thought he should take. And without looking at me or anything, he simply said very quietly when I finished, he said "I am not you" (laughs). And that was the greatest lesson I learned. Isn't that marvelous (laughs)?

I am, if I may say so, a good teacher, but I don't teach. Instead, I write books and do my work, and I think of my books as my teaching, and I think of my work as an example of what I would teach. I prefer that way to the classroom because it reaches more people, and no one has to enroll (laughs)!

[Question: Can you talk more about the relationship between your writing and teaching? And, how did you start to write?]

After giving up the ministry [in 1930–31], I thought I would be a writer, and in hindsight I think the reason we want to write is because that's the only thing that schools teach us to do, really. They teach us not only to write but to read. They used to call education "reading, and writing, and arithmetic," and now of course it must have changed a great deal with computers, but the only thing that you really learn after you've been educated in the public school system is to write, so I thought I'd be a writer. And I told my parents that and said I should go to Europe instead of to school because a writer needed this experience, something to write about. And school, of course, is not an interesting thing to write about, so I went off to Europe, and it was there that I discovered music and painting. I gave up the notion of writing, temporarily, and painting later, because when I decided to concentrate on music I gave up both writing and painting. The paintings exist somewhere. I generally gave them away. I don't know where the painting is that I gave to Richard Bulig, but that was perhaps the most interesting one, and it wasn't that interesting.

I felt that I had made so many changes in music, that I had a responsibility to teach at the New School, so I did, but I never even made enough money to pay for the travel from Stony Point [in Rockland Country, New York] to the school, so it was more like a contribution to the school. Ideally — I was so poor then — ideally I would have made a little bit of money and could have had a reason for teaching to make money, but it didn't work out that way.

Your other question is, "How did you start to write?" I did such strange things that people asked me to explain why I was doing what I was doing, and so I generally wrote the text — as I explain somewhere [for example, "Composition As Process" (1958) in *Silence* (1961, 18–56)] — in the same way that I was writing music, so that would give an example rather than an explanation. Then I began to assume that if anyone was interested in my work that he would study it chronologically, and so I don't repeat the directions from one piece to the next, so that you really had to know the work — the history of the work — in order to know what was going on. Not entirely, but partially.

At the time I was at the New School, I was definitely shifting from object to process, and so I was talking, probably, about process. And now I'm bringing about a process that includes objects. [An example of this is *Euro-peras 1 & 2* (1987), discussed in Chapter 8.]

[Question: Did you have any idea at the time when you were teaching at the New School that these classes would become a direct influence in the development of performance art, as in Happenings or Fluxus?]

I wasn't thinking along those lines. We were just having the classes. I don't think they thought that either at Black Mountain, but all the classes at Black Mountain were very important later on.

APPENDIX 2

JOHN CAGE ON *THEATRE PIECE*

(The following comments by John Cage are transcribed from a taped interview on May 12, 1988. These extended comments on a specific score page
from *Theatre Piece*, reproduced in Fig. 48, provide a rare documentation of
how Cage himself would approach doing one of his indeterminate notations.
Interestingly, he would not discuss any performances of *Theatre Piece* with
specific examples, preserving an evocative and open-ended approach for

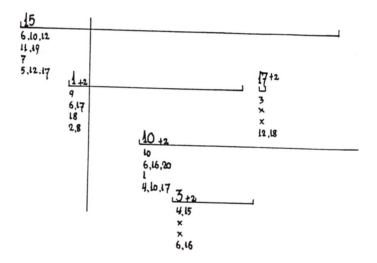

Fig. 48.   A page from *Theatre Piece*, score part I, © 1960 Henmar Press Inc. Discussed
by John Cage on May 12, 1988.

others to take. Most of the questions have been edited out, and appear in square brackets. The square brackets within Cage's comments are to clarify the specific parts of the notation on the page referred to. The three words "pencil," "swim," and "slide" were not given by Cage. He asked for suggestions after his own first example of "rose." The three other words thus appear in square brackets, and should not be thought of as purely representative of words that Cage might choose.)

[Question: I know that you prefer that the individual performer find his own way of using your indeterminate notations, but could you explain how you would approach using this page from *Theatre Piece*?]

This is in space equal to time, and there are two systems. And this [15 at the top] begins before the bracket [the first system] — you would have to begin earlier according to how you measure the time, so you can actually measure it one way or another. I probably just used one [time] ruler when I performed it in Japan in 1962. I gave these [rulers] as different ways of measuring — or you could make your own ruler — but it is measured time.

And you would have made decks of cards with nouns and verbs on them which you would be willing to be engaged in. And so you'd find this out [referring to the numbers below a horizontal line] if you had any questions about it. You could list your questions and the possible answers, and then use these numbers to answer the questions.

At a " + 2" you have to add two cards to the deck. And here [at 14 in the second bracket, or second system] you add three and take away two. So first you would know what this number was [at 1 in the first bracket], and then after that you would bring two cards in from the deck that was available to do new things. The small numbers underneath are to answer questions. You make lists, you wouldn't have to have decks, because the answers wouldn't have to be shuffled.

Answers can not be taken from the original deck of twenty [nouns and verbs] because they don't refer to the questions. Out of the cards that you have are nouns and verbs, and if you want to know what color a chair is, for instance, say that is your question — is it just any old chair?, or is it colored? and what color is it? — then you would have to list twenty colors, and then you would find out which color it was because it would be the sixth. Or, in this case [15 at the top] if you said what color is it?, you'd get three numbers [6, 10, 12], which would be three colors. It has to be painted three colors, if that was your question.

[Question: Doesn't this encourage performers to take the easy way out by making their interpretation of the score itself to be open-ended?]

No, because you put nouns and verbs that you're willing to be involved with in a deck, and then you've turned them upside down so that you don't know which one is which. And when you choose something from that — and you don't know what it is — there's no way of your knowing what 15 used at the same time as 1, as 10, as 3 is going to be, what kind of actions that's going to result in. You have no way of knowing!

Say 15 is "rose" and 1 is ["pencil"] and 10 is ["swim"] and 3 is ["slide"], and you're faced with the problem of a rose, a pencil, and swimming, and sliding. How are you going to do that? And how are you going to do it in the right time relationship? *What* are you going to do, in fact? If sliding comes after swim, comes after pencil, comes after rose, how are you going to work that out? And when questions arise, when you finally get a notion of what you might do, and then you wonder whether it's this way of that way, or is it to the right or the left, and so forth, then you can answer those questions.

I've rarely seen people do this well. They mostly do it in such a way that they don't have to confront a new experience. They almost never do. When I gave the example with *Water Walk* [1959], which I wrote out, I gave the example of how that kind of thing can be done. I wanted a lot of activity in a short period of time. I wanted something really quite extraordinary — which almost nobody does who works with this material — but very little serious work has been done on it, to my experience.

APPENDIX 3

DAVID TUDOR'S 1960 PERFORMANCE OF
THEATRE PIECE

David Tudor's notes for his performance of *Theatre Piece* in 1960 provide the most complete documentation of any performer or any performance of this work. Tudor's performance notes are in two versions. The first is a set of typed pages which include a typed version of the complete eighteen-page score with Cage's performance instruction, plus Tudor's own notes on timings and actions. The second set is a hand-written copy of the actions and timings on rectangular cards that were carried about and referred to during the actual performance. For purposes of documentation, only the typed version is summarized here, because it is the more detailed of the two.

The first page lists the events and durations. Tudor used ten pages from the eighteen total pages in his score part. Each of the ten pages would thus equal three minutes, making the total of thirty minutes for a complete performance. The next three-and-an-eighth pages are a typed version of all eighteen pages in Cage's score, listing the timing and duration of an event, the numbers assigned in both Cage's score with also Tudor's newly assigned number, and the four sets of score numbers to be used in answering questions. The timings and durations listed by Tudor reveal that he used the top ruler on the transparency (100 seconds) to measure the time. In his final, hand-written performance notes, however, the events have different timings, none of which correspond to any of Cage's time rulers. Tudor most probably made his own time ruler after first making the initial typed score readings. The final page of the typed notes is the set of Cage's instructions for *Theatre Piece*, dated January, 1960. Tudor's scrupulously detailed notes and realizations do not mention which of the eight score parts he worked from, but this is easily discovered through cursory analysis.

The set of Cage's instructions dated January, 1960, and retyped by Tudor for his own reference, appear as follows:

> Large nos. within brackets refer to a gamut of 20 nouns and/or verbs chosen by the performer. Brackets refer to time (rulers may be changed at any points), within which an action may be made. Any amount of the bracket may be used. Preparation for the action may be made at any time (outside or within the bracket); and any necessary and relevant actions following are also free with respect to time. A program of action is to be prepared using as much or as little of the material provided (horizontally and vertically) as wished.

If any questions arise as to what is to be done, 4 may be asked, provided they are posed in such a way that a number or numbers (1–20) will provide an answer. X is no answer (Performer's free choice). None of the answers given may be used in response to more than a single question.

Pages may be performed in any order.

Each performer is who he is (e.g. performing musician, dancer, singer), but he is also performing a piece of theatrical music. Music is here understood to mean the production of sounds. Thus a performer's decision as to what he is to do will often be determined by whether he thus makes a sound.

A performer may include other performers in his gamut (as nouns).

For performance, part may be memorized, or read from cards carried about or placed at useful points. Actions may be timed for reference to a stopwatch carried or by reference to clocks placed on the stage.

There is no conductor or director. A rehearsal will have the purpose of removing physically dangerous obstacles that may arise due to the unpredictability involved.

Lighting will be general. Alterations of this may be included in a performer's gamut (as verbs).

These instructions do not differ very much from the published version, but are important documentation for comparison. The original instruction does not give any indication of how long the performance is to last, while the published version states that *Theatre Piece* is to be thirty minutes. The original performance length of thirty minutes was probably the duration agreed upon by the original participants, and this detail was then included in the revised, published instruction. The most significant difference between the two is that the published version instructs the performer to write each noun or verb on a card and place these face-down, manipulating them according to the score pages like a solitaire game. This added feature was incorporated by Cage into the published instruction as a result of Tudor's personal approach to the score.

Tudor made a deck of cards numbered from 1 through 112. This home-made deck is found among his *Theatre Pieces* papers, but there is no corresponding list of nouns or verbs. What is documented is that, by using the deck of 112 cards, 46 different actions resulted, done 72 times. These are listed below in cross-reference to both the typed and hand-written score realizations in the following manner: the left column shows the number of times an event occurs, the second column shows the original card number Tudor assigned to the event, and the third column is the notation of the action or object used:

```
1 – 1      squeaker hammer
2 – 3      big beater on bass strings
2 – 4      jack in the box
3 – 5      coil
1 – 6      rubber hammer
```

1 – 11	*wipe keys*
3 – 12	*exploding matches*
1 – 13	*turtle*
1 – 14	*mustard snake*
3 – 16	*big beater sound–board*
3 – 17	*atoms*
2 – 18	*mouse*
2 – 20	*fire alarm*
3 – 22	*dipsy car*
5 – 23	*rubber whistle*
1 – 25	*wipe strings*
3 – 26	*money in bank*
1 – 29	*confetti*
1 – 30	*recording 1 (music)*
3 – 33	*glass*
1 – 36	*beater right case*
1 – 40	*tea*
2 – 41	*Japanese whistle*
2 – 43	*plastic under*
2 – 44	*trem. plastic rod*
1 – 49	*shoe squeaker*
1 – 50	*small scope*
1 – 53	*balloon squeaker*
1 – 64	*beater const. bar (bs.)*
1 – 65	*dart*
1 – 69	*saucer*
2 – 74	*flash pad*
1 – 79	*bird*
1 – 82	*beater metal plate*
1 – 84	*bubble horn*
1 – 86	*plastic gliss.*
1 – 91	*recording 2 (speech)*
1 – 96	*beater const. bar (tea)*
1 – 98	*chicken (alto)*
1 – 99	*ball on strings*
1 – 100	*plastic sound–board*
1 – 102	*cracked record*
1 – 104	*chirping bird*
1 – 105	*trem. mobile*
1 – 110	*beater under*
1 – 112	*big scope*

From Tudor's notes, one can backtrack to find which score, and which pages, he used. This is a somewhat laborious process, for one must go through each of the eighteen pages of the eight *Theatre Piece* score parts. Fortunately, Tudor's notes contain the relevant information — he used score number III. The first of the pages that Tudor used is reproduced in Fig. 49.

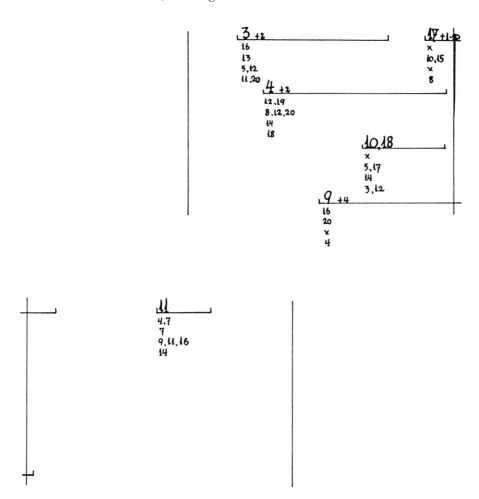

Fig. 49.   A page from *Theatre Piece* (1960), score part III, chosen by David Tudor for the beginning of his simultaneous solo in the first performance of *Theatre Piece* on March 7, 1960; © 1977 Henmar Press Inc.

The two different timings for events that Tudor assigned in the typed and hand-written versions is a thorny issue as yet unresolved. David Tudor could not answer this question, but stressed, after both of us trying and suggesting various ways to measure, that the numbers he came up with were proportions within which to work, and that it does not mean that an action takes place for a specific duration, but only that an action is to occur *within* that time. Many of the sound objects, mentioned above in Tudor's events list, are manipulated or mechanical toys, which he recalls as a simple solution to being required, according to Cage's score, to be able to make as many actions, as many sounds, as possible within the measured time.

The following ten brackets of Fig. 50 are a short-hand version of
Tudor's performance notes with the ten pages used from *Theatre Piece* score
part III. These notations are read in this manner: each of Cage's two systems
(or, two brackets) per page are renotated into one continuous bracket; horizontal lines appear according to relative spatial proportions; numbers above a
line appear as in Cage's score; and numbers below a line give Tudor's
numbers of events according to his deck of 112 cards, as listed above. The
first renotated bracket is of the page from Cage's score reproduced in Fig. 49,
and should be compared by the reader with the renotated version.

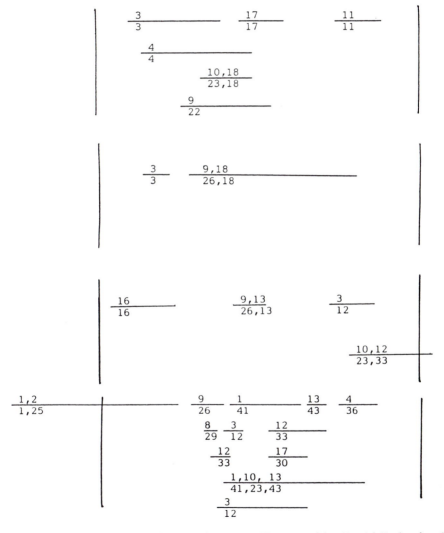

Fig. 50.   The ten pages from *Theatre Piece*, part III, as used by David Tudor for the
first performance: each of Cage's original pages are renotated as one bracket;
summary by author made from access to materials courtesy of David Tudor.

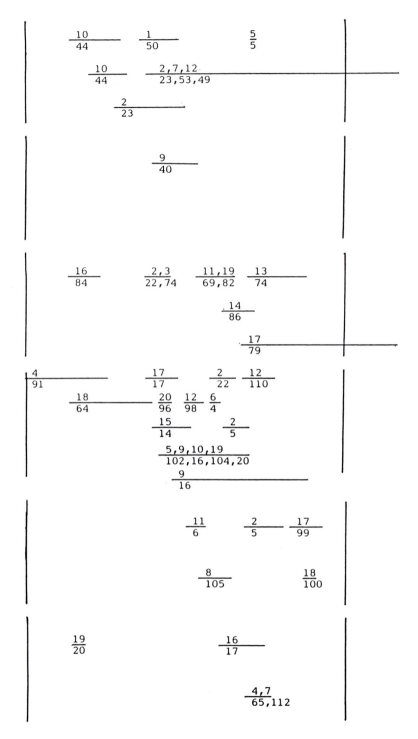

Fig. 50.   (*Continued*)

APPENDIX 4

SONG BOOKS SOLOS 9, 61, AND 87
IN PERFORMANCE

The following material is the manner that Solos 9, 61, and 87 in *Song Books* are performed by the American Music/Theatre Group. These three solos are rather lengthy, and thus do not have the original score reproduced for space considerations. Solos 9, 61, and 87 are notated in the same manner as Solo 7, which is reproduced in Fig. 28 and discussed briefly in Chapter 7. The events in the score appear at the left, and are appended with remarks by the individual performers involved.

The instructions for Solo 9 state that the performer not perform "for longer than four minutes and thirty-two seconds" (Cage 1970a, 32). Toby Twining performs Solo 9 in the following manner:

– loss of interest – I express loss of interest by reading a magazine silently to myself and then setting it down;

– dog – I get down on all fours and sniff around;

– lively ringing little trills of fox-colored sparrows – I chose not to do this, as Cage says in the instructions you can do all or none of the material;

– "a novel, powerful rich strain" like a new bird – I do a vocal sound imitating a loon;

– deep suffering – I grouped this with the action above, as in the score, by alternating the loon sounds with low grunting sounds of somebody in deep pain;

+ "Changer de peau" – I don't perform this;

– loss of interest – I read a newspaer silently to myself, then put it down;

+ un chapeau haut de forme, une large lavallière – I put on a large yellow felt sombrero for about one minute;

+ difficulty – I do the following action in the score;

+ take your temperature. Give yourself another (each hour). – I have a thermometer, an aspirin bottle filled with "tic-tacs" [a commercial brand of tiny breath candy], and a watch. I take my temperature, look at the watch, then swallow some pills with water. The "difficulty" is that I do it like I have palsy;

– the blowing of wind – I combine this with the action below in the score;

+ a rose – I have a real rose as a prop. I stroke the air with it like a wand, and blow on it;

+ flyswatter – after using the rose, I repeat the action with a flyswatter. I use the same quality of gesture, and am pretty sure I sniff the flyswatter as well – I like irony;

+ speed – I use the flyswatter as fast as I can, as if to catch flies;

– popular music – this is done by quoting "bubblegum" songs such as "Apple, Peaches, Pumpkin Pie," or "Wooley-Bully." Sometimes I improvise a Bobby McFerrin-type scat style;

– loss of interest – I start these pop tunes and quickly loose interest. Another way I did this was at the Pierre Hotel – I read a magazine, and quickly got bored;

– solfeggio exercises – I sing exercises, like "Do-Re-Mi-Fa-So;"

+ Terrible Anger – I throw a temper-tantrum for five to ten seconds, then stare out into the performance space. (Twining 1989 and 1990)

Solo 61 is to be performed for no longer than "nine minutes and twenty-eight seconds" (Cage 1970a, 228). Phyllis Bruce performs Solo 61 in the following manner:

+ listen – I try to listen to something going on at another station [another soloist], sometimes cupping the hand over the ear. But it is more effective if truly listening;

+ "They stoop to rise." – I thought through that in terms of ritual. Sometimes it comes off. Preferably it is best when it feels natural. I do a knee-bend with the hands extended and go down to the knees. The head goes down, then I rise and stretch tall;

– laugh – I retreat in a quiet way;

+ Orient – I take several steps forward in prayer position, bowing slightly;

– Sea Captain – I look through a "pair of binoculars" in pantomine. I found that using a prop breaks the continuity, breaks the flow;

+ Begin Again – I start with " + listen" again;

– wings calmly opening and closing – I take a step or so back. This takes a longer time to establish. I am a big bird;

+ fill a glass with water very full – I literally do it, but not overlapping with the previous activity, as in the score. It is a focused event, and one of the hardest things to do;

+ wren (lurking, restless, chirping) – I'm in a crouched position, working as a vagrant might work, for about one minute. Then I get restless, and I chirp like a bird, doing bird movements;

+ Sea Captain – I do this in the same way as above;

– piano – I usually play a simple piece from memory, usually "Jesus Loves Me;"

" + the animal nature of men – I get lascivious, and interact with another performer, and go after Neely. At the end I imagine there is blood on my fingers;

+ blood – this overlaps with the above;

– travelling – I do a shuffle-dance step, like "Shuffle Off To Buffalo," a reference to Vaudeville;

– newspaper – I sit and silently read something to myself;

+ Charleston – I do the "Charleston." That was Neely's choice;

– do some mathematics on your fingers – I just literally think of an exercise and use my fingers to count;

– sound of the first frog in spring – I take a step backward, making a low, gutteral sound of a frog in spring, like "brapp, be-brupp, be-brupp;"

– *nightingale* – I *make a bird sound;*

– *smoke* – I'm *stepping back, and put my arms up to try to get smoke away from me;*

– *applaud* – I *take another step back, and make a small applause, sort of delighted with myself;*

– *"a genoux"* – I *do a prayer gesture and, kneeling, make the sign of the cross;*

+ *wren (lurking, restless, chirping)* – I *step forward and get down and try to get the feeling of that bird, though I doubt if a bird would have those feelings (laughs);*

– *listen* – *while down, I move the body posture back and do active listening;*

– *"They stoop to rise"* – I *step back, kneeling down as doing in exercise class, rolling up gradually;*

+ *Sea Captain* – I *step forward, salute, and "look over the deck for anything that might be on the horizon;"*

– *do some mathematics on your fingers* – I *step back and repeat the above gesture of adding;*

– *"a genoux"* – I *step back and do the sign of the cross, kneeling;*

+ *amused* – I *step forward and give a facial expression of amusement;*

– *play soldiers* – I *have a toy machine gun, and get down on the floor, crawling from left to right, firing it;*

– *hesitation* – I *sort of "freeze" in the middle of firing. My head and shoulders are up, and the stomach is flat, poised to shoot. I freeze for a few seconds. That's the end.*
(P. Bruce 1989 and 1990)

Solo 87 is to be performed for no longer than "nine minutes and twenty-four seconds" (Cage 1970a, 297). Neely Bruce performs Solo 87 for approximately eight-and-a-half minutes in the following manner:

+ *look for something in your pocket or pulse* – *this is overlapped with Solo 46, where I make hoe cakes, so I'm already cooking. I get the change out of my pocket, from which I'm going to make my collection of twelve pennies further on;*

– *wood duck* – I *make a vocal "quack;"*

– *elegance* – I *make a circular gesture with my arms that I think is "elegant;"*

– *death* – I *drop my head as if I suddenly died;*

+ *tears* – I *sort of extravagantly, with my right hand, wipe a tear from my right eye;*

– *locate a straight line between two points* – I *put the first two fingers of my left hand on the table where the cooking is, and using the index finger of my right hand, locate the points between my fingers on the table-top;*

– *make a collection of 12 things* – I *count out the twelve pennies on the table;*

– *measuring* – I *measure different things, usually with a carpenter's metal tape measure. Sometimes I measure the distance from the table-top to the floor, but if something going on is interesting, I measure that. Once I measured David Barron's height;*

– *give a lecture* – I *read a short paragraph from Carrie Jacobs-Bond's column "Friendly Preachments From Hollywood" in the 1920s. Phyllis has a clipping collection. This is the beginning of a column installment about thinking positive thoughts at breakfast. [Carrie Jacobs-Bond is a rather obscure person today, but was a popular song writer in the early twentieth century, perhaps best remembered for her songs "I Love You Truly" (1906) and "A Perfect Day" (1910) (Jacobs-Bond 1925).];*

– back — I turn my back to the audience;

+ open a book — the book I have is a large copy of the Jerusalem Bible. I'm facing up-stage with my back to the audience. The book is large, so the opening and closing is a real moment;

+ failure — I look dejected;

– raised shoulders — I raise my shoulders, but in a completely mechanical way. I make a conscious effort to make the action separate from an emotional connotation, even though the audience might interpret this action as an emotional statement;

– dance — I do a little dance separately, then;

+ open a book — I open the Jerusalem Bible, facing the audience;

+ raised shoulders — I raise my shoulders again;

– money — I take the collection of twelve pennies that are on the table and put them back in my pocket;

+ shadow — I observe my shadow, looking down on the floor where it is;

– a vertical line — I don't do that action;

+ chase — I run in place;

+ Debussy — this changes from performance to performance. I chose three pieces that related to American music — "General Lavine — eccentric," "Minstrels," and "Golliwog's Cakewalk" — and the three pieces that relate to nature — "The Snow Is Dancing," "Brouillards (Fog)," and "Bruyeres (Heaths)." Then I chose one page from each piece by chance, and then decided which would be appropriate to the theatre pieces in the Song Books. I have a sheaf of these, including other piano pieces by Debussy. You have to shift gears with this;

– seduce — I go over to Phyllis, kneel on one knee, and sing the opening of "Là ci darem la mano" from Mozart's Don Giovanni;

+ shadow — I observe my shadow again;

– a pure melody — usually I sing something like "Frere Jaques;"

+ sing like a factory "far enough to be musical" — I do a "vocal fry." You slow down your singing so that you hear the individual components of what you are singing. [This is making an extended tone at one's lowest use of the vocal chords, and sounds "very gravely."] If I'm near a microphone, I do this into it, otherwise it is hard to hear;

– seduce — the same as above;

+ make a collection of 12 things — I put the pennies back on the table. I'm not sure I always do it, because you don't have to do all these things, according to Cage's instructions;

+ solitary reflections — I sort of look wistfully into the distance, stage-right, and "muse;"

+ Debussy — I play a different page;

– "se mettre à plat-ventre" — I put myself flat on my stomach and lie full-front on the floor by the piano, then go back and;

– Debussy — I play another page;

+ *open a book — the same action as above. I must cross back from the piano to the table to get the Bible;*

+ *chase — again, I run in place;*

+ *"a sound that creeps into the ears so gradually that most do not observe it, and so our ears are gradually accustomed to the sound, and perchance we do not perceive it when at length it has become very much louder and more general." — I begin to breathe into the microphone, and I gradually make the breath louder and louder;*

– *ice — I have an ice-bucket, and take a piece of ice out and eat it. Sometimes I don't use ice, because you can't always find ice. I also have taken the ice-bucket and put it away under the other table [not the cooking table];*

– *religion — I read something from the Bible;*

– *chase — I run in place;*

+ *syncopation — I do different things. I've clapped my hands, or have sung an improvisation like "de-doo-de-doo," but not as a quotation from some other piece;*

– *low voice — I sing quietly on a low tone;*

+ *mushroom — I don't do this action;*

– *"se mettre à plat-ventre" — it works out that the previous several events are at the music stand, so I move from right to left or to the music stand and do a grand prostration. [This is an important gesture in the traditional Catholic Church as well as in Tibetan Buddhism.]*

– *"se mettre à plat-ventre" — I do the above action again;*

+ *solitary reflection — I look up musingly, at stage right. (N. Bruce 1991)*

APPENDIX 5

A *DIALOGUE* SCORE BY JOHN CAGE

The following is a previously unpublished score by John Cage for one of his *Dialogue* performances. This was discovered among his unpublished papers. The original is either lost or was given to someone, for Cage's copy is a photocopy. It apparently was written in ink, and consists of four lined pages measuring 8½ by 11 inches.

Although this score has no accompanying date, the content follows very closely the performance descriptions of *Dialogue* at the Denver Art Museum on October 30, 1978. One review characterizes this event as:

> *Many people ... were chatting with their neighbors and generally looking around when a man slid a table to the middle of the floor, turned around and pushed it back again.*
>
> *The man pushing the table wore a blue shirt out at the waist, blue jeans and moccasins. The people who didn't know he was John Cage assumed he was a stagehand working on the set and kept on talking but others began listening because the noise the table made was the opening salvo in the performance ...*
>
> *Suddenly, Merce Cunningham squirted in from the side and lay with his forehead pressed against the tile floor and his long arms spread. Nothing happened. There was no motion for a few moments, and there was complete silence.*
>
> *Cage walked to a counter and set an electric pot of water boiling and put a microphone to his throat.*
>
> *Then while Cunningham danced, Cage slurped down a soft drink. The microphone amplified his swallowing so that each glug and slurp filled the room with loud noise. (Caldwell 1978)*

Another review of this performance adds that Cage put on a pair of eyeglasses, answered a telephone "with garbled language," and moved a serving tray and stand across the floor. At times he also walked up and down a staircase, alternately using a dog or penguin mask. The review continues:

> *Cunningham is a commanding figure ... He moves with presence and falls more eloquently than anyone.*
>
> *Fluttering hands rivet the eyes, stalking, stiff walks suggest a menacing personage, pitiless ...*
>
> *Each time Cunningham appeared, it was with a different costume: white top and charcoal bottom, turquoise top, white suit with gloves, blue top, trench coat (involving a curiously humorous episode of a man returning to a lunch counter for a cracker and peanut butter), and a jump suit. (Giffin 1978)*

As is typical with reviews of other *Dialogue* events, Cage's performance is noted in less detail than Cunningham's actions.

The following score is, therefore, an important document not only of the basic content Cage employed in various instances of *Dialogue*, but also indicative of Cage's own type of events for a *Theatre Piece*-type performance.

There are several indeterminacies and particular notations which must be explained. In the section I title "Preliminary Notes," the first line includes "No mask 33–64" which is a reference to *I Ching* hexagrams used to make this composition; however there is no accompanying list of *I Ching* hexagrams used to make this specific work. The floor-plan of nine posts for objects has no indication of where the audience would be. From the other five *Dialogue* scores, all with similar floor-plans, three place the audience at the top of the figure; one places the audience at the bottom of the figure; and one has two floor-plans, which show the audience at the top, and then the bottom. I would guess that the audience is at the top of this specific floor-plan.

The readings listed are probably from *Empty Words*, but from the page numbers listed, only pages "25" and "34" correspond to spoken text in the published version. Quite possibly the page numbers Cage was referring to were from his original manuscript or typescript. In the actual performance section of the score, there are no indications of when the telephone will ring, nor when he will read or chant the five text selections. Possibly Cage had someone call on the telephone five different times through the hour, thus using the "telephone interruptions" as an instance of non-preconceived cues/timings, to further exemplify his aesthetic blurring distinctions between art and life.

Finally, the preliminary notes state that there are ten possible whistles to be employed. In the actual performance only five different whistles were used, and what they were is not identified.

The "Performance Score" section is the actual content of Cage's performance. The two masks he employed are very explicitly noted as being a dog and a penguin. The actual objects used are not identified, but probably were various items found on the premises previous to the performance, as Cage notes earlier to "Identify the objects/Practice the sounds."

Reading the score thus is a very straight-forward matter. My editing is minimal. Sections of text that were crossed-out in the hand-written version appear in square brackets. Material that does not appear in the original is identified by being italicized within brackets. Unfortunately Cage did not make — in this or the other *Dialogue* scores — any indication of the duration for individual events within the total hour. While many indeterminacies are contained within the score, and many unanswered questions remain, it is nonetheless an exemplary demonstration of Cage's concise and minimalist charm.

[DIALOGUE]

[Preliminary Notes]

Dog Mask downstairs
Coffee pot
8 objects (9 posts)

No mask 33–64
Make 3 copies (up & downstairs & kitchen)
Identify the objects
Practice the sounds

3 o	6 o	9 o
2 o	5 o	8 o
1 o	4 o	7 o

answering telephone (reading I) (Chanting IV) (no mask)
   Read 4 times 2, 4, 2 *[3?]*, 5
   Chant once 1

1st Reading	=	24″	Page 42	4th & 5th stanzas
2nd ″	=	16″	Page 34	6, 7, 8, & 9th ″
3rd ″	=	32″	Page 29	(last 2 stanzas)
4th ″	=	*[?″]*	Page 41	(last stanza & first 4 of pg. 42)
Chant	=	First column pg. 25 at 45″		

Drinking with throat mike (no mask)   Beer, tea, water
Door Sd. at top of stairs
Whistles (10)

[Performance Score]

Move object 1 to Post 9 without mask.

Go to Bar & drink water (with throat mike).

Start coffee pot without mask.

Repeat coffee pot with Dog mask (empty pot & flush with
   cold water before plugging in).

Make cup of tea. (Remove mask) downstairs.

Whistle #10 (upstairs).

Move object 5 to Post 1.

Go upstairs (wearing Dog mask) & make door noises.
   (Leave *[Dog]* Mask upstairs and stay there.)

Whistle #6 (upstairs).

Drink some tea.

Flush coffee pot (no mask) & start it again.

Move object 6 to post 6 (no mask).

Go upstairs & make noise. (Put on Penguin mask.)

Make more door noises. Then go down stairs leaving
[Penguin] mask there.

Drink more tea.

Go upstairs & whistle 9.

Make door noise.

Whistle 3.

Move object 3 to Post 6 (without mask).

[Drink beer.] Flush & start coffee pot (without mask).

Drink more tea.

Go upstairs to make door sound (wearing Penguin mask).
Leave mask there.

Move object 7 to Post 8 without mask.

[Go upstairs to m] Drink beer.

Go upstairs to make door sound.

Whistle 6.

Move object 4 to Post 4 (wearing P. mask).

Return upstairs, remove P. *[mask]* & whistle 1.

Go downstairs wearing Dog mask, flush pot, & start.
Remove *[Dog]* mask.

Make & Drink tea.

Go upstairs Wearing Dog mask. Make door sd. Change D *[Dog]*
to Penguin mask.

Move object 2 to Post 6 (wearing P. mask).

Flush & start coffee pot   ″   ″   ″   .

Go upstairs to make door sound ″   ″ ″ .

After pause make door sound again. Leave *[Penguin]* mask.

Go downstairs. Flush & start coffee pot (no mask).

Go upstairs. Whistle 5. Put on P mask.

Move object 8 to Post 5 (wearing P.).

Move object 7 (at Post 8) to Post 3 (wearing P.).

Go upstairs. Remove *[Penguin]* mask. Whistle 10.

Move object 5 (at Post 1) to Post 9 without mask.

Go upstairs & make door sound (wearing P. *[)]*. (Go down
    a little & back up.)

Whistle 3.

Flush & start coffee pot (no mask).

[Go back] Drink beer.

Flush & start coffee pot (no mask).

Drink water.

Whistle 3.

APPENDIX 6

FRANCES OTT ALLEN'S EXPERIENCES
OF *HPSCHD*

(The following is an edited version of a Journal entry, made in collaboration with its author, Frances Ott Allen, relating her personal experiences of *HPSCHD* at the University of Illinois, Urbana-Champaign, on May 16, 1969. Allen's account of the performance is the most complete, single view of the entire evening, and includes several details not found in any other source. The floorplan from this Journal entry appears as Fig. 33 in Chapter 6. In her letter to me dated May 28, 1990, she notes that "parading" is "a reference to the Beatles' *Hard Day's Night* — the grandfather's advice to Ringo.")

HPSCHD on as we all walk in. First impression: interesting and exciting. We walk down through the empty seats to the center. The sounds are strange. Large sheets of clear plastic are hung in rows above a center circle — slides and movies are being projected on the plastic. Between rows of plastic, floodlights shine down into the circle. There are four or six podiums with harpsichords — people playing them — each a different piece. Slides are also being projected on screens around the outside edge. The crowd seems to gravitate toward the center — under the floodlights.

We walk around the center area several times — it's very pleasant — like "parading" on a Sunday. Everyone walks around and smiles. You see them like people on the street — wondering what they are doing, thinking, what brings them here. You share part of a moment. I ask myself what's so great about this, and though I am enjoying it now, how long can it hold my interest — the continuous sound — always different but the same, and the sheets of plastic with colored and black-and-white pictures. But the question evaporates and I don't even realize it at the time and my interest is absorbed.

All around the hall are speakers. Each one emits a sound now and then. Some are high squeaks and peeps and others are low drones — all manner of random sounds come from hundreds of places — it's like the random sounds of civilization and all through it there is a tinkling hint of harpsichord — a humanity to cling to.

I was wearing my red and blue dress. Suddenly a floodlight of black light lit it strangely. "Look at your dress" Roy said — and then light skipped off playing here and there. Around 8 p.m. or so smocks were passed out at one area of the circle — mythological figures printed on them. The dark print became bright florescent color under the lights. With your smock on you assumed a new identity. People look at each other's bright pictures. I am a goatherd with two goats, Roy a warrior fighting a hydra. The black spotlight catches people at the edge of the circle and in the seats, and playfully and at random shows a beautiful color here, another there.

About 9 I felt it was very mysterious — the center floodlights changed from blue to red, then to yellowish white. After a long period of blue, the red then yellow was like a new day, then the blue would come again.

Sometimes in the center under the lights (especially the yellow) the dark corners of the stadium seemed like outer space — so black and far away. It was like being on a small planet sitting in space. You could get a feeling too of being in space and seeing a planet from high in the seats. A globe covered with pieces of mirror somewhere reflected little flecks of light that moved and shone like distant stars. Then again the center reminded me of a city and the seats outside of suburbs — it especially seemed that way under the blue light from the seats.

Now and then some sounds or gongs — like thunder, very threatening. It was especially strange to be in the center when these sounds occurred — they seemed to tell of some great catastrophe or warn of impending doom. But through it life went on — the tinkling harpsichord and all the other sounds and people talking and all the colorful slides and movies and movement.

About 10 o'clock movie-makers were noticeable and also a number of people "performing" for them. Between 9:30 and 11 there was also a sort of Happening: many people had been sitting in the center on the concrete floor under the sheets, watching the projections. A small, slightly built fellow with dark shoulder-length hair, a blue shirt and dark jeans whistled on a leaf and danced in and around. He disappeared, then sometime later danced in again whistling. Now he danced mainly with his arms, swaying, reaching toward people — trying to get them to respond, to reach toward him in the same rhythm, never touching, and hands reached toward him. Later I saw him again hopping among those seated — holding hands together, a guy and girl — sometimes including himself, a three-person hug. Then he began whistling again in rhythm — many of the people in the center clapped along — it grew in intensity, finally he threw up his arms with a scream and disappeared out of the crowd.

Also for a time a number of people sitting there threw wads of paper up into the air again and again — it was interesting in the colored light — from the seats high up it looked like sodapop effervescence. Some kids also sat blowing soap bubbles.

In one corner a silkscreen printed all night — a Beethoven-type face on smocks — many people brought T-shirts, which the printers printed for them.

11:15 to 11:45 we sat and watched from high in the seats. For a long time a blue spotlight shone on a harpsichordist — the center was lit red — very colorful — sort of decadent color.

The sounds went on forever — like the universe — the stars and the planets and the sounds of someone somewhere.

Then we walk back down and around the circle at midnight, the center lights change quickly — red, blue, red, blue, red, blue — then white lights on all over the hall and the music stops. It's all over and it's like it never happened — like may be only in your mind. Mr. Cage in a blue suit is standing by a harpsichord. People all around applaud — some to talk to him or get an autograph.

LIST OF REFERENCES

(Note: all of John Cage's compositions previous to 1960 are listed by year of composition rather than year of publication. Most of the pre-1960 works that have been published are copyrighted 1960 by Henmar Press Inc.)

About music furthered in the Italian tradition/Quaderni Perugini di Musica Contemporanea 1992 *Die Neue Zürcher Zeitung*, 11/12 July. Translated by Laura Kuhn; C. F. Peters files, New York.

Allen, Frances Ott 1969 Unpublished journal entry of 17 May on *HPSCHD*, sent to the author 2 May, 1989.

Anarchy with a Beat. 1960 *Time*, 21 March, 46.

Arnbom, Arne 1966 *Variations V*. 50 min. black & white sound film. Hamburg: Nord-deutscher Rundfunk. Film and Videocassette available from the Merce Cunningham Foundation.

Artaud, Antonin 1958 *The Theater and Its Double*. Translated by Mary Caroline Richards. New York: Grove Press Inc.

Attali, Jacques 1985 *Noise: The Political Economy of Music*. Translated by Brian Massumi. Minneapolis: University of Minnesota Press.

Atwood, David 1971 *WGBH-TV*. 28 min. color sound film. Boston: WGBH-TV. Available on rental from C. F. Peters.

Avignone, June 1985 Expect the Unexpected. *The (Bergen, N.J.) News*, 8 April.

Avshalomoff, Jack 1940 Cage Percussion Players ... A Review. *The Reed College Quest*, 16 February.

Barron, David 1990 Interview by author, 27 April, New York.

Battcock, Gregory, ed. 1981 Paik and Moorman Perform Cage. In *Breaking the Sound Barrior: A Critical Anthology of the New Music*, 142–149. New York: E. P. Dutton.

Behrens, Jack; and Gayle Young 1992 Notes to *Europera 5* excerpt; CD accompanying *Musicworks 52*, Winter.

Berger, Arthur 1951 New Music Society: "Imaginary Landscape" No. 4 for 12 Radios Heard. *The New York Herald Tribune*, 12 May.

Bird, Bonnie 1991 Interview by author, 10 June, New York.

Block, Rene 1980 Der Summe aller Klänge ist grau. In *Für Augen und Ohren*, ed. Werner Düttmann and Ulrich Eckhart, 103–146. Berlin: Akademie der Kunste und Berliner Festspiele.

Bowen, Meirion 1990 Cage and the anti-opera. *The Guardian*, 19 June.

Brecht, George 1966 *Chance-Imagery*. New York: Great Bear.

Brockman, John 1966 "Theatre, Engineering": All the Fun Was Backstage. *The Village Voice*, 27 October.

Brooks, William 1982 Choice & change in Cage's recent music. In *A John Cage Reader in celebration of his 70th birthday*, ed. Peter Gena, Jonathan Brent, and Don Gillespie, 82–100. New York: C. F. Peters Corporation.

1984 Album liner notes to John Cage's *Sixteen Dances*, performed by New Music Concerts. New York: Musical Observations, Inc.

Brown, Anthony 1974 An Interview with Dennis Russell Davies and John Cage. **Asterisk* Vol 1, no. 1 (December): 20–25.

Brown, Carolyn 1960 Unpublished letter to her parents 8 March, sent to the author 5 May 1989.

1989 Telephone interview by author, 5 May.

Brown, Norman O. 1989 John Cage. In *John Cage at Seventy-Five*, ed. Richard Fleming and William Duckworth, 97–118. Lewisburg, Pa.: Bucknell University Press.

Bruce, Neely 1989 Interview by author, 3 April, New York.

1991 Telephone interview by author, 21 January.

Bruce, Phyllis 1989 Telephone interview by author, 10 May.

1990 Telephone interview by author, 18 October.

Cadieu, Martine 1970 Les journees de musique contemporaine a Paris. *Les Lettres Francaises*, 4 November.

Cage, John 1936 *Trio*. New York: Henmar Press Inc.

1938 *The Marriage at the Eiffel Tower*. Unpublished score in the collection of the John Cage Estate, housed at the New York Public Library.

1939a *First Construction (in Metal)*. New York: Henmar Press Inc.

1939b *Imaginary Landscape No. 1*. New York: Henmar Press Inc.

1940a *Bacchanale*. New York: Henmar Press Inc.

1940b *Living Room Music*. New York: Henmar Press Inc.

1940c Program notes for Reed College concert performed by the Cage Percussion Players 14 February. In the John Cage Archive, Northwestern University.

1942a *The City Wears a Slouch Hat*. New York: Henmar Press Inc.

1942b *Credo in Us*. New York: Henmar Press Inc.

1942c *Totem Ancestor*. New York: Henmar Press Inc.

1942d *The Wonderful Widow of Eighteen Springs*. New York: Henmar Press Inc.

1943 *She is Asleep*. New York: Henmar Press Inc.

1944a *Four Walls*. New York: Henmar Press Inc.

1944b *Root of an Unfocus*. New York: Henmar Press Inc.

1944c *A Valentine out of Season*. New York: Henmar Press Inc.

1946 *Two Pieces*. New York: Henmar Press Inc.

1947 *The Seasons*. New York: Henmar Press Inc.

1946–48 *Sonatas and Interludes*. New York: Henmar Press Inc.

1950 *String Quartet in Four Parts*. New York: Henmar Press Inc.

1951a *Concerto for Prepared Piano and Orchestra*. New York: Henmar Press Inc.

1951b *Imaginary Landscape No. 4 (March No. 2)*. New York: Henmar Press Inc.

1951c *Music of Changes*. New York: Henmar Press Inc.

1951d *Sixteen Dances*. New York: Henmar Press Inc.

1952a *Imaginary Landscape No. 5*. New York: Henmar Press Inc.

1952b *Imaginary Landscape No. 5.* Tape recording in possession of Jean Erdman, New York.
1952c Projector Part in Black Mountain untitled event; unpublished, in the composer's papers.
1952d *Water Music.* New York: Henmar Press Inc.
1952e Unpublished work notes for *Water Music,* titled "6 W. 12," in the New York Public Library, MN3 Am. 1952.
1952f *Williams Mix.* Unpublished score, in the collection of the Margarete Roeder Gallery, New York.
1953a *4'33".* In *Source* Vol. 1, no. 3 (July 1967): 46–55.
1953b *4'33".* New York: Henmar Press Inc. (1993).
1957 *Winter Music.* New York: Henmar Press Inc.
1957–58 *Concert for Piano and Orchestra.* New York: Henmar Press Inc.
1958a *Fontana Mix.* New York: Henmar Press Inc.
1958b *Music Walk.* New York: Henmar Press Inc.
1958c *Music Walk* realization, unpublished in the collection of the composer.
1958d *The 25-Year Retrospective Concert of the Music of John Cage.* A three-record set with score excerpts and notes by the composer, recorded in performance at Town Hall, New York, 15 May. New York: George Avakian.
1958e *Variations I.* New York: Henmar Press Inc.
1959a *Indeterminacy.* A two-record set with notes by the composer. New York: Folkways Recordings.
1959b *Sounds of Venice.* New York: Henmar Press Inc.
1959c *Water Walk.* New York: Henmar Press Inc.
1959d *Water Walk* composition notes, unpublished in the collection of the composer.
1960a *Cartridge Music.* New York: Henmar Press Inc.
1960b *Cartridge Music* realization, unpublished in the collection of the composer.
1960c *4'33"* (typed version). New York: Henmar Press Inc.
1960d *Solo for Voice 2.* New York: Henmar Press Inc.
1960e *Theatre Piece.* New York: Henmar Press Inc.
1961 *Silence.* Middletown, Conn.: Wesleyan University Press.
1962a Liner notes to the recording of *Cartridge Music,* performed by the composer and David Tudor. New York: Time Records.
1962b *0'00".* Unpublished scores and notes, in the collection of the composer.
1962c *0'00" (4'33" No. 2).* New York: Henmar Press Inc.
1963a *Variations III.* New York: Henmar Press Inc.
1963b *Variations III* realization, unpublished in the collection of the composer.
1963c *Variations IV.* New York: Henmar Press Inc.
1964 *Variations IV, Vol. 1 & 2.* Two records, issued separately, of the composer and David Tudor performing *Variations IV* at the Feigen/Palmer Gallery, Los Angeles, on 12 January. Los Angeles: Everest Records.
1965a *Rozart Mix.* New York: Henmar Press Inc.
1965b *Variations V.* New York: Henmar Press Inc.
1966 *Variations VI.* New York: Henmar Press Inc.
1967 *A Year from Monday.* Middletown, Conn.: Wesleyan University Press.

1969 *Cheap Imitation.* New York: Henmar Press Inc.

1970a *Song Books.* New York: Henmar Press Inc.

1970b *Song Books Instructions.* New York: Henmar Press Inc.

ca. 1970 [*Dialogue.*] Untitled manuscript, in a folder marked "pre-1976," in the John Cage Archive, Northwestern University.

ca. 1971 *Atlas Eclipticalis, Winter Music, and Cartridge Music.* Phonograph recording conducted by Rainer Riehn, performed by Ensemble Musica Negativa. Hamburg: Deutsche Grammophon.

1971 *WGBH–TV.* New York: Henmar Press Inc.

1973 *M.* Middletown, Conn.: Wesleyan University Press.

1974 *Score (40 Drawings by Thoreau) and 23 Parts for any Instruments and/or Voices, Twelve Haiku followed by a Recording of the Dawn at Stony Point, New York, Aug. 6, 1974.* New York: Henmar Press Inc.

1975 *Child of Tree.* New York: Henmar Press Inc.

1976a *Apartment House 1776.* New York: Henmar Press Inc.

1976b *Branches.* New York: Henmar Press Inc.

1976c *Cheap Imitation.* Live performance by the composer, recorded 7 March at Mills College, Oakland, Ca. Italy: Cramps Records.

1976d *Renga.* New York: Henmar Press Inc.

1976e *Song Books with Empty Words III.* Phonograph recording conducted by Clytus Gottwald, and performed by the Schola Cantorum, with the composer reading *Empty Words III.* Mainz: Wergo.

1977 *Inlets.* New York: Henmar Press Inc.

ca. 1978 Five *Dialogue* scores, unpublished in the collection of the composer.

1978 *Variations VIII.* New York: Henmar Press Inc.

1979a *Empty Words.* Middletown, Conn.: Wesleyan University Press.

1979b _____ , _____ _____ *CIRCUS ON* _____ . New York: Henmar Press Inc.

ca. 1980 *4'33".* Phonograph recording performed by Gianni-Emilio Simonetti. Italy: Cramps.

ca. 1982 *4'33".* Holograph recording performed by the composer. Available on rental from C. F. Peters, New York.

1982a *House Full of Music.* Unpublished notes in the collection of the composer.

1982b Interview by author, 2 December, New York.

1983a *HV.* Series of thirty-six monoprints. Oakland, Ca.: Crown Point Press.

1983b *X.* Middletown, Conn.: Wesleyan University Press.

1984 *Music Circus for Children of Torino.* Unpublished notes in the collection of the composer.

1985a Liner notes to *Atlas Eclipticalis with Winter Music.* A four-record set conducted by the composer, performed by The New Performance Group. Kew Gardens, N.Y.: Mode Ltd.

1985b *Roaratorio, an Irish Circus on Finnegans Wake,* ed. Klaus Schöning. Königstein: Athenäum.

ca. 1986 *4'33",* handwritten revision of 1960 typed score version. New York: Henmar Press Inc.

1986a Work notes for *Europeras 1 & 2*, collection of the composer.

1986b Interview by author, 9 April, New York.

1987a *Empty Words Part IV*. A two-record set performed by the composer. Cologne: Michael F. Bauer.

1987b Work notes for *Europeras 1 & 2*, collection of the composer.

1987c Program notes to *Europeras 1 & 2*, 12 December. Frankfurt: Frankfurt Oper.

1987d *Europeras 1 & 2*. New York: Henmar Press Inc.

1987e Interview by author, 9 October, New York.

1987f Program for *Musicircus*, 6 September, Los Angeles.

1988a Program notes for American performance of *Europeras 1 & 2*. Purchase, N.Y.: Pepsico Summerfare.

1988b Interview by author, 12 May, New York.

1989a *4'33"*. CD recording performed by the Amadinda Percussion Group. Budapest: Hungaraton.

1989b *ONE³*. Unpublished notes, in the collection of the composer.

1990a Interview by author, 10 August, New York.

1990b *I-VI: MethodStructureIntentionDisciplineNotationIndeterminacyInterpenetration ImitationDevotionCircumstancesVariableStructureNonunderstandingContingencyIn-consistencyPerformance*. Cambridge, Mass.: Harvard University Press.

1991a *Cartridge Music*. CD recording performed by David Tudor, Takehisa Kosugi, and Michael Pugliese. Kew Gardens, N.Y.: Mode.

1991b *FOUR³*. New York: Henmar Press Inc.

1991c *4'33"*. CD recording, Wayne Marshall, piano. Perivale, Middlesex, England: Floating Earth.

1992a A Composer's Confessions. *Musicworks* 52 (spring): 6–15.

1992b *Europera 5*. Recorded excerpt, performed by Jane Leibel, Darryl Edwards, Jack Behrens, and Noel Martin. CD accompanying *Musicworks* 52.

1992c *FOUR⁶*. Performed by Joan La Barbara, voice; William Winant, percussion; Leonard Stein, piano; and John Cage, voice; at Central Park, New York, 23 July. Tape recording courtesy of Joan La Barbara.

1992d *ONE¹²*. Unpublished notes, in the collection of the composer.

1993 *4'33"*. Performed by Frank Zappa, in the 2-CD anthology *A Chance Operation: The John Cage Tribute*. Westbury, N.Y.: Koch International Classics.

1994a *Apartment House 1776*. In the CD *John Cage: Orchestra Works I*, performed by the New England Conservatory Philharmonia. New York: Mode.

1994b *Europera 5*. CD recording of the world premiere. New York: Mode.

1995 *Europeras 3 & 4*. Two-CD set of the 1993 Long Beach Opera production. New York: Mode.

Cage, John; and Daniel Charles 1981 *For the Birds*. Boston: Marion Boyars.

Cage, John; and Andrew Culver 1990 *Europeras 3 & 4*. Composition by Cage; and textual notes by Culver. New York: Henmar Press Inc.

1991 *Europera 5*. Composition by Cage; and textual notes by Culver. New York: Henmar Press Inc.

Cage, John; and Lejaren Hiller 1969 *HPSCHD*. Phonograph recording with computer printout, performed by Antoinette Vischer, David Tudor, and Neely Bruce. New York: Nonesuch.

Cage, John; and Kathleen Hoover 1959 *Virgil Thomson: His Life and Music*. New York: Thomas Yoseloff.

Cage, John; and Alison Knowles, eds. 1969 *Notations*. New York: Something Else Press.

Cage, John; and Lois Long 1982 *Mud Book*. New York: Abrams.

Cage, John; and William Russell 1939 Percussion Music and Its Relation to the Modern Dance. *The Dance Observer* (October): 226, 274.

Cage Speech Is Termed "Astounding". 1964 *The LSU Daily Reveille* (Baton Rouge, La.): 10 January.

Cage: Variations IV, Vol. 2. 1969 *High Fidelity Magazine* (February): 84.

Cage-y: opera guyed. 1988 *The New York Post*, 18 July.

Caldwell, Larry 1978 Show Features Common Sounds. *The Daily Camera* (Boulder, Col.), 31 October.

Calendar 1952 Black Mountain College Calendar for August. Photocopy courtesy of David Vaughan.

Campana, Deborah 1985 Form and Structure in the Music of John Cage. Ph.D. dissertation, Northwestern University.

Cernovitch, Nicholas 1989 Telephone interview by author, 7 May.

Close, Roy M. 1978 Cunningham-Cage "event" well planned. *The Minneapolis Star*, 17 October.

Cocteau, Jean 1964 *The Wedding on the Eiffel Tower*. In *Modern French Theatre*, edited and translated by Michael Benedikt and George E. Wellwarth, 101–115. New York: E. P. Dutton & Co., Inc.

Cohn, Robert Greer 1949 *Mallarmé's Un Coup de Dés: an exegesis*. New Haven, Conn.: Yale University Press.

Composing by Knucklebone. 1962 *Time*, 13 April, 55.

Cope, David H. 1981 *New Directions In Music*, 3rd. ed. Dubuque, Iowa: Wm. C. Brown Company.

Corner, Philip 1989 Interview by author, 1 April, New York.

Cowell, Henry 1938 *The Marriage at the Eiffel Tower*. Unpublished score in the Notations Archive, Northwestern University.

1952 Current Chronicle — New York. *The Musical Quarterly* Vol. XXXVIII, no. 1 (January): 126–136.

Culver, Andrew 1988 Interview by author, 23 November, New York.

1992 Interview by author, 20 October, New York.

1993a Sample computer print-out for *ONE*^{12}, sent to the author.

1993b Telephone interview by author, 1 July.

Cunningham, Merce 1944 *Four Walls*. 6 min. color silent film, collection of the Merce Cunningham Dance Foundation Archive.

1964 *Story*. Produced by Finnish Television and directed by Hakki Seppala. 20 min. black & white sound film. Available on film and videocassette from the Merce Cunningham Foundation.

1968 *Changes*. New York: Something Else Press.

1982 A collaborative process between music and dance. In *A John Cage Reader in celebration of his 70th birthday*, ed. Peter Gena, Jonathan Brent, and Don Gillespie, 107–120. New York C. F. Peters Corporation.

1985 *The Dancer and the Dance*, in conversation with Jacqueline Lesschaeve. New York: Boyars.

1989a *Changing Steps*. Choreography by Merce Cunningham, video directed by Cunningham and Elliot Caplan. New York: Merce Cunningham Dance Foundation.

1989b Interview by author, 18 August, New York.

Darter, Tom 1982 Interview with John Cage. *Keyboard Magazine* (October): 18–29.

Daseler, Robert 1970 John Cage Remains Heretic's Heretic in Heretical Times. *The Middletown (Conn.) Press*, 10 April.

Driver, Paul 1990 Glass moves a little darkly. *The (London) Sunday Times*, 24 June.

Duberman, Martin 1972 *Black Mountain: An Exploration in Community*. New York: E. P. Dutton & Co., Inc.

Duchamp, Marcel 1960 *The Bride Stripped Bare By Her Bachelors, Even*. Translated by George Heard Hamilton. New York: George Wittenborn Inc.

1973 *The Writings of Marcel Duchamp*. Edited by Michel Sanovillet and Elmer Peterson. New York: Da Capo Press, Inc.

Dunn, Robert, ed. 1962 *John Cage Cataloque*. New York: C. F. Peters Corporation.

Durner, Leah 1988 John Cage: Past & Future in *Europeras 1 & 2*. *Ear* Vol. 13, no. 2 (April): 10–11; 13.

Dworkin, Andy 1992 "A Smashing Success": More than 1,000 took part in week-long tribute to John Cage. *The Stanford Daily*, 4 February.

Dyer, Richard 1976 The Boston Symphony Orchestra. *The Boston Evening Globe*, 1 October.

Erdman, Jean 1989 Interview by author, 11 April, New York.

Ericson, Raymond 1961 Assorted Sounds Heard in Concert. *The New York Times*, 21 April.

Faxon, Grace B. 1913 *The School Year: An Assemblage of Modern Material for Everyday Use in the Schoolroom*. Dansville, N.Y.: F. A. Owen Publishing Company.

Fine, Douglas J. 1992 The Music of Noise: Composer John Cage makes his own sound. *The Peninsula Times Tribune*, 24 January.

Flanagan, Ray 1967 John Cage Releases His "Chance Theories." *The (Allentown, Pa) Morning Call*, 23 February.

Flanagan, William, 1960 A 3-Ring Circus of Lunacy Is This Musical Premiere. *The New York Herald-Tribune*, 8 March.

Francis, John Richard 1976 Structure in the Solo Piano Music of John Cage. Ph.D dissertation, Florida State University.

Gann, Kyle 1992 Cagemusicircus!. *The Village Voice*, 17 November.

Gena, Peter; and Jonathan Brent 1982 Recordings of Cage's Music. In *A John Cage Reader in celebration of his 70th birthday*, ed. Peter Gena, Jonathan Brent, and Don Gillespie, 202–207. New York: C. F. Peters Corporation.

Giffin, Glenn 1978 "Dialogue" Provides Absorbing Evening. *The Denver Post*, 31 October.

Gillespie, Don 1988 Interview by author, November, New York.

Gluck, Grace 1966 Disharmony at the Armory. *The New York Times*, 30 October.

Golea, Antoine 1970 Musicale Internationale De La Musique Au Cirque. *Carrefour de Idees* (Paris), 4 November.

Goldstein, Malcolm 1988 *Sounding the Full Circle.* Sheffield, Vt.: Malcolm Goldstein.

1989 Interview by author, 5 April, New York.

Goodman, Peter 1988 John Cage's Wild Collage. *Newsday*, 16 July.

Gouvels, Georgette 1988 John Cage stages meaningful madness. *The Fannett Westchester*, 16 July.

Gray, Francine du Plessix 1990 Black Mountain: The Breaking (Making) of a Writer. In *Black Mountain College: Sprouted Seeds*, ed. Mervin Lane, 300–311. Knoxville: University of Tennessee Press.

Green, Stanley 1971 *Ring Bells! Sing Songs!: Broadway Musicals of the 1930s.* New Rochelle, N.Y.: Arling House.

Greenaway, Peter 1982 *John Cage: A Music Circus.* 55 min. film documentary. London: BBC.

Griffiths, Paul 1982 *Cage.* London: Oxford University Press.

Groenfeldt, Tom 1985 The Impatient Sounds of Silence. *The (Bergen, N.J.) Record*, 29 March.

Guest, Ann Hutchinson 1984 *Dance Notation: The process of recording movement on paper.* New York: Dance Horizons.

Guzzo, Louis R. 1962 Cage's Electronic Music Amazes and Amuses. *The Seattle Times*, 27 September.

Haas, Joseph 1969 A Happening with John Cage. *The Chicago Daily News*, 10 May.

Hakim, Eleanor 1979 Cage in Paris. Unpublished article in the John Cage Archive, Northwestern University.

Hamm, Charles 1980 John Cage. In *The New Grove Dictionary of Music and Musicians*, ed. Stanley Sadie, 597–603. London: Macmillan Publishers Limited.

Hancock, Jane 1985 Arp's Chance Collages. In *Dada Dimensions*, ed. Stephen C. Foster, 47–82. Ann Arbor, Mich.: UMI Research Press.

Harding, James 1975 *Erik Satie.* London: Secker & Warburg.

Harris, Charlene, ed. 1988 John Cage in Frankfurt. Story no. 15182 on *European Journal*, English transcript of news program on Oregon Public Television.

Harris, Gary 1989 Interview by author, 5 September, New York.

Harris, Mary Emma 1987 *The Arts at Black Mountain College.* Cambridge, Mass.: The MIT Press.

Harrison, Jay S. 1966 "Dear Sirs: Here's Some Stravinsky to Act By" (subtitled "Memo to Sir Laurence, Sir John and Sir Ralph"). *The New York Post*, 16 July.

Henck, Herbert, ed. 1985 *Ansätze zur Musik der Gegenwart Jahrbuch, Band 5 (1984/85).* Cologne: Neuland.

Hendrick, Kimmis 1972 Mushrooms — and listening. *The Christian Science Monitor*, 9 September.

Herbort, Heinz Josef 1987 Die Oper uberlebt (alles). *Die Zeit* (Hamburg), 18 December.

Hines, Thomas S. 1994 "Then Not Yet 'Cage' ": The Los Angeles Years, 1912–1938. In *John Cage: Composed in America*, ed. Marjorie Perloff and Charles Junkerman, 65–99. Chicago: The University of Chicago Press.

Horowitz, Joseph 1977 Cage and Grete Sultan Collaborate on Program. *The New York Times*, 25 October.

Horvath, Adam 1992 "Europera 5": Yet Another John Cage Puzzle. *New York Newsday*, 24 August.

Husarik, Stephen 1983 John Cage and Lejaren Hiller: HPSCHD, 1969. *American Music* Vol. 1, no. 2 (Summer), 1–21.

Huang Po 1958 *The Zen Teaching of Huang Po: On the Transmission of Mind.* Translated by John Blofeld. New York: Grove Press, Inc.

Hulten, Pontus, ed. 1993 *Marcel Duchamp: Work and Life.* Texts by Jennifer Gough-Cooper and Jacques Caumont. Cambridge, Mass.: The MIT Press.

It It Music? 1963 *Newsweek*, 2 September, 53.

Ives, Charles 1972 *Memos.* Edited by John Kirkpatrick. New York: W. W. Norton & Company, Inc.

Jacobs-Bond, Carrie 1925 *Songs Everybody Sings.* Boston: Carrie Jacobs-Bond & Son.

James, Carol P. 1989 Duchamp's Silent Noise/Music for the Deaf. In *Marcel Duchamp: Artist of the Century*, ed. Rudolf Kuengli and Francis M. Naumann, 106–126. Cambridge, Mass.: The MIT Press.

Johnson, Tom 1973 Manning the radio stations. *The Village Voice*, 13 December.

1978 The Content of John Cage. *The Village Voice*, 9 January.

Johnston, Ben 1989 Telephone interview by author, 31 August.

Johnston, Jill 1991 Telephone interview by author, 11 January.

Johnstone, Will B.; and Jack Suhl 1942 Bach, Beethoven, Brahms and Beer. *The (New York) World-Telegraph*, 6 March.

Jones, Caroline A. 1993 Finishing School: John Cage and the Abstract Expressionist Ego. In *Critical Inquiry* Vol. 19, no 4 (Summer), 628–665.

Jou, Tsung Hwa 1984 *The Tao of I Ching.* Sciota, Pa.: Tai Chi Foundation.

Joyce, James 1939 *Finnegans Wake.* New York: The Viking Press.

Jungheinrich, Hans-Klaus 1987 Arien-Faden im kulinarischen Labyrinth. *Frankfurter Rundschau*, 14 December.

Junkerman, Charles 1993 Modeling Anarchy: The Example of John Cage's Musicircus. In *The Chicago Review* Vol. 38, no. 4 (Winter), 153–168.

Kaplan, Stuart R. 1971 *Tarot Classic.* New York: U. S. Games Systems, Inc.

Kaprow, Allan 1966 *Assemblage, Environments & Happenings.* New York: Abrams.

1989 Telephone interview by author, 4 April.

Kennedy, John; and Charles Wood 1990 Made in America: The Music of William Russell. Program notes for a concert by Essential Music at Florence Gould Hall, New York, 24 February.

1992 Rare Cage. Program notes for a concert by Essential Music at Greenwich House Auditorium, New York, 16 April.

Kenyon, Nicholas 1990 Just like opera up for the cup. *The (London) Observer*, 24 June.

Kirby, Michael 1965 *Happenings: An Illustrated Anthology.* New York: E. P. Dutton & Co., Inc.

1969 *The Art of Time.* New York: E. P. Dutton & Co., Inc.

1971 *Futurist Performace.* New York: E. P. Dutton & Co., Inc.

1987 *A Formalist Theatre*. Philadelphia: University of Pennsylvania Press.

1990 Written note to author, May.

Kirby, Michael; and Richard Schechner 1965 An Interview with John Cage. In *Tulane Drama Review* Vol. 10, no. 2 (Winter), 50–72.

Klein, Howard 1966 Music: Stravinsky's Own. *The New York Times*, 16 July.

Klüver, Billy 1988 Notes for John Cage. Unpublished oral presentation given at Wesleyan University, 27 February. In the John Cage Archive, Northwestern University.

Klüver, Billy; Julie Martin; and Barbara Rose 1972 *Pavilion*. New York: E. P. Dutton & Co., Inc.

Kneit, Tibor 1982 Spiel mit der Substanz. *Der Tages Spiegel* (Berlin), 12 December.

Knowles, Alison 1989 Interview by author, 3 May, New York.

Koch, Gerhard R. 1987 Der babylonische Sprachführer: Uraufführung von John Cages ''Europeras 1 & 2'' im Frankfurter Schauspielhaus. *Frankfurter Allgemeine Zeitung*, 14 December.

Kosman, Joshua 1992 Stanford's Big Splash For Cage. *The San Francisco Chronicle*, 25 January.

Kostelanetz, Richard 1969 They All Came to Cage's ''Circus''. *The New York Times*, 25 May.

1970 *A John Cage Reader*, ed. New York: RK Editions.

1980a *Scenarios: Scripts to Perform*, ed. New York: Assembling Press.

1980b *The Theatre of Mixed-Means: An Introduction to Happenings, Kinetic Environments and Other Mixed-Means Presentations*. New York: RK Editions.

1987 John Cage. In *High Performance #38*, Vol. 10, no. 2, 20–29.

1988a *Conversing with Cage*, ed. New York: Limelight.

1988b John Cage's First Opera, Written by the Numbers. *The New York Times*, 10 July.

Kosugi, Takehisa 1991 Inquiry by author, 19 March, New York.

Kotik, Petr 1990 Telephone interview by author, 27 February.

Kotz, Mary Lynn 1990 *Rauschenberg/Art and Life*. New York: Harry N. Abrams, Inc.

Kragland, John 1966 John Cage: musical McLuhan. *The Globe and Mail* (Toronto), 13 May.

Kramer, Jonathan D. 1988 *The Time of Music: New Meanings, New Temporalities, New Listening Strategies*. New York: Schirmer Books.

Kremen, Irwin 1992 Telephone interview, 23 October.

Kubota, Shigeko 1970 *Marcel Duchamp and John Cage*. Tokyo: Takeyoshi Miyazawa.

Kuhn, Laura Diane 1992 John Cage's *Europeras 1 & 2*: The Musical Means of Revolution. Ph.D. dissertation, The University of California, Los Angeles.

Kuhn, Marsha 1969 HPSCHD! Woweee!. *The Daily Illini* (Urbana-Champaign, Ill.). 6 May.

La Barbara, Joan 1993 Telephone interview by author, 1 May.

La Hay, Wauhillau 1942 Radio's Pioneers Air 'Columbia Workshop': WBBM Originates Novel Program Today for Ultramodern Ears. *The Chicago Sun*, 31 May.

Lenel, Ludwig 1977 Recollection told to author during the spring semester at Muhlenberg College, Allentown, Pa.

"Little" Magazine Gets a Bit Boost at Gotham Mart. 1976 *The New York Times*, 9 January.

Look, No Hands! And It's Music. 1954 *The New York Times*, 15 April.

Lucier, Alvin 1988 Notes in the Margin. Unpublished oral presentation given at Wesleyan University, 11 February. In the John Cage Archive, Northwestern University.

1989 Telephone interview by author, 31 May.

Mac Low, Jackson 1972 *Stanzas For Iris Lezak*. New York: Something Else Press.

1978 The Poetics of Chance & the Politics of Simultaneous Spontaneity, or the Sacred Heart of Jesus (Revised & Abridged). In *Talking Poetics from Naropa Institute* Vol. I, ed. Anne Waldman and Marilyn Webb, 171–194. Boulder, Col.: Shambhala Publications, Inc.

Malina, Judith 1989 Interview by author, 2 March, New York.

Mallarmé, Stéphane 1982 *Selected Poetry and Prose*. Edited by Mary Ann Caws. New York: New Directions.

McKay, George 1938 *Marriage at the Eiffel Tower*. Unpublished score in the Notations Archive, Northwestern University.

Mekas, Jonas 1966 Musical Journal. *The Village Voice*, 27 October.

Mikhashoff, Yvar 1993 Telephone interview by author, 14 June.

Miller, Allan; and Vivian Perlis 1990 *I Have Nothing to Say, And I Am Saying It*. 55 min. video documentary on John Cage. New York: PBS.

Montague, Stephen 1982 Significant Silences of a Musical Anarchist. *Classical Music*, 22 May, 11.

1985 John Cage at Seventy-Five: An Interview. *American Music* Vol. 3, no. 2 (Summer), 205–216.

Moore, Barbara 1992 Telephone conversation, 12 August.

Mozart, Wolfgang Amadeus 1973 *Melody Dicer (Musikalishes Würfelspiel)*. New York: Carousel Publishing Corp.

Music. 1949 *Time*, 24 January, 36.

Music: A Long, Long, Long Night (and Day) at the Piano. 1963 *The New York Times*, 11 September.

"Musicircus" Has It All Mixed In. 1970 *The Daily Telegraph* (London), 29 October.

Myers, Rolla H. 1968 *Erik Satie*. New York: Dover Publications, Inc.

Naumann, Francis M. 1989 Marcel Duchamp: A Reconciliation of Opposites. In *Marcel Duchamp: Artist of the Century*, ed. Rudolf Kuegli and Francis M. Naumann, 20–40. Cambridge, Mass.: The MIT Press.

Nelson, Richard 1989 Telephone interview by author, 7 May.

Nes Kirby, Victoria 1972 George Ribemont-Dessaignes. *The Drama Review* Vol. 16, no. 1 (March), 104–109.

Oestreich, James R. 1992 Empty Chairs In Honor of Cage. *The New York Times*, 17 August.

Olson, Charles 1966 *Selected Writings*. Edited by Robert Creeley. New York: New Directions.

Parmenter, Ross 1958 Music: Experimenter (Zounds! Sounds by) John Cage at Town Hall. *The New York Times*, 16 May.

1963 Music: Avant-Garde Sound Mosaic. *The New York Times*, 22 August.

Patchen, Kenneth 1942 *The City Wears A Slouch Hat*. Mimeographed typescript with annotations by John Cage. In the John Cage Archive, Northwestern University.

1977 *Patchen's Lost Plays: Don't Look Now and The City Wears A Slouch Hat*. Edited by Richard G. Morgan. Santa Barbara, Ca.: Capra Press.

Patchen, Kenneth; and John Cage 1942 *The City Wears A Slouch Hat*. Cassette recording in private collection from the original 78 r.p.m. recording of the live broadcast, WBBM, C.B.S., Chicago, 31 May.

Percussion Concert: Band bangs things to make music. 1943 *Life*, 15 March, 42; 44.

Perloff, Marjorie 1981 *The Poetics of Indeterminacy: Rimbaud to Cage*. Princeton, N.J.: Princeton University Press.

1982 "Unimpededness and Interpenentration": the poetic of John Cage. In *A John Cage Reader in celebration of his 70th birthday*, ed. Peter Gena, Jonathan Brent, and Don Gillespie, 4–16. New York: C. F. Peters Corporation.

1989 Music for Words Perhaps: Reading/Hearing/Seeing John Cage's *Roaratorio*. In *Postmodern Genres*, ed. Marjorie Perloff, 193–228. Norman: University of Oklahoma Press.

1991 *Radical Artifice: Writing Poetry in the Age of Media*. Chicago: The University of Chicago Press.

Perrin, Peter 1989 Interview by author, 29 March, New York.

Petkus, Janetta 1986 The Songs of John Cage (1931–1970). Ph.D. dissertation, The University of Connecticut.

Popper, Karl R. 1982 *The Open Universe: An Argument for Indeterminism*. Edited by W. W. Bartley, III. Totowa, N. J.: Rowland and Littlefield.

Porter, Andrew 1976 Musical Events. *The New Yorker*, 29 November, 146–153.

1988 Musical Events. *The New Yorker*, 8 August, 67–69.

Porzio, Michele 1992 A White Cage Inside Four Walls: Silence in 1944. In *Musicworks* 52 (Spring), 28–37.

Pritchett, James W. 1988 The Development of Chance Techniques in the Music of John Cage, 1950–1956. Ph.D. dissertation, New York University.

1989 Understanding John Cage's Chance Music: An Analytical Approach. In *John Cage at Seventy-Five*, ed. Richard Fleming and William Duckworth, 249–261. Lewisburg, Pa.: Bucknell University Press.

1993 The music of John Cage. Cambridge, UK: Cambridge University Press.

Program 1952 Maverick Concert Hall, Woodstock, New York; 29 August. In the John Cage Archive, Northwestern University.

1960 Circle In The Square Theatre, New York, 7 March. In the John Cage Archive, Northwestern University.

1973 2 evenings of John Cage at The Kitchen, New York; 7, 8 December. Courtesy of Don Gillespie.

1976 Assorted programs for *Renga with Apartment House 1776*. In the files of C. F. Peters Corporation, New York.

1985 4 Walls at the Asia Society, Lila Acheson Wallace Auditorium, New York, 17 May. In the files of C. F. Peters.

1992a Summergarden, the Museum of Modern Art, New York, 3 July–29 August. Paul Zukofsky, artistic director.

1992b Cagemusicircus, at Symphony Space, New York, Nov. 1.

Pschera, Alexander 1991 Vorstoss als Methode. *Rhein–Neckar–Zeitung* (Heidelberg), 14 November.

Read, Gardner 1969 *Music Notation: A Manual of Modern Practice.* Boston: Crescendo Publishers.

Reps, Paul n.d. *Zen Flesh, Zen Bones: A Collection of Zen & Pre-Zen Writings.* New York: Anchor Books.

Revill, David 1992 *The Roaring Silence, John Cage: A Life.* New York: Arcade Publishing.

Richards, Mary Caroline 1989 Interview by author, 13 April, Kimberton, Pa.

Ripin, Edwin M. 1980 Prepared Piano. In *The New Grove Dictionary of Music and Musicians,* ed. Stanley Sadie, 216. London: Macmillan Publishers Limited.

Rockwell, John 1973 Music: 2 Composers for the Theater. *The New York Times,* 9 December.

1988 John Cage's Quasi Opera Has American Premiere. *The New York Times,* 16 July.

Ross, Alex 1992 Classical Music in Review. *The New York Times,* 7 November.

Roth, Williams; and Moira Roth 1973 John Cage on Marcel Duchamp: An Interview. *Art in America* Nov.–Dec., 72–79.

Rothstein, Edward 1992 Classical Music/1992: The Year In the Arts. *The New York Times,* 27 December.

Round About. ca. 1939 Unidentified newspaper clipping. In the John Cage Archive, Northwestern University.

Russell, William 1993 "Made In America": The Complete Works. CD Recording performed by Essential Music. Kew Gardens, N.Y.: Mode.

Russett, Robert; and Cecile Starr 1976 *Experimental Animation: An Illustrated Anthology.* New York: Van Nostrand Reinhold Company.

Sabatini, Arthur J. 1989 Silent Performances: On Reading John Cage. In *John Cage at Seventy-Five,* ed. Richard Fleming and William Duckworth, 74–96. Lewisburg, Pa.: Bucknell University Press.

Salzman, Eric 1989 Liner notes to *John Cage: Four Walls.* CD recording performed by Richard Bunger, piano; and Jill Clayton, voice. New York: Tomato.

Sandow, Gregory 1982 The Cage Style. *The Village Voice,* 11 May.

Sayre, Henry M. 1989 *The Object of Performance: The American Avant-Garde Since 1970.* Chicago: The University of Chicago Press.

Schechner, Richard 1973 *Experimental Theatre.* New York: Hawthorn Books.

Schmitt, Natalie Crohn 1982 John Cage, nature and theater. In *A John Cage Reader in celebration of his 70th birthday,* ed. Peter Gena, Jonathan Brent, and Don Gillespie, 17–37. New York: C. F. Peters Corporation.

Schneider, Marcel 1970 Les impenetrables desseins de John Cage. *Le Figaro* (Paris), 28 October.

Schneider, Pierre 1970 Paris: Savoring All Kinds of Silence. *The New York Times,* 16 November.

Schonberg, Harold C. 1960 The Far-Out Pianist. *Harper's Magazine,* June, 49–54.

Schüren, Dieter 1982 Gummikeile im Klavier. *Die Welt* (Bonn), 28 April.

Shapiro, David 1985 On Collaboration in Art: A Conversation with John Cage. *RES* 10 (Fall), 103–116.

Siff, Nancy 1959 Concert Review. *The Village Voice*, 15 April.

Silence, Sound in Composition Are Stressed. 1951 *The Hartford Times*, 14 March.

Smith, Michael 1965 Theatre Journal. *The Village Voice*, 16 September.

Smith, Stuart Saunders 1992 On Performance: Having Words with John Cage. In *Percussive Notes*, February, 48–52.

Smoliar, Stephen 1987 Happy Birthday, John Cage. Associated Press newscopy, 7 September. In the John Cage Archive, Northwestern University.

Snyder, Ellsworth 1970 John Cage and Music Since World War II: A Study in Applied Aesthetics. Ph.D. dissertation, The University of Wisconsin.

1989 Telephone interview by author, 1 July.

1993 Telephone interview by author, 23 January.

Snyder, Ellsworth; and Anne d'Harnoncourt 1982 Biographical chronology. In *A John Cage Reader in celebration of his 70th birthday*, ed. Peter Gena, Jonathan Brent, and Don Gillespie, 184–193. New York: C. F. Peters Corporation.

Sollberger, Harvey 1974 Liner notes to *Percussion Music: Works by Varèse, Colgrass, Cowell, Saperstein, Oak*. Phonograph recording performed by The New Jersey Percussion Ensemble. New York: Nonesuch.

Sontag, Susan 1982 *A Susan Sontag Reader*. New York: Farrar, Straus, Giroux, Inc.

Stein, Jean; and George Plimpton 1982 *Edie, An American Biography*. New York: Alfred A. Knopf.

Stevenson, Robert 1982 John Cage on His 70th Birthday: West Coast Background. In *Inter-American Music Review* Vol. V, no. 1 (Fall), 3–17.

Strindberg, August 1968 The New Arts, or the Role of Chance in Artistic Creation. In *Inferno, Alone and Other Writings*, ed. Evert Sprinchorn, 97–103. Garden City, N.Y.: Anchor Books.

Sultan, Grete 1989 Interview by author, 10 April, New York.

Suzuki, Daisetz T. 1959 *Zen and Japanese Culture*. Princeton, N.J.: Princeton University Press.

Swed, Mark 1988a John Cage's Opera of Chaos. *The Wall Street Journal*, 26 February.

1988b Celebration of Chaos: John Cage's first opera comes to PepsiCo Summerfare on July 14. *Opera News* Vol. 53, no. 1, July, 30–31.

1992 John Cage: A Last Salute. In *American Record Guide* November/December, 22–24.

Sweeney, John S. 1988 Cage's opera collage is "mind ventillating". *The Greenwich (Conn.) Times*, 16 July.

Tame, David 1984 *The Secret Power of Music*. New York: Destiny Books.

Tan, Margaret Leng 1989a Interview by author, 16 March, New York.

1989b "Taking a Nap, I Pound the Rice": Eastern Influences on John Cage. In *John Cage at Seventy-Five*, ed. Richard Fleming and William Duckworth, 34–58. Lewisburg, Pa.: Bucknell University Press.

1990 Telephone conversation with author, 5 January.

1993 Telephone interview by author, 19 August.

Taruskin, Richard 1993 No Ear For Music. In *The New Republic*, 15 March, 26–35.

Taylor, Markland 1988 Cage's "Europeras 1 & 2" pokes fun at grand opera. *The New Haven (Conn.) Register*, 16 July.

Tenney, James 1989 Telephone interview by author, 4 April.

Thaler, Lotte 1987 Friedfertiger Hand zur sanften Anarchie. *Frankfurter Allgemeine Zeitung*, 11 December.

Thomson, Virgil 1945 Music. *The New York Herald–Tribune*, 22 January.

1960 John Cage Late and Early. In *The Saturday Review* Vol. 43, 30 January, 38–39.

Thoreau, Henry David 1968 *The Variorum Walden and Civil Disobedience*, ed. Walter Harding. New York: Washington Square Press.

Tomkins, Calvin 1968 *The Bride and the Bachelors*. New York: Penguin Books.

Tudor, David 1958 Unpublished realization of *Music Walk*, in the collection of David Tudor.

1960a Unpublished realization of *Cartridge Music*, in the collection of David Tudor.

1960b Unpublished realization of *Theatre Piece*, in the collection of David Tudor.

1982 Unpublished realization of *4'33"*, in the collection of David Tudor.

1989a Interview by author, 8 March, New York.

1989b Interview by author, 21 June, Stony Point, New York.

1989c Interview by author, 21 August, Stony Point, New York.

1993 Telephone interview by author, 17 September.

Twining, Toby 1989 Telephone interview by author, 23 August.

1990 Telephone interview by author, 24 October.

Tzara, Tristan 1981 *Seven Dada Manifestos and Lampisteries*. Translated by Barbara Wright. New York: Riverrun Press Inc.

Urmetzer, Reinhold 1979 Arzenei gegen Schlaflosigkeit: Szenische Musik mit der Gruppe The-Ge-Ano in Stuttgart. *Stuttgarter Zeitung*, 28 June.

van Emmerik, Ivo; and Ron Ford 1989 John Cage in the Hague: A Theatre of Songs. Translated by Ron Ford. In *Key Notes* 25, 15–17.

von Berswordt-Wallrabe, Kornelia 1992 John Cage: On Aspects of emptiness and disappearance. In *John Cage: Arbeiten auf Papier*, 15–20. Wiesbaden: Nassauischer Kunstverein/Galerie Ressel.

Variations VII. 1966 Unpublished performance notes by an engineer. In the John Cage Archive, Northwestern University.

Vaughan, David 1989 Conversation with author, November, New York.

1991 Notes to *Cartridge Music* CD recording. Kew Gardens, N.Y.: Mode.

Waldman, Anne; and Marilyn Webb 1978 John Cage, *Empty Words with Relevant Material*. In *Talking Poetics from Naropa Institute* Vol. I, ed. Anne Waldman and Marilyn Webb, 195–220. Boulder, Col.: Shambhala Publications, Inc.

Wilhelm, Richard 1967 *The I Ching, or Book of Changes*. Translated by Cary F. Baynes from Wilhelm's German translation from Chinese. Princeton, N.J.: Princeton University Press.

Willis, Thomas 1969 Urbana Happening in Solar Setting. *The Chicago Tribune*, 18 May.

Wittgenstein, Ludwig 1922 *Tractatus Logico–Philosophicus*. Translated by C. K. Ogden. London: Routledge & Kegan Paul LTD.

Wolff, Christian 1989 Telephone interview by author, 7 May.

Yates, Peter 1964 Music Review. *Vogue*, 1 October, 22.

1967 *Twentieth Century Music: Its Evolution from the End of the Harmonic Era into the Present Era of Sound.* New York: Pantheon Books.

Yesterday's Revolution. 1960 *Time*, 10 October, 59.

Zierolf, Robert 1983 Indeterminacy in Musical Form. Ph.D. dissertation, The University of Cincinnati.

Zumstein, Bruce 1967 Musicircus Rocks Stock Pavilion. *The Daily Illini* (Urbana-Champaign, Ill.), 18 May.

INDEX OF CAGE'S WORKS

GENERAL INDEX